T0301433

Truth and Progress in Economic Knowledge

Truth and Progress in Economic Knowledge

Roger E. Backhouse

Professor of the History and Philosophy of Economics
The University of Birmingham, UK

Edward Elgar
Cheltenham, UK • Lyme, US

Published by
Edward Elgar Publishing Limited
8 Lansdown Place
Cheltenham
Glos GL50 2HU

Edward Elgar Publishing, Inc.
1 Pinnacle Hill Road
Lyme
NH 03768
US

A catalogue record for this book
is available from the British Library

Library of Congress Cataloguing in Publication Data
Backhouse, Roger
    Truth and progress in economic knowledge / Roger E. Backhouse.
    (Advances in economic methodology)
    Includes bibliographical references and index.
    1. Economics—Methodology. I. Title. II. Series.
    HB131.B33   1997
    330—dc21   97–12142
                                                            CIP

ISBN 1 85278 691 4

Printed and bound in Great Britain by
Biddles Limited, Guildford and King's Lynn

Contents

List of Figures and Tables

FIGURES

TABLE

Preface

The initial reaction of some readers to a book that is sceptical about post-modernism, that asks questions about progress in economic thought, and that views philosophers such as Popper and Lakatos in a fairly favourable light, will be that it must be old-fashioned, seeking to turn back the methodological clock a decade or more. Such a reading of this book, however, would be a mistake (assuming, of course, that I have expressed myself adequately). The book does view Popper and Lakatos favourably (though not uncritically), it does focus on the concept of progress, and it does offer criticisms of contemporary economics, even endorsing a perspective on the subject that goes back as far as Alfred Marshall. But it does not simply take ready-made philosophy of science and apply it to economics. Ideas taken from Popper and Lakatos, along with Kuhn, Peirce, Laudan and Hacking, are used to establish that there are ways in which we can think about progress in economic thought that are not vulnerable to post-modernist arguments. The nearest to a straight 'application' of philosophy of science to economics is the use made of Lakatos, but it is the Lakatos of *Proofs and Refutations*, not the Lakatos of the methodology of scientific research programmes. The end result is, therefore, very far from a conventional Lakatosian perspective.

One way to locate this book in the methodological literature is to compare it with two recent books: Hausman's *Inexact and Separate Science of Economics* (1992) and Kincaid's *Philosophical Foundations of the Social Sciences* (1996), the latter of which appeared too late for me to take its arguments into account when writing the main text of this book.

Hausman's *Inexact and Separate Science of Economics* would appear to be poles apart from this book.[1] It is very critical of Popper and

---

[1] For more detailed discussions of Hausman's book, on which these paragraphs draw, see Backhouse (1995) and (1997d).

vii

Lakatos, advocating instead a modified version of Mill's inexact deductive method. However, despite our very different attitudes to these three philosophers, my perspective on economic methodology offered here has much in common with Hausman's.[2] The difference is that where Hausman emphasizes his disagreements with falsificationism, arguing that if its defects are put right nothing survives, I focus on what can be learned from Popper and Lakatos.[3] Though we take different routes, our destinations are not far apart. We both engage in empirical philosophy of science; we both view scientific knowledge as corrigible; we both attach importance to empirical criticism and theories being open to such criticism; we both accept that epistemology should be concerned with the growth of knowledge; and we both consider it legitimate and important to draw normative conclusions. Though I am not convinced Hausman has made the case for some of his recommendations (devoting more resources to data-gathering and experimental economics, and to the development of new statistical techniques), many of them are aimed at strengthening the empirical side of the discipline, something I endorse.

Setting aside the differences between our treatment of falsificationism, the most significant difference between Hausman's book and mine is that he focuses far more on economic theory, whereas I devote much more attention to econometrics. The reason for my emphasis is that if the question of empirical progress is central to any appraisal of economics, or any normative judgements, it is vital to examine economists' empirical practices, for it is through these that theories are brought into contact with empirical evidence. On this point, however, the two books complement each other. Hausman explores economists' reactions to certain experimental results in great detail, whereas I explore the way various types of non-experimental and econometric evidence are used. There no disagreement between us on these issues. Hausman provides a list of recommendations for improving the economics, whereas I prefer, on the whole, to leave the book's normative implications implicit. The main problem with our discussion of these issues is that neither of us does much more than scratch the surface of the problem, for it

---

[2] This is no coincidence, for I have learned much from Hausman during the period when I have been writing this book.

[3] C.f. Backhouse (1994c).

is a vast one, requiring much more research than has been done so far.

In contrast with Hausman, Kincaid focuses on the social sciences as a whole, not simply on economics, arguing the case for naturalism (the doctrine that the methods of natural science can be applied to social science) and holism (the doctrine that social phenomena cannot be analysed in purely individualistic terms). This book is directly concerned with neither of these issues, but it shares two common features with Kincaid's book.

1. Though we both see great value in the analysis of rhetoric, Kincaid and I are both critical of what he calls currently trendy forms of scepticism and irrationalism (Kincaid, 1996, p. 5).
2. We is willing to accept the notion of 'good science', even though this may be difficult to capture within a formal methodological scheme.

In order to develop a methodology based on these views, Kincaid draws primarily on Quine. Though I draw on the work of other philosophers, reading Kuhn very differently from Kincaid (I focus on the Postscript to *The Structure of Scientific Revolutions*, not on the first edition), the conclusions we reach are very similar.

In addition, the two books reach compatible conclusions. Kincaid's recommendations take the form of a list of barriers to good science, which includes the following (Kincaid, 1996, pp. 261–2).

1. Failure to investigate *ceteris paribus* clauses in the ways necessary to prove theories trustworthy.
2. Failure to rule out competing hypotheses.
3. Failure to do 'fair' tests.
4. Not searching for new sources of data and not acknowledging the weaknesses in existing data.
5. Treating correlations as an end in themselves, rather than as evidence for causal explanations.
6. An over-emphasis on grand, highly abstract, theory.
7. Confusing a simplified, heuristic model with real explanation.[4]

---

[4] Two other barriers have been omitted on the grounds that they are clearly not relevant to economics.

Kincaid urges economists to avoid these pitfalls, in order to improve the empirical practices of economics. I have no objections whatsoever to such advice – it would be endorsed by many economists, but I contend that such values do not take us far enough. It is, I suggest, necessary to look in much more detail at the problems involved in testing economic theories. This is what is attempted in the closing chapters of this book.

The most general conclusion to emerge from these chapters is that the conventional division of labour, in which economic theorists, starting from general assumptions such as rationality, propose hypotheses to be tested, whilst econometricians, drawing above all on statistical theory, test those theories and establish empirical generalizations, seems unlikely to be successful. The main reason for this is that replication, which is absolutely fundamental to establishing empirical generalizations or testing theories, is an *economic*, not a statistical problem. Economic criteria, therefore, enter into the process of testing, and not simply at the stage of proposing hypotheses to be tested. In addition, economic theories need to be informed by economic data and the practicalities of testing, if there is to be effective interaction between theories and data. Such interaction is vital if economics is to exhibit empirical progress.

Acknowledgements

Though all the material has been extensively revised, some of the material in Chapters 2–4 and 6 has been taken from Backhouse (1992c), (1992d) and (1993). Chapter 2 is a greatly expanded version (by a factor of around 10) of Backhouse (1992a). I am indebted to numerous friends who commented on the many drafts of these papers and to others who have supplied me with ideas, material and comments on other material in the book. The list of people to whom I am indebted is very long. Individual chapters and the papers on which some of them are based were read by Charles Bazerman, Vivienne Brown, Bruce Caldwell, Sheila Dow, Daniel Hammond, Willie Henderson, Wade Hands, David Hendry, Chris Hookway, Kevin Hoover, Uskali Mäki, Diedre McCloskey, Judith Mehta, Philip Mirowski, Philippe Mongin, Paul Wendt and Nancy Wulwick. Mark Blaug read numerous drafts and provided encouragement and invaluable advice at every stage. Warren Samuels convinced me that an early draft was so unsatisfactory that I needed to start again, virtually from scratch. Bob Coats, Daniel Hausman, Denis O'Brien and Tom Mayer provided immensely detailed criticisms of a draft of the whole book, without which many errors would not have been eliminated and many improvements not have been made. Drafts of various chapters were presented to meetings of the History of Economics Society, the Veblen Society, the Royal Economic Society, an International Network for Economic Method session at ASSA, the Dublin Economic Workshop, and seminars at the University of Birmingham, Erasmus University Rotterdam, the University of East Anglia, the University of Sheffield, the London School of Economics, and Wake Forest University. I am grateful to all these audiences for their attention and for the criticism and, equally important, the encouragement that they have provided. It goes without saying that they should not be blamed for the results, some of which they may hardly recognize.

1. Introduction

1.1 OBJECTIONS TO THE CONCEPT OF PROGRESS IN ECONOMICS

Truth and progress are now, in many quarters, unfashionable concepts to use in the context of economics. Unlike in the 1960s, when Keynesian economics seemed to offer the key to prosperity and economists were generally optimistic about the prospects for their discipline,[1] economics is widely seen to have failed. Economists are blamed for the many of the policy disasters of the past 25 years, these ranging from the poor macroeconomic performance of most European and North American economies since the 1970s' oil shocks to the disastrous consequences, at least in terms of unemployment and social cohesion, of stabilization policies and structural adjustment programmes in developing countries and in the countries of the former Soviet bloc. Many commentators have drawn the conclusion that the fault lies with the economic theories upon which economic policies are based.

Truth and progress have also fallen out of fashion in the literature on economic methodology, but for a very different set of reasons, going under loosely-defined labels such as 'post-positivism' and 'post-modernism'. 'Post-positivism' stems above all from Thomas Kuhn's *Structure of Scientific Revolutions* (1962/70). Where the prevailing orthodoxy (evolved out of logical positivism) had sought to understand science in terms of a set of general logical categories, Kuhn argued that science had to be analysed in terms of paradigms – historically-specific matrices of metaphysical presuppositions and other commitments. The history of science involved, he claimed, a series of paradigms, interspersed with what he termed scientific revolutions. Two aspects of this vision were of crucial importance.

---

[1] See, for example, O'Brien (1974), pp. 10–11.

1. It undermined the notion of progress in science, except within specific paradigms. The meanings of scientific terms and concepts were dependent on the paradigm, and when this changed so did the meanings. This meant that it might be impossible to compare scientific theories across paradigms – Kuhn's incommensurability thesis.
2. Science had to be understood as a social process. Normal science and scientific revolutions could be understood only in the context of science as a professional activity.

Though Kuhn did not move as far in this direction as many of those who took up his ideas (indeed, as is explained in Chapter 5, he argued that science exhibited progress in a way that other types of intellectual activity did not) his work contributed to an undermining of the notion that science was characterized by progress, establishing in its place the idea that knowledge was historically specific. Rather than search for general principles underlying the growth of scientific knowledge, it is claimed that all we can do is to examine how knowledge is produced in specific settings. Philosophy of science becomes a much more localized enterprise.

Post-modernism takes such ideas a stage further. Where Kuhn argued that scientific knowledge was the property of specific scientific communities, post-modernism argues that this is true of all knowledge. Science has to be viewed as one of many types of discourse. It occupies no privileged position. This is a version of what Laudan (1984, p. 30) has termed 'cognitive egalitarianism'. Furthermore, there is no possibility of finding general rules governing the creation of knowledge, for that would imply an ability to stand outside society, obtaining a 'God's eye' view, something that is clearly impossible. The notions of truth and progress in any absolute sense cannot be sustained.

Such post-positivist and post-modernist ideas have been used to mount a critique of the whole project of economic methodology, by which is meant the process of uncovering, or establishing rules governing the growth of economic knowledge. This argument against thinking of progress in economic knowledge has very different origins from the argument, discussed in the opening paragraph, that economics has failed to exhibit any progress. Indeed, arguing that the subject has failed implies that there *are* standards against which it can be judged. The two arguments, however, can reinforce each other. If economics were clearly successful, this would make post-modernist arguments less compelling. Arguments about the impossibility of making general statements about the nature of scientific knowledge are attractive to those who wish to argue that orthodox methodology is flawed, and such arguments in turn would be harder to make if economics were clearly progressive. In addition, arguments about the failure of economics are frequently used as evidence for post-modernist arguments about methodology.

Amongst historians of economics the issue of progress has been widely debated in the context of so-called 'Whig' history. This debate has centred on whether it is appropriate to read the past from the perspective of present-day ideas. The opponents of 'Whig' history argue that it is important to read past writings against the contexts in which they were written, and that the concerns of past economists, their presuppositions and beliefs may be very different from those of present-day economists. In its most extreme form, this position denies that there can be progress in economic thought: there are merely changes in the questions.[2]

1.2 THE VIEW FROM WITHIN THE ECONOMIC MAINSTREAM[3]

And yet, despite all these developments, many economists see their subject very differently. When asked to defend contemporary economics they argue that it has made immense progress. In their view, economics has developed techniques of analysis that differentiate it sharply from 'soft' disciplines, such as philosophy, political science, sociology, history and most of the humanities. In such disciplines there are perennial issues over which people argue: it is the absence of progress that means one can learn, say, political philosophy by studying Hobbes and Locke. Economics, in contrast, is believed to have moved beyond this stage, the application of mathematical techniques having transformed the subject into a

---

[2] This is discussed at length in Backhouse (1995), Chapters 1–3.

[3] The qualification 'from within the economic mainstream' is inserted to allow for the existence of substantial numbers of economists who would strongly dissent from the views expressed in this section. Though no formal definition of the mainstream will be provided, its use, in this context, does not result in any ambiguities.

cumulative discipline, in which progress is self-evident to anyone familiar with the literature. Thus Hahn (1992a) could, without irony, describe the theory of industrial organisation of only two decades previously as 'stone age theory'. Similarly, Debreu refers to 'dazzling mathematical developments', pointing out that the rigor of modern theory stands 'in sharp contrast to the standards of reasoning that were accepted in the late 1930s' (1991, p. 3). Economists, it is widely held, need read only the most recent journal articles. Unlike philosophers or political scientists, the cumulative nature of the discipline means that economics can be undertaken without knowledge or understanding of the writings of previous generations.

There are two aspects to this transformation of economics. The first is the mathematization of economic theory – the analysis of economic problems through formal models of individual choice. Individuals are, almost universally, modelled as optimizing agents in a variety of tightly-specified environments (perfect competition, monopolistic competition, monopoly, co-operative and non-cooperative games). The second is econometrics, involving the analysis of statistical data through formal estimation of quantitative relationships under the assumption that the data can be modelled as being generated by an underlying probability distribution. These two strands of modern economics clearly have much in common (notably the use of formal mathematical techniques), and it can be argued that they reinforce each other: mathematical techniques and other conceptual advances can often be transferred from one to the other; the existence of econometrics means that theorizing can (most of the time) be separated from formal testing, and vice versa. It can also be argued, however, that the integration of the two has been much less satisfactory than many of the pioneers of such methods anticipated, and much less than some of the rhetoric claims.

Despite its importance, however, the concept of progress underlying these developments has remained largely unanalysed. For most practising economic theorists (using the term in the peculiar sense that it is understood amongst economists, as referring to someone who undertakes mathematical analysis of systems of individual optimization[4]) and econometricians, the existence of

---

4   C.f. Mayer (1995), p. 51.

progress is too obvious to require discussion and it has, despite its importance in economists' rhetoric, remained largely unanalysed.

One exception to this is Blaug (1994) who has addressed the question of whether there is empirical progress in economics. He draws a distinction between theoretical progress and empirical progress. Theoretical progress is heuristic progress: greater conceptual clarity and analytical innovations. Empirical progress, Blaug contends, 'is a much more elusive idea than theoretical progress', but involves 'a deeper grasp of the inner springs of economic behaviour and hence of the operations of the economic system' (Blaug, 1994, pp. 116–17). He goes on to link this with the ability to make qualitative and quantitative predictions. The track record of economics, he suggests, is mixed: unlike some critics, he points to numerous examples of empirical progress; but at the same time many supposed advances in the subject have involved no more than theoretical progress which, if it contributes nothing to empirical progress, is of little value.[5]

1.3   THE ARGUMENT TO FOLLOW

The aims of this book are (1) to argue that methodology matters for economics, (2) that there are interesting and important questions that can be asked about the nature of truth and progress in economic thought, and (3) to point to ways in which these questions might be answered.

The first stage is to defend the thesis that methodology matters. This involves taking on not only the 'practical' objections to methodology raised by economists, but also the philosophical case made by McCloskey and Weintraub and other 'postmodern' critics of methodology.[6] The former task is undertaken in Chapter 2, the main evidence being examples in which the methodological choices made by economists had a significant, and not necessarily beneficial, impact on the way particular branches of the subject developed. The latter task is the subject of Chapters 3 and 4.

The book then turns, in Chapters 5 to 8, to a number of ways in which it is possible to think about truth and progress in science.

---

[5] Another exception is Bliss (1986), discussed on page 99 below.

[6] As is explained below, the term 'postmodern' is used fairly loosely here.

Chapter 5 discusses Kuhn, often taken to be the arch-relativist in recent philosophy of science. It points out how, because he took for granted the pervasiveness of certain values and the ability of empirical evidence to constrain scientific theories, Kuhn *was* able to speak of progress, even across paradigms, and even though he did not hold a correspondence theory of truth. Chapter 6 takes this argument further through drawing on the pragmatist tradition, notably the work of Peirce. For Peirce, progress resulted from following a particular method – the method of science. Two important characteristics of this method, Peirce claimed, were realism (the doctrine that there is a world external to our experience of it, and that we can know it) and experimentation (doing things and finding out their consequences). Chapter 7 discusses the view of truth and progress found in the Popperian tradition, whilst Chapter 8 sums up by providing a survey of ways in which the concept of progress can be understood. Various forms of theoretical and empirical progress are distinguished, and the point is made that these two types of progress are not independent of each other.

Having established various ways in which progress can be understood, the focus shifts to specific problems arising in economics. The first question to be addressed is that of whether it is right to regard economics as an empirical science at all. Chapter 9 addresses Rosenberg's claim that economics should be considered a branch of contractarian political philosophy, and the claims of economists, as diverse as McCloskey and Lawson, who have argued that prediction is impossible in economics, a view which is hard to reconcile with the claim that economics should be an empirical science. The chapter concludes with a discussion of the prediction of novel facts as an appraisal criterion.

Theoretical progress is considered in Chapter 10. After discussing several ways in others have tried to make sense of theoretical progress in economics, it is argued that the most useful one is what Lakatos calls 'informal' mathematics. Though this provides an account of theoretical progress, however, the process is guided by 'intuitive' understandings of the phenomena that appear in the theory. Because these understandings are informed by empirical evidence, theoretical progress cannot be discussed in isolation. Theoretical and empirical progress are connected.

The nature of the argument then changes. Rather than seek to characterize empirical progress in general, Chapters 11 to 13 discuss some of the key issues that arise in relating economic theories to empirical evidence, paying particular attention to econometrics. Chapter 11 is concerned with replication and the establishment of economic facts. In natural sciences, replication is fundamental, for it is the process whereby scientists establish that the phenomena they are dealing with are indeed features of the natural world: that they are not artefacts of the particular experimental procedures followed by individual scientists. Replication is fundamental to any claim to be producing reliable knowledge. This chapter explores what might be the equivalent in economics. The next stage, in Chapter 12, is to consider the problems that arise in testing economic theories: in testing *explanations* of economic phenomena. The use of formal econometric techniques is considered in relation to more informal methods of testing theories, such as those advocated by Friedman.

Finally, in Chapter 13, attention is turned to the way in which empirical evidence, ranging from descriptions of institutions to formal econometric results, is used by some economic theorists. This chapter supports the view, argued in Chapter 10, that theory and empirical work cannot be separated, for replication emerges as an *economic*, not a purely econometric problem. Even if econometricians do not replicate results as much as one might like, the way in which economists use econometric results goes some way (though admittedly not far enough) towards remedying this. More important, replication is something that can occur at a variety of levels, which means that it is not a purely statistical problem.

Chapter 13 concludes with a section on the successes of economics. In part, the reason for this is to make the point that, though the state of contemporary economics may leave much to be desired, not everything is wrong. Considering some examples of successes points to some of the problems that arise elsewhere. The message implicit in these chapters is an appeal for a more empirically orientated economics. Though not expressed in falsificationist language, and though it does not presume to tell economists how to set about the task, this message is similar in spirit to Blaug's (1980/92) conclusion that where economists have sought to test theories, the result has been progress in the subject.

2.   Why methodology?

2.1   THE CASE AGAINST METHODOLOGY

The practical objection

The practical objection to methodology has been forcefully stated by Frank Hahn. Invited, on the occasion of his retirement, to offer some reflections for the RES Newsletter, he chose to cast them in the form of advice to the young. After warning young economists to 'garner the great pleasures of discovery' while they can, he went on to

> advise everyone to ignore cries of 'economics in crisis', to avoid discussion of 'mathematics in economics' like the plague, and to give no thought at all to 'methodology'. (Hahn, 1992a)

When challenged (Backhouse, 1992a), Hahn responded that his critique of methodology was 'empirically and not theoretically based' (Hahn, 1992b). The literature on methodology is, he contended, sterile and of 'uniformly poor quality'. Reading methodology may entertain, but it is a distraction from serious work.

It was in a similar vein that Irving Fisher, in his Presidential address to the American Statistical Association, wrote:

> It has long seemed to me that students of the social sciences, especially sociology and economics, have spent too much time in discussing what they call methodology. I have usually felt that the man who essays to tell the rest of us how to solve knotty problems would be more convincing if first he proved out his alleged method by solving a few himself. Apparently those would-be authorities who are forever telling others how to get results to not get any important results themselves. (quoted in King, 1992)

Methodology, according to Hahn and Fisher, is at best a waste of time that might better be spent actually doing economics. At worst, its effects are positively harmful. Thus Hahn was critical of what he called 'positivist proselytising' and the demands of 'American Popperians' for predictions. Predictions, he contends are at present beyond us and, in any case are far less important than understanding.

The historian's objection

The 'historian's' objection to methodology takes such arguments a step further. The argument runs in two stages.

1. Economists have not followed the prescriptions of any methodology.
2. Economists have had good reasons for behaving as they have.
3. The attempt to fit economics into any philosophical scheme is, therefore, misguided.

It follows that economic methodology, understood as the attempt to establish rules governing the successful conduct of economic inquiry, is not only futile but dangerous. Reading the past through the lens of philosophy results in distorted, over-simplified, 'thin' history.

The reason for this is that the world is, so the argument runs, too complex to fit into a (necessarily) simple philosophical framework. As McCloskey puts it,

> One can imagine a world, perhaps, in which the growth of knowledge was interestingly philosophizable. But it doesn't seem to be our world. (McCloskey, 1988b, p. 245)

Philosophy is thin, he claims, because of the thinness of the questions it asks. It fails to take account of the rich variety of history and is thus a poor guide to either the history of economic thought or economics itself. McCloskey concludes that the only rules to be followed are the ethical rules that govern any conversation – Habermas's *Sprachethik*.

The philosopher Paul Feyerabend went even further:

It is clear, then, that the idea of a fixed method, or of a fixed theory of rationality, rests on too naive a view of man and his social surroundings. To those who look at the rich material provided by history, and who are not intent on impoverishing it in order to please their lower instincts, their craving for intellectual security in the form of clarity, precision, 'objectivity', 'truth', it will become clear that there is only *one* principle that can be defended under *all* circumstances and in *all* stages of human development. It is the principle: *anything goes*. (Feyerabend, 1975/88, p. 19)

Methodology, fostering the illusion that it may be possible to establish universal rules governing scientific inquiry, is dangerous, for it arbitrarily restricts the process of inquiry.

The post-modernist objection

The leading critic of methodology, since his influential article in 1983, is McCloskey. His claim, in short, is that any 'Methodology' must be based on the assumption that the 'Methodologist' has privileged access to knowledge, for without this the 'Methodologist' would not be in a position to offer economists advice on how to undertake their work.[1] Such a God's eye position, McCloskey points out, is simply not available. His conclusion is that those who study economic arguments (we can hardly call them methodologists!)

---

[1] McCloskey reinforces this with many supporting arguments. These include the following. (1) Cartesian doubt is inefficient, for it is not necessary to check everything. (2) People might have found something interesting to say about truth, but they have not. (3) The rhetoric of science has produced many good studies of episodes in science, but methodology has produced very few. (4) Prediction in economics is impossible, otherwise economists would be rich. (5) Anyone who discovered a formula for scientific success would become a scientific millionaire, which (given the absence of such scientific millionaires) implies that such formulae have not been found.

The last two arguments are versions of what McCloskey calls 'The American Question'.

It [a serious prediction] must answer again the American Question: If you're so smart why aren't you rich? At the margin (because that is where economics works) and on average (because some people are lucky) the industry of making economic predictions, which includes universities, earns only normal returns. (McCloskey, 1983, p. 488).

This point is discussed on page 110 below.

should therefore abandon 'Methodology' in favour of rhetoric – in favour of analysing the means economists actually use to persuade one another. The purpose of analysing rhetoric is not to appraise, but to help economists understand one another better – to improve the 'conversation' amongst economists.

In many expositions of his argument, McCloskey presents it as directed against what he chooses to call 'modernism', a perspective based on the notion 'that all sure knowledge is modelled on the early 20th century's understanding of certain pieces of 19th century physics' (McCloskey, 1983, p. 484). Modernism constitutes the 'official rhetoric' of economics – it describes what economists *claim* they are doing (though in practice they do not conform to its precepts. McCloskey characterizes (caricatures?) modernism in terms of eleven precepts.

(1) Prediction (and control) is the goal of science. (2) Only the observable implications (or predictions) matter to its truth. (3) Observability entails objective, reproducible experiments. (4) If (and only if) an experimental implication of a theory proves false is the theory proved false. (5) Objectivity is to be treasured; subjective 'observation' (introspection) is not scientific knowledge. (6) Kelvin's Dictum: 'When you cannot express it in numbers, your knowledge is of a meagre and unsatisfactory kind.' (7) Introspection, metaphysical belief, aesthetics, and the like may well figure in the discovery of an hypothesis but cannot figure in its justification. (8) It is the business of methodology to demarcate scientific reasoning from non-scientific, positive from normative. (9) A scientific explanation brings an event under a covering law. (10) Scientists, for instance economic scientists, have nothing to say as scientists about values, whether of morality or art. (11) Hume's Fork: 'When we run over libraries, persuaded of these principles, what havoc must we make? If we take in our hand any volume – of divinity or school metaphysics, for instance – let us ask, *Does it contain any abstract reasoning concerning quantity or number?* No. *Does it contain any experimental reasoning concerning matter of fact and existence?* No. Commit it then to the flames, for it can contain nothing but sophistry and illusion.' (McCloskey, 1983, pp. 484–5)

His argument is, somewhat controversially(?), that 'a large majority of economists' believes all eleven propositions, whereas 'few' philosophers believe even half of them, with a 'substantial, respectable and growing' minority of philosophers believing none of them.

The main feature of modernism, McCloskey claims, is the search for *certain* knowledge.

> Modernism gleams diamond-hard from many facets, and the word can be fully defined only in use. But in a preliminary way it can be said to be, as the literary critic Wayne Booth has put it, the notion that we know only what we cannot doubt and cannot know what we can merely assent to. ... Philosophically speaking, modernism is the program of Descartes, regnant in philosophy since the seventeenth century, to build knowledge on a foundation of radical doubt. (McCloskey, 1986, p. 5)

Using arguments taken from pragmatist philosophy, rhetoric, literary criticism and sociology of scientific knowledge McCloskey argues that there can be no such thing as absolutely certain knowledge – there are no secure 'foundations' for knowledge – which means that the modernist project collapses. He draws the conclusion that as there is no knowledge that is free from doubt, it follows that 'any method is arrogant and presumptuous' (McCloskey, 1983, p. 490).

> Einstein remarked that 'whoever undertakes to set himself up as a judge in the field of Truth and Knowledge is shipwrecked by the laughter of the gods'. ... Any methodology that is lawmaking and limiting will have this risible effect. (McCloskey, 1986, p. 20)

Economists, McCloskey claims, cling to modernism in the false belief that its precepts are followed in other sciences. Fortunately, however, they ignore them in practice, because otherwise economic inquiry would be impossible.

Whilst McCloskey's arguments undoubtedly fall within the post-modernist camp, however, they fail to capture the radical nature of the post-modernist critique of methodology. To see this we need to broaden the definition of modernism to include the following (based on Klamer, 1987; and Dow, 1992):

1. A break with the past involving: (a) the search for universal theories; (b) a commitment to the idea of progress, with each generation using all that is useful from the past;
2. Formalism, with a preference for axiomatic, reductionist, dualist reasoning and the use of mathematics;

3. Compartmentalization (for example, between positive and normative, and between disciplines) and a turning inwards involving, amongst other things, the use of jargon and self-referential discourse.

This alternative definition, though compatible with McCloskey's, relates modernism more clearly to developments in art, including music and architecture. Its three elements can be related by arguing that modernism is centred on the metaphor of the machine. This metaphor gives rise to the three essential characteristics of modernism: foundationalism (the notion that it is possible to find secure, certain, foundations on which knowledge can be based); objectivism (seeing the object of study as separate from the observer); and control (as a machine is controlled).[2]

Post-modernism, as its name implies, involves a reaction against modernism. Post-modernism recognizes the impossibility of achieving certain knowledge and involves a movement away from unifying theories towards a more pluralist approach, with different theories and methods being seen as appropriate for different problems. Wendt (1990, pp. 53–4), for example, characterizes post-modernism as an anti-modernist program calling for discourse studies, which is characterized by, amongst other features: 'multiple knowledges or discourses, with incommensurability and persistent or irreducible differences among them'; 'the discursive production of subjects, which decenters the individual'; irrationality, contradiction, the arbitrary, play and surprise; knowledge as unstable and ever changing; the unmeasurable and guesswork, rejecting content and system; and deconstructing modernism and modernist discourse.

The post-modernist critique of economic methodology, therefore, is part of a much wider critique of knowledge in general. It is thus much more radical than either the practical or the historical critiques of methodology outlined above, drawing on these as well as non philosophical arguments concerning the nature of knowledge. To answer the post-modernist critique of methodology it is necessary to consider these philosophical arguments in more detail, as is done in Chapter 3. Before then, however, there are some preliminary responses that need to be made: that methodology is (for better or worse) unavoidable; that methodology does matter; and that anti-

---

[2] See Wendt (1990), p. 49.

methodology is conservative in the sense of defending the status quo.

2.2   METHODOLOGY IS UNAVOIDABLE

Objecting to methodology on any of these grounds implies that methodology is avoidable – that economists could, if they chose, get on with doing economics unhampered by methodology. But this is unrealistic. One can say of methodology what Blaug said of the history of economic thought.

> The history of economic thought is irrepressible. It would survive even if it were banned: like the writing of books banned in the society described by Ray Bradbury in Fahrenheit 451, it would be carried on in secret underground organizations. Many economists denigrate the history of economics but, in fact, they have deluded ideas about the history of their own subject. After all whenever anyone has a new idea in economics, whenever anyone hankers to start a new movement or school of thought, what is the first thing he or she does? Why, it is to rummage the attic of past ideas to establish an appropriate pedigree for the new departure. (Blaug, 1991, p. x)

There are several points here. The first is that, like it or not, there will always be economists who wish to engage in explicit discussion of methodology. Robbins, Friedman, Koopmans, Samuelson, Lipsey and Hendry – eminent economists who, in Fisher's words, have proved their ability to solve a few knotty economic problems themselves – have all chosen to write on methodology, presumably because they thought there were important things that needed to be said. Amongst economists wishing to make the case for abandoning orthodoxy, the practice of not only seeking to establish a pedigree for the new departure, but also seeking to argue that it involves a methodological break with the past, is almost universal. It is hard to imagine Austrian economics, Institutionalist economics, Marxist economics, or post-Keynesian economics shorn of any statements about methodology. The challenge to orthodox methodology is an integral part of all such movements.

But the irresistibility of methodology extends beyond this. Even those who actively denigrate methodology make methodological statements. Hahn's 'Reflections' provides a good example. Within his half-page article we find the following claims.

[1] Indeed, the questioning of almost everything, for instance the rationality postulate, is not a sign of crisis but of vigorous endeavour.

[2] Of course all theories contain predictions, but testing these has not yet been a conspicuous success. I do not find that depressing.

[3] If I were not confined to one page I would go on to sing the praises of 'understanding'.

[4] You put your faith in selection: if it [the use of mathematics in economics] turns out to be as futile as some believe then its use will wither, if not it will continue to grow. (Hahn, 1992a)

These claims are all methodological. They have all been discussed in the methodology literature. Though Hahn appears to consider them obvious, none of them is uncontroversial. Each one of them raises philosophical issues.

A major reason why economists who express such disdain for methodology nonetheless make methodological pronouncements is a desire to generalize. Economists, and in particular economic theorists, are trained to generalize, so it is inevitable that they make generalizations when they consider what is going on in their own discipline. Generalizations about practices within the discipline are, almost by definition, methodological statements. The only way they could be avoided would be if economists were *completely* unreflective about what they were doing. This is clearly impossible. For a start, teaching would be severely handicapped if economists were unable to offer students advice on how economic inquiries might be conducted.[3]

Even if economists were able to refrain from explicit discussion of methodology, however, they have, of necessity, to make methodological judgements in the course of their work. If economists are to refrain from methodology, it follows that such implicit methodology must, along with any explicit methodological statements that economists 'inadvertently' or 'misguidedly' make, remain unanalysed. The dangers of this are obvious – they are just as great as the dangers of refusing to analyse assumptions made in

---

[3] Even the advice, 'To solve a problem, write down a suitable model, collect data and then estimate or test the model using best-practice econometric techniques' involves making a methodological statement, and is ruled out by Hahn's advice.

economic theories.[4] But if we were to accept that economists should
abstain from methodology, where should we draw the line between
assertions that are methodological (and to be ignored) and those that
are not (and which merit discussion)? There is no satisfactory way to
draw such a line. The argument has to be a pragmatic one – that
economists believe that certain types of discussion have led, and will
lead, nowhere.

To counter this, it is necessary to show that methodology does, in
practice, make a significant difference to the way economists
undertake their work, and that explicit methodological analysis
might change this for the better. To show this, we consider two
examples: recent developments in macroeconomics and industrial
economics. These examples are chosen for two reasons. The first is
that their centrality and relevance to contemporary economics are
indisputable. The second is that they are cases where the path taken
by economists has followed from a clearly-defined methodological
choice. In discussing all three examples the emphasis is on problems
that economists' methodological choices have caused. This emphasis
arises because critics of methodology demand that methodology be
able to improve the way in which economics is undertaken. It is
crucial, therefore, to choose cases where methodological choices may
have had adverse consequences, for it is by mitigating these that
methodological analysis might have had a beneficial impact.

---

[4] In a discussion of the dangerous distance between general equilibrium theory and the
real world, Morishima cites the example of Japanese mathematics in the Tokugawa
period as a cautionary tale.

> though it had attained a high level of sophistication, [Japanese mathematics] came
> to a wretched end due to its total absence of interaction with natural science. It
> turned into a technique for the setting of puzzles, and the *wasan* [mathematics]
> scholars were reduced to being the playmates of culture-loving samurai and
> members of the newly risen merchant class, just like the masters of the tea
> ceremony, of flower arrangement and of the *haiku*. At the same time, the
> mathematics itself regressed. The following words by John von Neumann can be
> read as a warning against decadence of this kind: 'At a great distance from its
> empirical source, or after much "abstract" inbreeding, a mathematical subject is in
> danger of degeneration' (Morishima, 1991, p. 70).

Though he does not use these words, Morishima argues that general equilibrium
theory needs to learn methodological lessons if it is not to degenerate.

2.3   METHODOLOGY MATTERS

Macroeconomics

Attitudes towards macroeconomic theory and policy have undergone a remarkable transformation since the mid 1970s. The main feature of this was the demise of Keynesianism, weakened by the monetarist attack of Friedman and his followers in the 1960s and 1970s and by the emerging problem of stagflation with which Keynesian economics was ill-equipped to deal. The critique of Keynesian economics was taken a stage further with the new classical macroeconomics, the establishment of the natural rate hypothesis and the absence of any permanent trade-off between inflation and unemployment, and the Lucas critique of macroeconomic policy making. The result has been a major change in macroeconomic thinking. Even with the revival of Keynesian economics since the mid 1980s, many of these changes have not been reversed.

The practical consequences of these changes are undeniable. But why did they come about? One possible answer is that the new theories fitted the empirical evidence better than did the Keynesian theories that went before. This was certainly true of the monetarism articulated by Friedman. Friedman's monetarism was, from the first, buttressed by extensive empirical evidence on money and prices, and in the 1970s it was able to provide an explanation, in a way Keynesian economics could not, of why capitalist economies were experiencing the problems they were, and of what governments should do about them. To a certain extent this was also true of the transformation in macroeconomics that followed the introduction of rational expectations in the mid 1970s. Theories based on rational expectations could explain anomalous empirical evidence. Dornbusch's (1976) model, for example, explained the apparent tendency of floating exchange rates, in a world of increasingly mobile capital, to overshoot their equilibrium values. The natural rate hypothesis, introduced by Friedman in 1967, but which really took off only when combined with the assumption of rational expectations, explained why the Phillips curve appeared to be unusable in designing macroeconomic policy.

There were, however, other ways in which economists could have read the available empirical evidence during this period. The variability of unemployment could, under the new macroeconomics, be accounted for only by assuming that the natural rate had changed. It would have been possible to read it as evidence against the natural rate hypothesis. The persistence of high unemployment in Europe during the 1980s could have been seen as undermining the assumptions of competitive markets and optimizing behaviour by participants in the labour market. The persistence of a business cycle could have been seen as undermining the notion that fluctuations in output were caused by unanticipated monetary shocks. Had economists wished to read the empirical record in a different way they could easily have done so: it would have been entirely plausible to argue that the new classical theories were decisively refuted by the macroeconomic experience of the 1970s and 1980s. Yet this did not happen.

The reason why this did not happen is that the standards by which economists judged macroeconomic theories underwent a profound transformation. Lucas and, later, most of the profession, accepted the assumption of individual rationality. Markets must clear, Lucas argued, because informed, rational agents would otherwise be turning down opportunities for profitable exchange. Expectations must be given by the mathematical expectation of the relevant variable, conditional on the information available to the agent, because no other assumption was compatible with the assumption of rationality: if expectations were not rational in this sense, agents would have an incentive to modify the mechanism whereby they formed their expectations. This assumption of complete rationality, and the implied need to disbelieve models in which key parameters had no foundation in optimizing behaviour, represents a clear methodological decision. As such it needs to be examined.

Economists often speak as though modern macroeconomic models, in which everything is grounded on optimizing behaviour, are completely rigorous. The implication is that they are thus inherently superior to models in which 'arbitrary' assumptions are made. Such beliefs are mistaken, for several reasons.

1. All macroeconomic models are simplifications in which many aspects of reality are ignored. There is no reason why, even if agents are optimizing in the 'true' model, their behaviour is necessarily described better by optimization in a simplified

model than by some other assumption (see McCallum, 1986). For example, problems of adverse selection may result in an equilibrium in which agents are rationed, and which, in some respects, is closer to what one might observe in a fix-price model than to what a simple market-clearing model would suggest.

2. Many modern macroeconomic models are representative agent models. This means that heterogeneity of agents is completely ruled out. Enough is known about aggregation for it to be certain that the conditions necessary for valid aggregation are, in practice, certain *not* to be met. There is therefore no reason to believe that aggregate behaviour in a world of heterogeneous agents will correspond to that of a representative agent.

3. There is much evidence to suggest that agents are not always rational. There is no logical reason why alternative behavioural assumptions should not be explored.

It may be that modern macroeconomic models come closer to being self-contained, consistent axiomatic systems than do models where the assumption of individual optimization is not followed so rigidly. But this is not the only way rigour can be defined.

Had macroeconomists made different methodological choices – and there are clearly other choices for which a strong case could have been made – the subject would have developed very differently. Methodology could, therefore, have made a difference. Economists might have been led to different ways of conceptualizing market behaviour, and to seeing the world very differently, perhaps with immense implications for policy making.

Industrial economics

Similar remarks can be made concerning recent developments in industrial economics. One of the main features of the literature on industrial economics in the past two decades has been the transformation of the subject by game theory. This transformation has been so radical as to cause Hahn to dub the theory that went before 'stone age' theory (Hahn, 1992a). We now have explanations of how numerous aspects of industrial organization can be explained in terms of optimizing behaviour. As with macroeconomics, however, these developments are the result of a methodological choice the rationale for which is open to question.

The nature of this choice has been clearly stated by Franklin Fisher, who reached the conclusion that,

> There is a strong tendency for even the best practitioners to concentrate on the analytically interesting questions rather than on the ones that really matter for the study of real-life industries. (Fisher, 1989, p. 123)

In this passage, 'analytically interesting questions' are defined in relation to the analytical (usually mathematical) techniques employed. The questions that 'really matter', Fisher contends, concern the circumstances (for example, degree of product differentiation, number of firms, ease of communication) under which oligopolists will achieve the co-operative, joint-profit-maximizing equilibrium. This would be what he terms a 'generalizing theory', a theory that 'proceeds from wide assumptions to inevitable consequences', or that tells us what must happen given background circumstances (Fisher, 1989, p. 117). The problem is that such general results are typically not available, for a characteristic of game theory, especially with repeated games, is a multiplicity of solutions. In general, almost anything can happen. He sums up the situation in the following words.

> A great many outcomes are known to be possible. The context in which the theory is set is important, with outcomes depending on what variables the oligopolists use and how they form conjectures about each other. A leading class of cases concerns the joint-maximization solution and when it will or will not be achieved. The answer to the latter question is also known to be very dependent on the context and experience of the oligopolists. (Fisher, 1989, p. 117)

The very same words, Fisher points out, could have been used to summarize the state of industrial economics in the early 1950s, long before the advent of game theory.

Fisher argues that this situation has arisen not by accident, but because industrial economists have pursued certain very specific strategies. Firstly, rather than develop 'generalizing theories' – theories that tell us what *must* happen, theorists have concentrated on what he calls 'exemplifying theory' – simple models, stripped down to the bare essentials in order to illustrate specific theoretical points. Exemplifying theory cannot tell us what must happen, merely what *might* happen. Secondly, mathematical considerations have also led to frequent analysis of normal-form games (where the theorist works with a matrix linking strategies directly to payoffs) rather than to extensive form games (specifying the entire decision-tree) and to the analysis of finite-horizon repeated games.

The reason for both these developments is the requirements of the mathematics. Models are stripped down in order to make the model mathematically tractable. The result, however, has been that economists have been led away from away from what Fisher sees as the fundamental issues: the relationship between background circumstances and outcomes in infinitely-repeated games.

Exemplifying theory is not useless. It can be useful in several ways:

1. As a source of counter-examples.
2. As a source of insights into mechanisms operating.
3. As a source of examples from which to generalize.

Fisher argues that because of the nature of the exemplifying theories that have been constructed, exemplifying theory has not provided a useful basis for the subsequent development of generalizing theory, and that it is unlikely to do so in future. His conclusion is, therefore, that 'one can reasonably question whether theorists are working on a useful research agenda' (Fisher, 1991, p. 209).

The point of citing Fisher here is not to argue that he is right (though his argument is very persuasive), but because he makes the point that, whether it is right or wrong, the evolution of industrial economics over the past two decades has been the result of a specific methodological choice that is open to question. It may be that economic theorists have made this choice with great wisdom, and that other paths would have been inferior, but other paths did exist and could legitimately have been chosen. For example, Bresnahan, in commenting on Fisher (1991), admits that certain types of valuable work are no longer undertaken.

> There were once books about an industry or about the same business practice in several industries by authors who knew price theory – that is all they needed; they didn't need to know any game theory. When they didn't understand something, they said, 'Yes, I don't understand this' and went on. This kind of book has largely disappeared. We see it from journalist. We see it from engineers. We see it from economists who disguise it as policy analysis –

but we don't see it as part of economic science any more, except in regulatory economics. Fisher is absolutely right. More of that kind of work, alongside systematic statistical evidence, would be very valuable. (Bresnahan, 1991, p. 227)

In other words, methodological choices have been made.[5] Had economists been more aware of these choices and their implications, it is arguable that the evolution of the subject might have been different.

2.4   ANTI-METHODOLOGY IS CONSERVATIVE

Economics, since its origins in the seventeenth century, has been concerned with understanding the world, and with the provision of advice to policy makers. Economists have posed and attempted to solve abstract problems, but it was always believed that these had some bearing on more practical concerns. During the last 50 years or so, however, the discipline has been transformed by the process Debreu (1991) has termed the 'mathematization' of economic theory. The crucial feature of this process has not been simply the use of mathematics, but the way standards have changed. As McCloskey (1991) has put it, economists have adopted the values of the math department. Perhaps the most striking illustration of this is provided in Debreu's presidential address where he brushes aside the criticisms of the subject made by Leontief and others with the remark that economics cannot be an empirical discipline, which means that the only criterion we have left is mathematical rigour.

At the centre of this process of 'mathematization' lies general equilibrium analysis, defined as the project which involves finding, subject to certain generally agreed constraints, sets of conditions under which it is possible to prove, with the appropriate degree of rigour, propositions such that equilibrium exists, is unique or is stable.[6] The models constructed in general equilibrium analysis

---

[5] Perhaps the work to which Bresnahan refers is too difficult for economists brought up with current methods of graduate training. Perhaps the reason for the neglect of such work is that it promises less rapid career advancement. In either case, it can be argued that an implicit methodological choice has been made.

[6] It is arguable that game theory has now displaced general equilibrium analysis from this role, but the present argument still stands.

(which are only a subset of general equilibrium models: see Blaug, 1992, Chapter 8) are acknowledgedly descriptive of no conceivable real-world economy. The intellectual values underlying general equilibrium analysis have, since the 1950s, gradually spread through the profession.

General equilibrium theory has, naturally, been strongly criticized. It has been criticized as being empirically empty (forbidding no state of the world, and yielding no predictions), for being based on unrealistic assumptions (perfect competition, individual rationality, complete markets, the absence of transactions costs), for being inconsistent with obvious facts about the world (the existence of money). To a limited extent these criticisms have been met by extending the theory (notably to deal with incomplete markets, certain forms of imperfect competition and limited increasing returns to scale), but there has remained the need to defend the theory against both heterodox and less-heterodox critics. Debreu's defence may appeal to mathematicians, but for most economists it is not a viable option. How then, could, general equilibrium analysis, and the 'mathematization' of economic theory be defended?

In the 1950s a powerful defence of neoclassical economic theory came from Fritz Machlup (1955), who argued that though much economic theory was not directly testable, it was indirectly testable. Economic theories should be viewed as part of a hypothetico-deductive system which generated testable propositions. When these derived propositions were tested, the propositions from which they were derived could be regarded as indirectly tested. This defence of neoclassical economic theory, however, had the attraction of appearing to be consistent with prevailing views in the philosophy of science, which in turn derived from logical positivism.[7] With the collapse of the 'received view' of the philosophy of science (see, for example, Suppe, 1977), however, such a defence of neoclassical economics lost much of its apparent philosophical respectability. Out of the proliferation of approaches to the philosophy of science that developed in the 1960s and 1970s, Lakatos's methodology of

---

[7] The relevance of indirect testing to profit maximization, however, is doubtful, for profit maximization is arguably both testable and inconsistent with much evidence. For the logical empiricists, arguments about indirect testing were used to defend the use of unobservable entities and untestable propositions. See Hausman (1992), pp. 158–62.

scientific research programmes proved attractive to economists. In a brilliant application of Lakatos's methodology, Weintraub (1985) argued that general equilibrium analysis could be defended as lying in the hard core of a empirically progressive research programme.

This situation, however, did not last long, Weintraub's position being criticized on several fronts. One criticism is to dispute the claim that the neo-Walrasian research programme is empirically progressive – that it leads to the prediction of novel facts that are subsequently corroborated. Weintraub (1988) made a bold attempt to argue that it was, but it was hardly convincing. Too much general equilibrium analysis deals with models that could not conceivably depict reality and are too general to generate any unambiguous predictions relating potentially measurable variables. It is hard to defend against the charge that it has no empirical content.[8]

Faced with this inability to defend abstract economic theory against the charge of empirical emptiness, post-modernism provides a way out. If there are no 'outside' standards that can be brought to bear (for no absolute standards are available) ideas have to be judged from within, by the community of those involved in general equilibrium analysis. Provided that such a community exists, objections can be dismissed as 'Methodological' and hence misconceived. The values of this community are decisive, and cannot be challenged.[9] The conservatism of such a view is emphasized by noting that it can be used to defend astrology or any other body of beliefs that is held by an identifiable community.

To say this is not to say that post-modernism inevitably supports the status quo. Far from it. Many supporters of a post-modern perspective are very critical of orthodoxy. Rather it is that post-modernism undermines certain types of criticism (notably criticism

---

8   Similar charges have been made against game theory (see p. 19).

9   Though he denies it (Weintraub, 1992), this is an interpretation that can be placed on Weintraub (1989 and 1991). See Backhouse (1992d). If we accept McCloskey's Chicago-style assumption that the economy of the intellect is running fine (see p. 32), this provides an even stronger defence of the status quo.

based on the notion that empirical evidence needs to be brought to bear, as directly as possible, on economic theories) as illegitimate. Given the vulnerability of orthodox economics to this type of criticism, this is particularly significant.

3. Postmodernism and methodology, I: Exposition

3.1 RORTY'S CRITIQUE OF EPISTEMOLOGY

The ideas used by post-modern critics of economic methodology have been taken from many sources. Though many of his ideas are not original (he acknowledges substantial debts to Wittgenstein, Heidegger and Dewey), one of the most important sources is Richard Rorty's *Philosophy and the Mirror of Nature* (1980). In this book and elsewhere Rorty provides a critique of epistemology which argues, not simply that specific theories about the nature of knowledge were wrong, but that the whole project of seeking to provide a theory of knowledge in general (and which can be used to pass judgement on specific claims to knowledge) is misconceived. [1]

Rorty's starting point is the argument that it is philosophy's claim to have access to the nature of knowledge in general – which rests on a particular notion of the mind and of mental processes – that underlies its claim to be able to pass judgement on the claims to knowledge made in other disciplines – whether in science, morality, art or religion.

> Philosophy can be foundational in respect to the rest of culture because culture is the assemblage of claims to knowledge, and philosophy adjudicates such claims. It can do so because it understands the foundations of knowledge, and it finds these foundations in a study of man-as-knower, of the 'mental processes' or the 'activity of representation' which make knowledge possible. (Rorty, 1980, p. 3)

---

[1] It should be noted that Rorty should probably not be classified as post-modern, for he does not take his ideas as far as others do. Though some philosophers (for example, Hacking, 1983) would not go so far, it is possible to see Rorty as a realist (see Devitt, 1991).

His aim is to show that such claims are unjustified.

> The aim of this book is to undermine the reader's confidence in 'the mind' as something about which one should have a 'philosophical' view, in 'knowledge' as something about which there ought to be a 'theory' and which has 'foundations', and in 'philosophy' as it has been conceived since Kant. (Rorty, 1980, p. 7)

Rorty argues that this position rests, crucially, on the metaphor of the mind as a mirror, which reflects nature, sometimes accurately, sometimes inaccurately.

> The picture which holds traditional philosophy captive is that of the mind as a great mirror, containing various representations – some accurate, some not – and capable of being studied by pure, nonempirical methods. (Rorty, 1980, p. 12)

Without such a metaphor, he continues, 'the notion of knowledge as accuracy of representation would not have suggested itself' (*ibid.*).

The flaw in this line of argument is, Rorty claims, that it rests on the notion of 'privileged access' – the notion that somehow the philosopher has some source of knowledge which is not subject to the problems that beset those whose quest for knowledge he is investigating – for no individual has any privileged, absolute source of knowledge outside itself. It is, he argues, meaningless to speak of knowledge as involving the accurate representation of nature because that presumes we know what nature is 'really' like – that we have access to a privileged source of knowledge. Even the concept of the mind as a distinct entity is undermined by the absence of any privileged access to knowledge for, Rorty argues, 'the purportedly metaphysical "problem of consciousness" is no more and no less than the epistemological "problem of privileged access" ' (Rorty, 1980, p. 69). We must, therefore, discard the notion of 'the mind as the Mirror of Nature' (Rorty, 1980, p. 170) and along with it the notion that it is useful to search for criteria for appraising the truth of claims to knowledge.

Rorty proposes that we replace the conception of knowledge as accurate representation – involving a confrontation between the mind and nature – with a view of knowledge as 'a matter of conversation and of social practice' (Rorty, 1980, p. 171). This involves abandoning the 'desire to find "foundations" to which one might cling, frameworks beyond which one must not stray, objects which impose themselves, representations which cannot be gainsaid' (Rorty, 1980, p. 315). To search for such a 'permanent neutral framework whose "structure" philosophy can display' is, Rorty argues, to accept the indefensible notion that the objects to be confronted by the mind, or the rules which constrain inquiry, are common to all discourse, or at least to every discourse on a given topic' (Rorty, 1980, pp. 315-6). In contrast, to view knowledge as the product arising out of a conversation is to accept its dependence on the rules and assumptions that govern that particular conversation. The justification of beliefs (and hence knowledge, if we view knowledge as justified beliefs) becomes a social phenomenon (Rorty, 1980, p. 9). The question of 'truth' becomes uninteresting.

> A pragmatist theory says that truth is not the sort of thing one should expect to have a philosophically interesting theory about. (Rorty, 1982/1987, p. 26)

The only constraints on inquiry are conversational ones. The task of philosophy becomes that of keeping the conversation going, not that of finding objective truth: conversation is 'the ultimate context within which knowledge is to be understood' (Rorty, 1980, pp. 377, 389). The role of the philosopher is thus that of the therapist, not the judge.[2]

3.2   RHETORIC AND METHODOLOGY

Explicit and implicit rhetoric

In the opening words of his article in the *Journal of Economic Literature*, McCloskey challenged economists to face up to the

---

[2] Rorty's pragmatist position has an important implication for the nature of philosophy, namely that one has to abandon the idea that there are certain perennial problems that constitute the 'central questions' in philosophy. To assume that there were such central questions, to which all 'great philosophers' must be seen as having offered answers, is to accept the notion that 'human activity ... takes place within a framework which can be isolated prior to the conclusion of inquiry' (Rorty, 1980, p. 8) – in other words, to assume privileged access to knowledge. Accepting this claim has enormous implications for the history of philosophy. The relevance of this for the history of economic thought is explored in Backhouse (1992b).

inconsistency between their methodological pronouncements and their actual practice.

> Economists do not follow the laws of enquiry their methodologies lay down. A good thing too. If they did they would stand silent on human capital, the law of demand, random walks down Wall Street, the elasticity of demand for gasoline, and most other matters about which they commonly speak. . . . Economists in fact argue on wider grounds, and should. Their genuine, workaday rhetoric, the way they argue inside their heads or their seminar rooms, diverges from the official rhetoric. (McCloskey, 1983, p. 482)

The 'official' rhetoric of economics, more appropriately (and less emotively) called its *explicit* rhetoric,[3] McCloskey argued, was positivist or modernist: 'an amalgam of logical positivism, behaviourism, operationalism, and the hypothetico-deductive model of science' (McCloskey, 1983, p. 484). Citing Wayne Booth, he argues that it is based on the notion that 'we know only what we cannot doubt, and cannot know what we can merely assent to' (*ibid.*; McCloskey, 1986, p. 5). According to this explicit methodology, scientific reasoning involved observable, objective, quantitative data produced by reproducible experiments. Other forms of argument are dismissed.

Contrasted with this is the methodology implicit in the arguments economists actually use. Here we find something very different, for economists seek to persuade each other using many arguments that have no place in their explicit methodology. To understand the principles that underlie economic inquiry as it is actually undertaken, therefore, we must look not at economists' explicit methodological pronouncements, but at how they actually argue – how they seek to persuade each other. In other words, to understand the nature of economics we must change our perspective and view economists as persuaders – we must engage in the analysis of rhetoric, not methodology. The term 'the rhetoric of economics' may thus refer either to the rhetorical practices of economists, or to the analysis of those practices.

---

[3] Although McCloskey proposes the terms 'explicit' and 'implicit' rhetoric as alternatives to 'official' and 'unofficial', he seems to prefer the latter.

Economists as persuaders

McCloskey stated that the purposes of his book *The Rhetoric of Economics* were to show that economists used rhetoric, and to study the nature of that rhetoric.

> The question is whether the scholar . . . speaks rhetorically. Does he try to persuade? It would seem so. . . . It seems on the face of it a reasonable hypothesis that economists are like other people in being talkers, who desire listeners when they go to the library or the laboratory as much as when they go to the office or the polls. The purpose here is to see if this is true, and to see if it is useful: to study the rhetoric of economic scholarship. (1986, p. xviii)

He makes it clear that rhetoric is not used in its pejorative sense (as in 'mere rhetoric') but deals with all of the means that people use to persuade each other. In view of its centrality, it is worth quoting several of the ways in which he defines rhetoric:

1. 'the art of probing what men believe they ought to believe, rather than proving what is true according to abstract methods' (Booth, 1974, p. xiii; quoted by McCloskey, 1983, p. 482, and 1986, p. 29);
2. 'the art of discovering good reasons, finding what really warrants assent, because any reasonable person ought to be persuaded' (Booth, 1974, p. xiv; quoted by McCloskey, 1983, p. 482, and 1986, p. 29);
3. 'careful weighing of more-or-less good reasons to arrive at more-or-less probable or plausible conclusions – none too secure but better than would be arrived at by chance or unthinking impulse' (Booth, 1974, p. 59; quoted by McCloskey, 1983, pp. 482–3, and 1986, p. 29);
4. the 'art of discovering warrantable beliefs and improving those beliefs in shared discourse' (Booth, 1974, p. xiii; quoted by McCloskey, 1983, p. 483, and 1986, p. 29), its purpose being not 'to talk someone else into a preconceived view; rather it must be to engage in mutual inquiry' (Booth, 1974, p. 59; quoted by McCloskey, *ibid.*);
5. 'the paying attention to one's audience' (McCloskey, 1986, p. xvii);
6. 'the proportioning of means to desires in speech' (McCloskey, 1986, p. xviii).

When defined in these ways, it is clear that economists do use rhetoric – indeed, how could they not do so? Similarly, it is obvious that economists use figures of speech and literary devices; that, as McCloskey puts it, the economist is 'self-evidently a linguistic actor' (1986, p. 57). Once the question has been posed, for example, it is obvious that economics is metaphorical, and that many of the metaphors used by economists are not simply ornamental. The interesting issue concerns *how* they seek to persuade: the *nature* of the literary and other devices they use, and the way they use them. It is because this is an important question, that economists need to take note of literary criticism.

> The service that literature can do for economics is to offer literary criticism as a model for self-understanding. . . . Chiefly it is concerned with making readers see how poets and novelists accomplish their results. An economic criticism of the sort exercised below is not a way of passing judgement on economics. It is a way of showing how it accomplishes its results. (McCloskey, 1986, p. xix)

McCloskey's brilliant analysis of texts by Samuelson, Becker, Solow, Muth and Fogel provides a taste of the insights that can be achieved using such methods.

Rhetoric and good conversation

If we adopt a rhetorical perspective, McCloskey argues, we start to think of economic discourse in terms of a conversation and this leads us to use a broader range of criteria with which to judge what constitutes good economics.

> What distinguishes good from bad in learned discourse, then, is not the adoption of a particular methodology, but the earnest and intelligent attempt to contribute to a conversation. (McCloskey, 1986, p. 27)

Whether or not a conversation is going well is not something that can be captured with simple methodological rules, but is something that one can recognize 'with ease' in one's own field. Furthermore, overlaps between fields are sufficient for one to be almost as sure about neighbouring fields. He then argues, in a rather opaque passage, that there is a market mechanism which maintains standards.

[E]xamining the overlap is what editors, referees, and members of research panels do. The overlaps of the overlaps, as Polanyi once observed, keep us all honest if some try to be. Q.E.D.: the overlapping conversations provide the standards. It is a market argument. There is no need for philosophical lawmaking or methodological regulation to keep the economy of the intellect running just fine. (McCloskey, 1986, p. 28)

The question of possible market failure is not addressed. He is simply adopting a standard Chicago position: '*Immo, civis Chicagonus sum, subspecies TP* (cf. Reder 1982)' (McCloskey, 1986, p. 9, n. 2). Reder's definition of 'tight prior equilibrium' theory, with which McCloskey here identifies himself, involves a commitment to the notion that the world is Pareto-efficient (or at least approximately so), a view to which many (most?) economists would not subscribe. It is hardly surprising, therefore, that he sees no need to appraise economic theorizing, and hence no need for methodology.[4]

Why should such arguments matter to economists? McCloskey argues that an awareness of the rhetorical nature of economic discourse will improve the conversation amongst economists. Economists would drop the facade of positivist methodology, making it easier to have an open discussion of what they are actually doing: 'If it understood its own way of conversing – its rhetoric – maybe some of its neurotic behaviour would stop, such as compulsive handwashing in statistical procedures' (McCloskey, 1986, p. xix).[5] The methodologist as critic gives way to the rhetorician as therapist.[6]

---

[4] If, on the other hand, we abandon this Chicago position, we find, at least *prima facie* evidence that 'the economy of the intellect' may not be running smoothly. Many economists believe that the structure of incentives in the profession works in a seriously imperfect manner (see, for example, Colander, 1991). In Britain, part of the problem (and it is important to stress that it is only part of the problem) rests with government, the research assessment exercises having a significant distortionary effect on academic research (for a brief account of these exercises, see Backhouse, 1997a).

[5] An approach that is very much in this spirit is Gerrard's analysis of the process of interpreting Keynes's *General Theory* (Gerrard, 1991). Drawing on hermeneutics, and particularly the work of Ricoeur, he points out that texts do not have single correct interpretations. The *General Theory* is, he argues, rich in interpretive content – the sign of a great work. Thus economists should not be concerned that different people interpret Keynes in different ways. Gerrard is thus trying to improve the conversation

3.3   LITERARY CRITICISM AND METHODOLOGY

Fish's critique of literary theory

'Theory', in literary criticism, is concerned with the nature and source of meaning in the interpretation of literary texts: is the text or the reader the source of meaning? Fish's answer is that it is neither of these, meanings being produced by interpretive communities:

> [I]t is interpretive communities, rather than either the text or the reader, that produce meanings .... Interpretive communities are made up of those who share interpretive strategies not for reading but for writing texts, for constituting their properties. (Fish, 1980, p. 14)

The claim that the text cannot be the source of meanings rests on the argument that what the reader sees in a text (*i.e.* the 'units of sense' to which the reader responds) is not 'in the text' but is 'always a function of the interpretive model one brings to bear' on it (Fish, 1980, p. 13). It follows that

> the text as an entity independent of interpretation and (ideally) responsible for its career drops out and is replaced by texts that are consequences of our interpretive activities. There are still formal patterns, but they do not lie innocently in the world; rather they are themselves constituted by an interpretive act. The facts one points to are still there (in a sense that would not be consoling to an objectivist) but only as the consequence of the interpretive (man-made) model that has called them into being. (Fish, 1980, p. 13)

We do not read a text and then interpret it according to some strategy: interpretive strategies determine the shape of the text. On the other hand, if texts are not the source of meanings, neither are

---

amongst interpreters of Keynes by using ideas from literary criticism to disabuse them of the false notion that texts have but a single correct interpretation.

[6] A second reason why the nature of economics discourse should be of concern to economists concerns education. During their education as economists, students learn more than simply a set of facts and techniques – they learn how to use a new language. Analysing this language can, it has been argued, suggest new ways of teaching the subject, improving the conversation between teachers and their students (see Henderson and Dudley-Evans, 1990; Klamer, 1990).

individuals: interpretive strategies are 'community property' which enable and limit the consciousness of individual members of the relevant community. It is wrong to think of individuals as standing apart from the communities to which they belong:

> since the thoughts an individual can think and the mental operations he can perform have their source in some or other interpretive community, he is as much a product of that community . . . as the meanings it enables him to produce. (Fish, 1980, p. 14)

Thus for Fish, neither the text nor the reader exists apart from the interpretive community. Meaning is thus neither subjective (totally dependent on the individual reader) nor objective (originating in the given text).

> An interpretive community is not objective because as a bundle of interests, of particular purposes and goals, its perspective is interested rather than neutral; but by the very same reasoning, the meanings and texts produced by an interpretive community are not subjective because they do not proceed from an isolated individual but from a public and conventional point of view. (Fish, 1980, p. 14)

Stability in interpretations is easily explained without positing stability in the texts: it is a consequence of stability in interpretive communities.

Weintraub's critique of economic 'Methodology'

Weintraub critique of economic methodology draws on Fish's critique of theory in literary criticism. Like McCloskey, Weintraub distinguishes between 'Methodology' (upper-case 'M') – a normative enterprise, and 'methodology' (lower-case 'm'), sometimes referred to as 'methodological discourse' – discussions amongst economists about the way they pursue their discipline. He draws an explicit parallel between 'Methodology' in economics and 'theory' in literary criticism, arguing that some simple substitutions can transform a definition of the latter into a definition of the former.

> By 'theory' we mean a special project in literary criticism: the attempt to govern the interpretation of particular texts by appealing to an account of

interpretation in general. (Knapp and Michaels, 1982, p. 723, quoted in Weintraub, 1989, p. 264)

By 'Methodology' we mean a special project in economics: the attempt to govern appraisal of particular economic theories by appealing to an account of theorizing in general. (Weintraub, 1989, p. 264)[7]

However, where McCloskey argues that replacing concern with 'Methodology' with the study of rhetoric can have beneficial effects, Weintraub's critique is more radical, for he argues that neither 'Methodology' nor 'Rhetoric' can have any implications for economic practice. His argument, in short, is that 'Methodology' is impossible and therefore cannot succeed; and that because it cannot succeed it cannot have consequences. For the same reasons, 'anti-Methodology' (as he prefers to term what McCloskey would call 'Rhetoric') cannot succeed either (Weintraub, 1989, p. 263). The essential point in his argument is that economic arguments should always be appraised from within economics, using economic arguments; never using arguments 'in Methodology' which come from outside economics. Weintraub echoes Rorty's arguments when he states that 'there *is* no position totally apart from the doing of economics which can inform the consideration of the doing of economics' (Weintraub, 1989, p. 272). In support of this, he quotes Fish's view of theory in literary criticism:

Theory cannot guide practice because its rules and procedures are no more than generalizations from practice's history (and from only a small piece of that history), and theory cannot reform practice because, rather than neutralizing interest, it begins and ends in interest and raises the imperatives of interest – of some local, particular, partisan project – to the status of universals. (Fish, 1985, pp. 438–9; quoted in Weintraub, 1989, p. 272)

Before considering these arguments in more detail, it is worth examining the way Weintraub works out his argument and some of the examples he uses. After defining 'Methodology'[8] he provides, in

---

7 Note that although Weintraub states that 'appraisal' is being substituted for 'interpretation', he substitutes 'appraisal' on the first occasion, and 'theorizing' on the second.

8 Given the house-style of the *Scandinavian Journal of Economics*, which is to capitalize the major words in headings, we do not know whether the heading is intended to read 'Methodology' or 'methodology', a major problem with this terminology.

a single paragraph, an account of 'Science' since the time of the Greeks in which the culmination of the history of philosophical inquiry is claimed to be Logical Positivism, according to which science is clearly demarcated from non-science, and in which 'the philosophy of science itself defines the epistemological enterprise, for only science provides us with True Knowledge, or warranted belief' (Weintraub, 1989, p. 265). This programme, he continues, implies two things: if economists think of themselves as 'Truth-seeking', they should think of themselves as scientists; and they should imitate 'in both fact and perception' the activities of science (Weintraub, 1989, p. 265).

Weintraub presents Methodology as the subdiscipline of economics comprising those economists who share the perspective of 'the Philosophy of Science'. In doing this (given his immediately preceding account of the philosophy of science) he defines 'Methodology' in such a way that it is the outgrowth of a foundationalist epistemology. Such a perspective is, he claims, shared by most economists. This has the effect of virtually equating 'Methodology' with Logical Positivism, a position that most philosophers have long since abandoned.

> Most economists, believing that claims about economic knowledge have no less epistemic, or truth, status than claims about physical, and chemical, and biological phenomena, are positivists in the sense that they believe there is a particular framework in which science's knowledge claims may be justified. (Weintraub, 1989, p. 266)[9]

Such foundationalist thinking, which is the basis of 'Methodology', leads to economists' believing that 'the Methodologist's arguments can have an effect on practice, can lead to a better way of doing economics' (*ibid*). In Fish's words,

> [T]hose who believe in the consequences of foundationalist theory are possessed by a hope – let us call it 'theory hope' – the hope that our claims to knowledge can be 'justified on the basis of some objective method of assessing such claims' rather than on the basis of the individual beliefs that have been derived from the accidents of education and experience. (Fish, 1985, p. 439; quoted in Weintraub, 1989, p. 266)

---

[9] It is worth noting that this is a somewhat unusual definition of positivism.

As examples of Methodologists he cites Terence Hutchison, Lawrence Boland and Mark Blaug.

After making this general point about the Positivist nature of most economists' thinking, Weintraub proceeds to examine the way in which 'Methodological' arguments are used in practice. He cites several examples. (1) Post Keynesians (such as Nicholas Kaldor, Paul Davidson and Douglas Vickers) oppose general equilibrium theory on the grounds that certain of the assumptions on which it rests are demonstrably irrelevant. Weintraub's interpretation is that,

> These writers acted as Methodologists because their critical position is developed from a perspective 'outside' economics, in this case from the epistemological theory of probabilistic knowledge. (Weintraub 1989, p. 267)

(2) Marxians who criticize neoclassical economics for its neglect of class, power, exploitation and social relations do so on the basis of categories derived from 'Hegelian historiographic tradition', something 'separate from either Marxian economic analysis or neoclassical analysis' (*ibid*). (3) The Austrian argument about methodological individualism is Methodological. (4) Paul Samuelson appealed to 'Operationalism', taken from the physicist Percy Bridgman. (5) Milton Friedman appealed to his 'methodology of positive economics'. (6) Keynes attacked Tinbergen on grounds that 'since the structures of the world change, time series analysis cannot possibly explain macroeconomic phenomena' (Weintraub, 1989, p. 268). (7) The 'Methodological' argument that 'the world is in disequilibrium, not equilibrium' is used to attack Lucas's view of unemployment.

In an italicized sentence, Weintraub comments that

> All these examples are associated with attempts to criticize existing economics as it is done by real economists, and are thus methodological in nature; but additionally all the particular criticisms are Methodological as they depend on a perspective outside economic analysis to criticize particular work in economics. (*ibid.*)

His argument rests on the assumption that there is a particular discourse community (or collection of related discourse communities) called economics, for it depends on being able to separate out those criticisms of particular economic theories that originate within economics from those that emanate from without.[10]

3.4   SOCIOLOGY OF SCIENTIFIC KNOWLEDGE

Sociology of scientific knowledge starts from the observation that scientific knowledge is inseparable from the beliefs of scientists. These beliefs, in turn, are dependent on the social context in which scientists are operating. The result is a potentially radical perspective from which *scientific knowledge itself* depends on the social setting in which it is developed. Scientific knowledge is seen not as objective, but as context-dependent. The sociology of scientific knowledge, therefore, goes substantially beyond the more traditional sociology of science that, though it used sociological analysis to explain scientists' practices, did not generally question the objectivity of scientific knowledge itself.

Sociology of scientific knowledge comprises a wide range of approaches, but common to all of them is the notion that scientific knowledge is constructed – negotiated within communities of scientists. Much work in the area is empirical, involving close observation of what goes on within scientific communities, whether in performing experiments or in writing scientific papers. Some go so far as to claim that they are merely applying the methods of science to science itself: 'I am an inductivist. ... My suggestion is simply that we transfer the instincts we have acquired in the laboratory to the study of knowledge itself' (Bloor, 1984, p. 83). This results in a perspective that is very different from the traditional or popular view of science. To see this consider two examples: the nature of scientific experiments and scientific facts.

The traditional view of scientific experiments is, very loosely, the following.[11]

1. Scientists disagree over a theory.
2. An experiment is performed to test the theory.

---

[10] C.f. Mäki (1994).

[11] This account, of course, overlooks numerous philosophical issues. It is, however, adequate for the argument that is to be based on it.

3. If the experiment is successful, it either confirms or refutes the theory.
4. Having seen the results of a successful experiment, scientists agree on whether the theory is correct or incorrect.

Experiments produce facts that constitute evidence for or against a theory. It is factual evidence that is the reason for consensus in science.

The sociological perspective described in the preceding paragraphs turns this relationship between facts and agreement upside-down. The problem with the traditional view is that it presumes agreement amongst scientists over what constitutes a valid test of a theory and over what constitutes a correctly-performed experiment. When scientists are agreed on fundamentals (within Kuhnian 'normal science') this will be the case, but when there is disagreement over fundamentals (where it really matters) there will be no agreement over the implications of experimental results. As an example, consider the famous observations made by Eddington in 1918 that allegedly confirmed Einstein's theory of relativity.[12]

Einstein's and Newton's theories both predicted that light rays would be affected by gravity, and that distant stars would appear to be displaced slightly when the sun is almost in front of them – the light rays from them have to pass very close to the sun and are deflected by its gravity. However, whilst the Newtonian theory predicts a deflection of 0.8 seconds of arc,[13] Einstein's theory predicted a deflection of 1.7 seconds. The brightness of the sun, however, means that stars cannot normally be seen when the sun is in front of them, which means observations can be made only during a solar eclipse. This was the reason why teams had to go to Brazil and West Africa, to two locations in the path of the eclipse. The evidence they brought back was read as confirming Einstein's theory. Their evidence could, however, have been interpreted completely differently.

---

[12] This account is taken from Collins and Pinch (1993). Such issues are discussed in more detail in section 11.2 below.

[13] A second of arc is 1/3600 of a degree.

1. In 1918 Einstein's theory of relativity was very poorly understood, in the sense that there was substantial disagreement about what it predicted. Even if his theory were correct, it was not clear that his calculations of the amount by which light would be reflected were correct.
2. The amount by which light was predicted to be deflected by the sun was *very* small. It was made even smaller by the fact that the closest stars that could in practice be observed were not adjacent to the sun but some distance away.
3. Large telescopes could not be moved to the required locations, which meant that ones used were comparatively small, without elaborate mechanisms for tracking the stars as the earth rotated. Because the telescopes were small, long exposures were needed.
4. Photographs taken during the eclipse had to be compared with ones taken when the sun was not present – at night, when temperatures, and hence possibly the focal length of the telescopes were slightly different.
5. The weather was not perfect.

In view of these problems, it is hardly surprising that the three telescopes used in the experiment gave different results. One gave results that suggested light was deflected more than Einstein's theory predicted (between 1.7 and 2.2 seconds), another than it was deflected much less (0.1 to 1.6 seconds), whilst the third was consistent with it (0.9 to 2.3 seconds).

The lesson to be drawn from this is that, though the experiment was immediately interpreted as confirming the theory of relativity, the evidence could legitimately have been interpreted differently. It was, in principle, not possible for the experiment to test simultaneously the theory of relativity, Einstein's use of the theory to predict the amount by which light rays would be deflected by the sun's gravity, and the accuracy of the experimental apparatus. To see the evidence as supporting the theory of relativity, evidence from two of the telescopes had to be disregarded.

The problem here is that the only way conclusively to prove the accuracy of the experimental apparatus is to show that it produces the correct results. But to know whether it produces the correct results, one needs to know what these are – in other words one needs to know the result that the experiment is seeking to establish.

Collins has called this problem 'the experimenter's regress'.[14] Its implication is that, where results are genuinely contested, arguments over the validity of an experiment and arguments over the correctness of a theory cannot be separated. Consensus has to be reached simultaneously over the validity and significance of the experimental evidence and the truth of the scientific theory.

This perspective affects the way we view scientific 'facts'. Scientific facts become what is agreed by the relevant community of scientists. Consensus is the basis for facts, not vice versa. It becomes possible, therefore, to speak of different degrees of facticity. Typically a successful scientific idea goes through a number of stages.[15]

1. A scientist proposes it in a journal article.
2. It is discussed in articles by other scientists.
3. It becomes cited as an established result in journal articles and in review articles.
4. It appears in textbooks.

At each stage the idea becomes closer to being accepted as a fact. In short, scientific ideas do not get incorporated into textbooks because they are facts. Rather, they are facts because they are accepted into textbooks.

3.5 CONCLUSIONS

The theme common to all the critiques of methodology outlined in this chapter is that knowledge is the property of specific communities and that it has to be understood as context-dependent. The absence of any knowledge that is not the property of a specific community is then taken to imply that there can be no objective, absolute knowledge that transcends discourse communities. From this, the conclusion is drawn that inquiries into the nature of knowledge in general are misconceived. Rorty applied such ideas to philosophy, attempting to undermine the idea of epistemology.

---

[14] This is discussed in more detail on page 138 below.

[15] Unsuccessful ideas, which far outnumber successful ones, never make it past the first or second stage.

Literary critics such as Fish have applied them to undermine the idea of 'theory' in literary criticism. Writers in the sociology of scientific knowledge have applied them to science. Postmodernism (the boundaries of which probably defy precise definition) applies them to all knowledge. This has been succinctly summed by Hands.

> In a nutshell, *relativism* [Kuhn, Feyerabend] says that *science* is not privileged, *postepistemology* [Rorty] says that *Philosophy* is not privileged, while *radical postmodernism* [postmodernism] says *nothing* is privileged. (Hands, 1993, p. 155)

Alternatively, Hands continued, these perspectives could be seen as relativism with respect to science, philosophy and 'the broad categories of Western intellectual life'.

This argument that the absence of any privileged source of knowledge undermines the idea of methodology rests on a specific view of what philosophy is. Philosophy, the argument runs, is assumed to offer insights into the nature of knowledge in general, which are then used to pass judgement on knowledge claims in particular fields. The methodologist is someone who takes these privileged, philosophical insights, and tells practitioners in a field how they should conduct their business. Given that philosophy is simply one discourse amongst others, this view is, its critics argue, simply unsustainable.

In the chapters that follow, the term 'postmodern' will be used as a convenient label for arguments of this type, even though some of the writers discussed should, arguably, not be so labelled. This should, however, cause no confusion. Earlier drafts used the term 'constructivism', citing the following definition.

> *Constructivism* The only independent reality is beyond the reach of our knowledge and language. A known world is partly constructed by the imposition of concepts. These concepts differ from (linguistic, social, scientific etc.) group to group, and hence the worlds of groups differ. Each world exists only relative to an imposition of concepts. (Devitt, 1991, p. 235)

Though the use of term has some advantages, it seemed preferable to use the more familiar term, postmodernism.

4. Postmodernism and methodology, II: Criticism

4.1 INTRODUCTION

The postmodern observation that knowledge has to be understood as the property of specific communities and as context-dependent, has led to many insights. Our view of science, it can plausibly be argued, will never be the same again. Within economics, McCloskey's urging those concerned with the nature of economics to study the way in which economists actually persuade one another, has opened up enormous and profitable areas of research. We have learned that there is much to be gained from viewing economics from the perspectives provided by rhetoric, literary criticism, linguistics and sociology. This is beyond dispute.

At the same time, however, there are reasons to think that the attack on methodology has gone too far. To quote Solow,

> I don't see how anything but good can come from studying how trained economists actually go about persuading one another. We will learn something about the strategy and tactics of their arguments. Self-knowledge might help to make the arguments better, or at least honest if they are not so. ... Nevertheless, I have to report a certain discomfort, a vague itch. It feels like my eclecticism warning me that Klamer and McCloskey are in grave danger of Going Too Far. To be specific, I worry that their version of the occupational disease is to drift into a belief that one mode of argument is as good as another. In this instance I side with Orwell's pigs: All arguments are equal, but some are more equal than others. For that reason I mistrust McCloskey's favourite image – borrowed from Rorty – of economics, or science generally, as an ongoing conversation. It seems *too* permissive. (Solow, 1988, pp. 32–3)

This chapter considers the most important of these reasons.[1]

4.2   A 'COMMON SENSE' RESPONSE TO POST-MODERNISM

Post-modernism argues that knowledge has to be understood in relation to specific discourse communities, and that there is nothing to be said about knowledge in general. This perspective shades rapidly into relativism: the doctrine that the real world, and evidence about it, do little to constrain our beliefs. All evidence, it is argued, is dependent on a conceptual framework, which undermines any claim to objectivity or to truth in anything other than a purely local sense. Although it may not be as satisfactory a response as we would like, it is quite coherent to argue that although we cannot refute these claims, they can be ignored. Consider the following argument about scepticism in philosophy.

> How important is it to defeat scepticism? How central is it to the tasks of epistemology? There is an attitude towards epistemological issues that can be expressed thus:
> Although we cannot answer the sceptical arguments, we are unconvinced by them. No one genuinely doubts his beliefs about his surroundings on the grounds that he cannot show that he is not a brain suspended in a vat of nutrients, sustained and manipulated by a brilliant scientist. Indeed, the more convinced we are that the arguments cannot be met head on, the more they look like pointless philosophical games. Consequently, let us leave them behind, and, making the best use we can of our knowledge of the history of science and the psychology of cognition, construct a plausible, scientifically informed, account of how we know as much as (we all agree) we do know.
> This view exploits the fact that our puzzlement by sceptical arguments is apparently 'insulated' from our first order practice of conducting inquiries and forming beliefs. Since they have no impact on this practice, we can ignore these arguments when we search for a philosophical understanding of our success in obtaining knowledge of reality. (Hookway, 1990, p. 130)[2]

---

[1] Other, more practical, reasons are discussed in Chapter 2.

[2] This passage is quoted to illustrate a point. It is not the position Hookway ends up supporting.

The challenge posed by scepticism to epistemology is not quite the same as the challenge to economic methodology posed by post-modernist arguments, but the parallels are sufficiently close that we could respond in a similar way. Whilst it is certainly the case that knowledge is constructed, and that much of our knowledge of economic events is conditioned by what we take for granted as members of particular discourse communities, it is going too far to argue that there is no such thing as empirical evidence. Post-modernist arguments end up treating all knowledge as similar in kind, whereas in practice this is not the case. Economic knowledge comprises statements which differ markedly as regards the certainty with which they are held. In many cases it may, *in practice*, be unproblematic to take the existence of objective empirical evidence for granted. We could then use our knowledge of contemporary economics and the history of economic thought, together with such ideas from philosophy or any other relevant discipline, to explore the nature of economic knowledge and to make such generalizations as we can concerning the way in which economic knowledge progresses. Though the results of such inquiries will always remain, to a greater or lesser extent, conjectural, there is no reason in principle why they should not be used as the basis for methodological prescriptions. Such prescriptions will, inevitably, be only as strong as the arguments on which they are based, but that is no reason why they should not be made and debated.

4.3   DISCOURSE COMMUNITIES AND THE PROBLEM OF REFLEXIVITY

In so far as they intended to be descriptive, the notion that there exist identifiable discourse communities is something to which it is hard to take exception. Clearly, there do exist different communities, sharing particular views and beliefs. Problems arise, however, when the attempt is made to *justify* knowledge claims with reference to such communities.[3]

---

[3] Of course, if one is prepared to make the *assumption* that the process of creating economic knowledge is working well, there is no need to ask such questions, and there is no need for methodology.

The first problem is that of how membership of the relevant discourse community is to be determined.[4] As Munz puts it,

> If knowledge is to be regarded as the prevailing state of mind in a convivial community, as Rorty has it, the real crux of the matter then is the question as to who is included and who is excluded in these communities. (1984, p. 211)

This question is vital because the definition of the community determines knowledge. If we accept Rorty's claim (1980, p. 38) that this is a matter of decision, then we simply regress one stage, for we have to ask what the criteria are. This, it can be argued, is a moral issue as much as a sociological one, for decisions as to what counts and does not count as knowledge cannot be taken in a vacuum. Without such a decision criterion, Rorty's claim to have avoided 'relativism' seems vacuous – given sufficient diversity of beliefs it is, surely, possible to define a discourse community such that knowledge is whatever one wishes it to be.

The answer that critics of methodology would give is that we are not free to define discourse communities as we like. There are, in any academic community, recognizable discourse communities, known to (or knowable by) workers in the relevant areas, and which can, in retrospect, be recognized by intellectual historians. This does not, however, solve the problem. It is not possible to take such communities as 'given', obviously recognizable, for this goes against the premise that there are no uninterpreted givens. If we simply say that 'qualified' people can agree on who these communities comprise, then we are left with the question of who is qualified to make the decision, and so on in an infinite regress. One coherent way out of the problem is to specify that the community must be such that its membership is agreed upon by all its members. This, however, means simply that a self-selected group is deciding what is, for it, knowledge. In some societies[5] this may present no problems, but in the democratic, pluralistic societies in the 1990s this hardly seems an acceptable solution to the problem.

The difficulty is not that defining the relevant communities is difficult, for in many cases this is comparatively straightforward. We could, for example, argue that the list of economists qualified to

---

[4] Rorty's 'conversation of mankind', is caricatured, mercilessly, by Munz (1984, pp. 229–38).

[5] Cambridge at one time? See Munz (1984) pp. 211–2.

judge work in a particular field comprises those who publish in the relevant specialist journals, or we could derive such a list using information on citations. It is rather than such an approach is inappropriate in a normative methodology. The influence of power on knowledge, an issue raised long ago in the context of Kuhn's paradigms, may be a fact of life, but it does not *justify* ideas. Defining truth as what the relevant community chooses to believe is, as was pointed out above, inherently conservative. It also ignores the issue that it should be the consumers, not the producers, who judge the value of an activity (see Hutchison, 1992).

These problems are related to the problem of 'reflexivity'. Take the sociology of scientific knowledge. This argues that scientific knowledge should not be seen as objective, but as context-dependent. But this should also apply to the sociology of scientific knowledge.

> The sociologists doing the SSK are a community of scientists; if what a community of scientists produces is constituted by its social context, then the output of the SSK will also be a product of, and is constituted by, its social context. As Alexander Rosenberg expresses it: 'This sort of sociology pulls itself down by its own boot straps'. (Hands, 1994, pp. 92, quoting Rosenberg, 1985, p. 379)

Though expressed in terms of the sociology of scientific knowledge, such arguments apply to any position that denies the existence of any absolute standards. Pure relativism, understood as the doctrine that there are no absolute standards, is self-refuting and is unsustainable.[6]

4.4   DISCOURSE COMMUNITIES AND METHODOLOGY

The argument that only members of discourse communities are qualified to pass judgement on the those communities' knowledge claims is the major argument used by those economists who argue that methodology is a doomed enterprise. As an example, take

---

[6] For a discussion of this problem, and how authors in the literature on the sociology of scientific knowledge deal with it, see Hands (1994).

Weintraub's interpretation of the debate between Kaldor and Hahn over general equilibrium theory.

> There is no instant rationality, no test we can apply which gives us a precise judgement about the worth of a particular bit of work in economics. . . . Kaldor appeared foolish in his exchange with Hahn about the significance of general equilibrium theory: Hahn knew about the theory, and knew about the community, while Kaldor instead had Methodological knowledge that no theory with certain characteristics was worth considering. . . . Kaldor's revealed preferences to the contrary notwithstanding, there is no shortcut to understanding Economics through Methodology. (Weintraub, 1989, p. 277)

Weintraub is claiming that methodology is a foolish enterprise because it is based on the presumption that methodologists are people who presume to know something special about knowledge, to have access to privileged information which is not accessible to 'ordinary' economists who do not study philosophy. This, however, is a caricature which collapses the moment it is examined.

Consider the following argument (where I have taken the liberty of describing the study of equality and wealth as economics, rather than politics, and those who undertake this activity as economists!)

> There is indeed something to be known about knowledge, just as there is something to be known about equality and wealth. There are many different opinions held by different people and all people interested in knowledge or [economics] must pay attention to these opinions and weigh them and evaluate them. Then there are some people who do not engage much in politics or in science themselves but who prefer to specialize in the question as to what we can know or how we can promote or, for that matter, prevent, social justice. Whether we call these specialists philosophers and [economists] or not does not really matter. The only thing that matters is the acceptance of the fact that there is something to be known about all these things; that it is better to know something about them than not to know anything about them; and finally, that practising scientists as well as ordinary citizens must sooner or later face up to the question as to what is known about knowledge or about strategies for promoting equality. (Munz, 1984, pp. 202–3, with amendments described in the text)

Specialists, including specialists in epistemology or economic methodology are simply those who choose to specialize in these questions. Einstein and Samuelson have reflected on the nature of knowledge, but we do not call them philosophers because they did not choose to specialize on this area.

It may be that methodologists have put forward their arguments, derived from philosophy, with great confidence, and as though they were logically compelling. But so too have many economists. Why should the method of conjecture and refutation not be permissible in methodology as well as in economics?

Having disposed of the argument that methodologists need claim any privileged position, what of the allegation that they seek to impose ideas from another discipline (philosophy)? The first point to make is that the argument rests on a particular definition of inter-disciplinary boundaries, but it is not clear that these are of any significance. Different discourse communities may in practice exist, but there is no reason, *a priori*, why ideas from one community should not be used in another. No economist, for example, is justified in disregarding a mathematician's criticism if she makes a mistake in differentiating a function. More significantly, disciplinary boundaries are constantly changing, with some of the most important scientific research taking place at those boundaries. To quote a leading authority on the organization of science,

> Scientific knowledge now tends to grow particularly vigorously in *interdisciplinary* areas, or to make particularly striking progress when it can be fitted together into a coherent *multidisciplinary*, conceptual scheme. (Ziman, 1994, p. 23)[7]

The second point concerns generalization. In any discipline there is always the question of how far it is appropriate to generalize, but we normally regard this as something that needs to be settled by considering the evidence. A similar case can be made here: we need to look in detail at the nature of economic knowledge to see how far concepts and issues that arise when we consider 'knowledge in general' are useful. There is no reason not to ask the question. Rorty would argue that by showing the inadequacy of the metaphor of mind as mirror he has shown that there is nothing of interest to be said about knowledge in general. The arguments presented above show that even if we accept Rorty's view of this metaphor, the

---

7 See also Ziman (1994), pp. 61–3.

conclusion that there is nothing of interest to say about methodology does not necessarily follow.

The final point that needs making about the role of the methodologist is that critics of 'Methodology' appear to equate it with simplistic recipes for success in economics. In other words, that claiming to understand something about the nature of economic knowledge is the same as claiming to know how to create new economic knowledge. Economists who claim to understand market behaviour in terms of profit-maximizing models, but who are prepared readily to admit that they cannot advise firms how to maximize profits ought not to make such a mistake.[8]

To illustrate these points, let us return to Weintraub's assessment of the controversy between Hahn and Kaldor. It is certainly plausible that, at least in the minds of most general equilibrium theorists, Hahn won the argument. Kaldor was objecting to general equilibrium theory on the grounds that its assumptions were unrealistic and he failed to appreciate that the methodological arguments (concerning the status and nature of general equilibrium theory) that Hahn would use to defend it would, as far as many economists were concerned, simply render his objections irrelevant. It could thus be argued that Hahn had a better understanding of the community within which general equilibrium theory was acceptable. Kaldor was an outsider to this community. In addition, he was objecting to general equilibrium theory on methodological grounds. It is very misleading to conclude from this, however, that Kaldor's argument failed because it was 'Methodological'.[9] Just as there is a community in which Hahn is seen to have won, there are other communities of economists (not just 'post-Keynesians') in which Kaldor's objections are been seen as decisive. Weintraub's judgement on the foolishness of Kaldor's challenge follows only if the judgement of the community of general equilibrium theorists is taken as correct, and that outsiders are not qualified to pass

---

[8] Similarly, Caldwell has argued that the goal of methodology is not to teach how to *do* economics.

[9] The word 'misleading' is used rather than 'wrong' because there is a sense in which Weintraub's argument is, almost trivially, correct. If we define as 'methodological' any arguments which are not acceptable to a given discourse community, then outsiders whose arguments are unacceptable to that community will always lose, and their arguments will always be 'methodological'. This, however, is a distorted usage of the term 'methodological'.

judgement on insiders' theories: in other words, if the *status quo* is accepted.

The lesson to be drawn from this debate is not that 'methodological' objections to a theory are foolish, but that if we are to have a constructive debate over the merits of an economic theory we need to state our objectives and the criteria we use to decide whether theories are helping us achieve those objectives. In other words, we need to discuss methodology.

The conclusion to be drawn from this is that methodology as traditionally understood, including methodology that draws on philosophy, even epistemology, is nothing other than, to use Weintraub's term, 'methodological discourse' which does not confine its horizons to those of a particular, arbitrarily defined discourse community that we call economics.[10] To term such activity 'Methodology' and to argue that it should wither away so that a blinkered form of 'methodology' can thrive would seem to be a wilfully misleading use of terminology. Had more precise terminology been employed, for example attacking not 'Methodology' or even 'prescriptive methodology', but rather, say, 'dogmatic, foundationalist methodology', the nature of the argument would have been much clearer. It would also have made it clearer that it applied to only a small part of the methodological literature.[11,12]

4.5   TAKING STOCK

Solow's instinct that, whilst they have much to offer, postmodern arguments have been taken too far, appears well justified. The implication of the criticisms discussed in this chapter is that discourse analysis (whether we see this as literary criticism, sociology of scientific knowledge, rhetorical analysis or whatever) and methodology are *complements*, not substitutes. There is a strong

---

[10] Weintraub's terminology is used because 'methodological discourse' is clearer than McCloskey's 'methodology' here, though the criticism applies as much to McCloskey – who used the argument first – as to Weintraub.

[11] It is tempting to argue that they are being inconsistent in trying to settle methodological disputes by appealing to 'Meta-Methodology' (with capital 'M').

[12] This view is compatible with Caldwell's position (see 1990).

case *for* undertaking discourse analysis, but the case against methodology – against bringing philosophical analysis to bear on questions of economic method – is not convincing.

5.   A historical perspective on science

5.1   SCIENCE AS A SOCIAL ACTIVITY

In the Introduction to *The Structure of Scientific Revolutions*, Kuhn clearly identifies his target as the textbook picture of science. Our image of science, he argued, 'has been drawn, even by scientists themselves, mainly from the study of finished scientific achievements as these are recorded in the classics and, more recently, in the textbooks from which each new scientific generation learns to practice its trade' (Kuhn, 1970, p. 1). Because the aim of such works is persuasive and pedagogic, they present science as progressing through the gradual and progressive accumulation of knowledge. Science is a cumulative enterprise, different from other types of human endeavour. From such a perspective the role of the history of science was seen as being to document this process.

Historians of science had discovered, however, that it was hard to fulfil this role: scientific knowledge could not be made to fit the picture of the gradual accretion of knowledge, and historians found it difficult to separate 'scientific' beliefs from what their predecessors had labelled error and superstition. They had, therefore, been driven to consider the social aspects of science, for the only way sense could be made of the historical record was to view science as a social activity, conducted along lines very different from those suggested by textbooks. Indeed, the very existence of textbooks is something that needs to be explained.

5.2 NORMAL SCIENCE AND SCIENTIFIC REVOLUTIONS

The centrality of normal science

Normal science is defined by Kuhn as 'research based upon one or more past scientific achievements, achievements that some particular scientific community acknowledges for a time as supplying the foundation for its further practice' (Kuhn, 1970, p. 10). It is the science found in textbooks – a body of accepted theory, illustrated by successful applications and supported by 'exemplary observations and experiments'. This view of science, and even the textbooks themselves, are possible only because scientists agree on the basic concepts and framework that are to be used. This framework of beliefs and presuppositions is regarded as so well-established that it is not open to question. It is what Kuhn, in *The Structure of Scientific Revolutions* called a 'paradigm theory' or simply 'paradigm', though in later work he adopted the term 'disciplinary matrix' in order to avoid ambiguities connected with the use of the term paradigm. To become members of the scientific community, students have to become proficient in working within the paradigm theory: they are trained not to think in ways that are inconsistent with it. 'Work under the paradigm can be conducted in no other way, and to desert the paradigm is to cease practising the science it defines' (Kuhn, 1970, p. 34).

If scientists do not question basic concepts and theories, of what does scientific research, within a period of normal science, consist? Kuhn's answer is a list of empirical and theoretical activities. Empirical work involves gathering facts, which falls into three categories.

1. Gathering facts that can be used to solve problems that may be important in their own right.
2. Gathering facts that are interesting only because they can be compared with the paradigm theory's predictions.
3. Gathering facts that are needed to resolve ambiguities in the paradigm theory, articulating it more clearly, thereby making it possible to use it to solve new problems. This includes establishing universal constants (such as the gravitational

constants, the speed of light, the electronic charge), quantitative laws (such as Boyle's Law, Coulomb's Law), and choosing between alternative ways of extending the theory.

In addition, there are three main categories of theoretical work.

1. Prediction of factual information that is of intrinsic value. It is worth noting that Kuhn points out that this will typically not be published in 'significant' scientific journals, for though such work is of major importance to the outside world, it is not central to the paradigm, and hence not so important to scientists themselves.
2. Prediction of results that can be compared with experimental evidence, and the derivation of such results with greater precision.
3. Reformulating the paradigm theory to be more uniform and less equivocal in its application to specific problems.

However, though Kuhn divides research into empirical and theoretical, the dividing line is not clear cut. The problems of paradigm articulation are simultaneously empirical and theoretical.

Normal science as puzzle solving

Normal science is puzzle-solving, where the relevant characteristic of a puzzle is that it involves solving a problem within the constraints imposed by certain well-defined rules. The range of acceptable solutions is known in advance, and failure to find an acceptable solution reflects badly on the experimenter, not on the paradigm. The rules governing normal science include accepted scientific laws, preferred types of instrumentation and how to use them, and the acceptance of certain metaphysical concepts and methodological rules. Yet these rules, though essential to the practice of normal science, frequently remain implicit. They are not taught directly, but are learned by practice, which is why textbooks contain examples of problems that students have to work through. In the course of their training, scientists learn to see resemblances between apparently diverse problems and to solve new problems by relating them to previously-solved ones. Methodology alone is insufficient: Kuhn refers to the insufficiency of methodological directives, by themselves, to dictate a unique substantive conclusion to many sorts of scientific questions. Instructed to examine electrical or chemical phenomena, the man who is ignorant of these fields but who knows what it is to be scientific may legitimately reach any one of a number of incompatible conclusions. (Kuhn 1970, pp. 3–4)

To achieve settled answers to scientific questions, tacit knowledge beyond what can be encapsulated in methodological rules, is required.

The importance of exemplars, or standard examples, however, extends far beyond this. Exemplars are fundamental to the structure of science because the scientific communities themselves (and hence periods of normal science) are normally established on the basis of specific scientific achievements – Aristotle's *Physica*, Newton's *Principia* or Lyell's *Geology*. Such works are both sufficiently unprecedented in their achievement to attract followers, and sufficiently open-ended to leave numerous problems for followers to solve. Normal science, therefore, is the result of scientists following the example set by a successful innovator. It is through following such an exemplar that the meanings of theoretical terms and many of the tacit rules governing science are established. Exemplars are, Kuhn contends, more fundamental than the rules of science, for they are the basis on which the rules and presuppositions of science are established. It is this which accounts for Kuhn's somewhat confusing use of the term paradigm to encompass, using the terminology he adopted in later work, both exemplars and disciplinary matrices. Disciplinary matrices, and hence normal science, cannot be conceived independently of the exemplars from which they are derived.

Scientific revolutions

Normal science does not aim at novelty in any fundamental sense, but at applying, articulating and extending a known paradigm. Yet novelty sometimes occurs – anomalies arise. Theories developed within the paradigm fail to solve problems they are expected to solve. Anomalies always exist, and for the most part they are either ignored, or viewed as problems awaiting solution. However, failure to solve an anomaly may become serious: it may concern a problem of particular practical importance or that raises doubts concerning a fundamental generalization within the paradigm, or it may simply have persisted for an inordinately long time. If such failure becomes sufficiently serious, a crisis may emerge.

When a crisis emerges, the paradigm is not abandoned – it cannot be abandoned unless there is a suitable alternative, for without any paradigm to guide research, science would be impossible – but *ad hoc* adjustments are made and versions of the paradigm theory proliferate. The rules of normal science are relaxed and become blurred. Scientific activity, which under normal science is purposeful and directed, becomes more random, as scientists search for solutions without the guidance provided by the paradigm. It is out of such searching that a new paradigm emerges. When this happens there is a scientific revolution, followed by a new period of normal science.

5.3   KUHN AND POSTMODERNISM

Recreating the world

Kuhn likened the change which accompanies a scientific revolution to a gestalt shift. There are changes in scientific theories, the meaning of established concepts and the standards that govern research. The list of permissible problems and explanations changes. Paradigms may thus be incommensurable: it is not possible to speak of one paradigm being better than another if they make use of different concepts to analyse different problems, judging the answers by different standards. Kuhn even went so far as to claim that paradigm changes created new worlds.

> Can it conceivably be an accident, for example, that Western astronomers first saw change in the previously immutable heavens during the half-century after Copernicus' new paradigm was first proposed? ... Using simple instruments, some as simple as a piece of thread, late sixteenth-century astronomers repeatedly discovered that comets wandered at will through the space previously reserved for the immutable planets and stars. The very ease and rapidity with which astronomers saw new things when looking at old objects with old instruments may make us wish to say that, after Copernicus, astronomers lived in a different world. In any case, their research responded as if this were the case. (Kuhn, 1970, pp. 116–17)

It is not simply that scientists see the world from a different perspective, for after a scientific revolution it is no longer possible to see the world in the old way. Once the moon has been seen as a satellite of the earth rather than as a planet, for example, the old view is seen as mistaken. The world in which scientists work is different after the revolution.

Though derived from history, this perspective on science has major implications for epistemology. Kuhn contrasts it with the traditional view according to which it is only the scientists' interpretation of observations that changes when a paradigm changes – that the scientists working in different paradigms see the same things, but see them differently. The traditional view, he argues, is part of an epistemological paradigm that goes back to Descartes. Though it was successful for a long time, this paradigm is undermined by historical studies of science.

The idea that science progresses through periods of normal science, separated from each other by paradigm shifts undermines the notion of any simple account of progress. Progress has to be defined in relation to some set of standards, but these standards are, for Kuhn, part of the paradigm. It is not possible to argue that standards are raised or lowered in the switch from one paradigm to another, for this would imply the existence of a set of external standards that does not exist. This absence of standards by which paradigm shifts can be judged means that the choice between paradigms cannot be settled by logic and experiment alone.

Progress through puzzle-solving

Seen from this perspective, Kuhn's epistemology appears close to the anti-epistemological position of Rorty and the sociology of scientific knowledge discussed in earlier chapters. Kuhn, however, reads his own work rather differently.[1]

Kuhn took for granted that science in general was dominated by certain values.[2]

1. Accuracy: within its domain a theory's consequences should agree with the results of existing experiments and observations.

---

[1] See the 'Postscript' to Kuhn (1970) and Kuhn (1977).
[2] This list is taken from Kuhn (1977), pp. 321–2.

2. Consistency: a theory should be consistent both internally and with other currently accepted theories applicable to related aspects of nature.
3. Scope: a theory's consequences should extend beyond the particular observations it was designed to explain.
4. Simplicity: a theory should bring order to otherwise isolated phenomena.
5. Fruitfulness: a theory should disclose new phenomena, or previously unnoticed relationships among already-known phenomena.

Without such values, science would have been very different. They are, however, 'values to be used in making choices rather than rules of choice'.

Given these values, Kuhn assumed that there were severe constraints on the theories scientists could adopt. Though he went on to say that they cannot determine beliefs completely, he observed that 'observation and experience can and must drastically restrict the range of admissible scientific belief, else there would be no science' (Kuhn, 1970, p. 4). Kuhn's position is, to this extent, empiricist.

This view that science was based on certain values, and that empirical evidence severely constrained theorizing, meant that Kuhn was able to speak of progress in science. Indeed, it was the existence of progress that marked science out from many other areas of inquiry.

> Though scientific development may resemble that in other fields more closely than has often been supposed, it is also strikingly different. To say, for example, that the sciences, at least after a certain point in their development, progress in a way that other fields do not, cannot have been all wrong, whatever progress itself may be. One of the objects of the book [*The Structure of Scientific Revolutions*] was to examine such differences and begin accounting for them. (Kuhn, 1970, p. 209)

The main difference is that scientists are puzzle-solvers: when confronted with a choice between theories, 'the demonstrated ability to set up and solve puzzles presented by nature is, in the case of value conflict, the dominant criterion for members of a scientific group' (Kuhn, 1970, p. 205). This commitment to puzzle-solving makes normal science possible, and leads to systematic attempts to increase empirical knowledge of nature. Without normal science, such activity would never occur and progress would be much less.

But what of the discontinuities and incommensurabilities that characterize scientific revolutions? Do they not undermine the notion of progress? Kuhn claims that they do not. Likening scientific theories to branches on an evolutionary tree, he argues as follows.

> Considering any two such theories, chosen from points not too near their origin, it should be easy to design a list of criteria that would enable an uncommitted observer to distinguish the earlier from the more recent theory time after time. Among the most useful would be: accuracy of prediction, particularly of quantitative prediction; the balance between esoteric and every-day subject matter; and the number of different problems solved. Less useful for this purpose, though also important determinants of scientific life, would be such values as simplicity, scope and compatibility with other specialities. Those lists are not yet the ones required, but *I have no doubt that they can be completed.* If they can, then scientific development is, like biological, *a unidirectional and irreversible process. Later scientific theories are better than earlier ones for solving puzzles in the often quite different environments to which they are applied.* (Kuhn, 1970, pp. 205–6, emphasis added).

He judges theories by their usefulness in discovering and solving puzzles about nature. According to this criterion there is not only progress within paradigms, but across paradigms. What he denies is that such progress constitutes progress in the sense of achieving 'a better representation of what nature is really like' (Kuhn, 1970, p. 206). He rejects the notion of correspondence between theory and reality – it is 'illusive in principle', for there is no theory-independent way to understand the world, and it is implausible in view of the historical record. To say this, however, is not to abandon the idea of progress, which can be understood perfectly well without such a view of truth.

5.4 PARADIGMS AND PROGRESS

Though economics has not been discussed in this chapter, the applicability of much of Kuhn's framework to contemporary economics is so clear as to require hardly any comment.

1. Economists are puzzle-solvers, with progress being achieved through neglecting many of the philosophical, metaphysical and empirical issues that concerned earlier generations.
2. Exemplars play a vital role in determining the direction in which research is undertaken, and in the training of students.
3. Economics exhibits many of the sociological characteristics that Kuhn attributes to normal science: the role of journals, with the bulk of work in the 'core' journals being addressed to concerns internal to the discipline, a generally accepted disciplinary matrix with dissenters not being taken seriously, a lack of concern with history.

There are difficulties in pinning down paradigms in economics very precisely, especially when we look back into the history of the subject,[3] but much contemporary economics is clearly Kuhnian normal science.

Yet Kuhn's analysis does not take us far enough. Reducing science to puzzle solving makes progress possible in the sense that it makes possible the building up of a far larger body of connected facts and explanations than would be possible without it, but this in itself does not *necessarily* constitute progress in an interesting sense. To call it progress requires that the knowledge built up within the paradigm is contributing to an understanding of the ostensible object of inquiry. In other words, it would (in principle) be possible to have the trappings of normal science – to have a research regulated by a paradigm – without 'real' science. In the sciences Kuhn discusses this is not a problem, but for economics this is one of the key issues.

On this point, Kuhn has two things to offer: his conviction that observation and experience 'drastically' constrain admissible beliefs; and the set of values that, he believes, underlie all science. Because he takes these things for granted, he fails to analyse either of them. This is crucial to any attempt to consider economics.

1. The extent to which, and the manner in which, observation and experiment (or any other type of empirical evidence) constrain admissible economic beliefs is highly contentious.
2. Kuhn lists five values underlying science, failing to explore the problems that may arise when they conflict with each other. One

---

[3] See, for example, Coats (1969).

of the problems with contemporary economics, many critics argue, is that the relative importance attached to different values has become distorted.[4]

It is necessary, therefore, to go beyond Kuhn in order to tackle these issues. Though Kuhn does, arguably, avoid relativism, the crucial arguments are insufficiently developed. In particular, they need to be explored much further in relation to specific problems that occur in economics.

---

[4] See Mayer (1993), Chapter 2; Leontief (1971).

6. The pragmatist tradition

6.1 INTRODUCTION

The first stage in the process of establishing an approach to economic methodology that takes account of postmodern or constructivist insights whilst avoiding the dangers of relativism, is to explore the pragmatist tradition more carefully. There are several reasons why this is important.

1. Rorty is a pragmatist, but though it can be argued that he manages to avoid relativism, the pragmatist tradition embraces a variety of positions, some of which imply a 'harder' view of science than his.
2. There are links between some varieties of pragmatism and the Popperian positions discussed in the following chapter.
3. Considering pragmatism throws up a range of ideas that will prove valuable in seeking to understand what is going on in economics.

Amongst the pragmatists, the key figure is C. S. Peirce, widely regarded as the founder of the pragmatist tradition.

For Peirce, pragmatism was a part of logic, for it provided a rule for clarifying the meaning of terms and concepts – it was a way to make our ideas clear. It was, Peirce argued, possible to distinguish between three grades of clarity.

1. *Recognizability*[1] A clear idea is one that can be recognized anywhere – that will not be confused with any other. But this does not take us very far, Peirce argued, for it involves a subjective feeling which may be mistaken.

---

[1] This is not Peirce's terminology, though the definition is his.

2. *Distinctness* This involves having an abstract definition of every important term, and having a clear apprehension of everything involved contained in the definition. The problem with this notion, attributed by Peirce to Leibnitz, is that it does not go far enough. Definitions may help us to set our ideas in order, but they do no more than that. 'Nothing new can ever be learned by analyzing definitions' (Peirce, 1878, p. 126).

3. *Practical bearing* The third grade of clarity involved knowing the practical consequences of an idea.

> It appears, then, that the rule for attaining the third grade of clearness of apprehension is as follows: Consider what effects, which might conceivably have practical bearings, we conceive the object of our conception to have. Then, our conception of these effects is the whole of our conception of the object. (Peirce, 1978, p. 132).

> It is impossible, Peirce argued, to have an idea of anything which relates to anything other than 'its sensible effects'.

This goes well beyond the claim that the meaning of an idea is illustrated or explained by its practical consequences. It is, Peirce contended, impossible to separate meaning and practical consequences: the two are virtually synonymous.

This idea that meaning, and hence knowledge, are linked to practice has been developed in different directions, but forms the basis of all varieties of pragmatism. Knowledge is seen as associated with activity: to know something is to have beliefs that work.

6.2   PEIRCE AND THE METHOD OF SCIENCE[2]

The fixation of belief

The pragmatic concept of meaning led Peirce to focus on beliefs and the process of inquiry – the process whereby beliefs were formed. Though he was concerned with logic – with rules for drawing true

---

[2] For accounts of Peirce in the context of economics see Hoover (1994), Backhouse (1994a) and Wible (1994).

conclusions from true premises – Peirce regarded beliefs as more fundamental than truth, for three reasons.

1. It is beliefs that lead to action. Without them, life is not possible. The link between beliefs and action is so close that, Peirce argued, beliefs can be identified by looking at actions. In the same way that he equated meaning with the practical consequences of an idea, he went so far as to claim that beliefs *are* habits.
2. The object of inquiry is not truth, but 'the settlement of opinion' or, as Peirce put it in the title of his article, 'The fixation of belief'.

> Hence, the sole object of inquiry is the settlement of opinion. We may fancy that this is not enough for us, and that we seek, not merely an opinion, but a true opinion. But put this fancy to the test, and it proves groundless; for as soon as a firm belief is reached we are entirely satisfied, whether the belief be true or false. . . . The most that can be maintained is, that we seek for a belief that we shall *think* to be true. But we think each one of our beliefs to be true, and, indeed, it is mere tautology to say so. (Peirce, 1877, p. 115)

3. To demonstrate a proposition it is not necessary to start from any 'ultimate and absolutely indubitable propositions'. All that is necessary is to start from propositions that are 'perfectly free from all actual doubt' (ibid.) – in other words, from firmly-held beliefs.

The opposite of belief is doubt – a state in which we lack the beliefs necessary for action.

> Doubt is an uneasy and dissatisfied state from which we struggle to free ourselves and pass into the state of belief; while the latter is a calm and satisfactory state which we do not wish to avoid, or to change to a belief in anything else. . . . the irritation of doubt causes a struggle to attain a state of belief. I shall term this struggle *inquiry*. (Peirce, 1877, p. 114)

The problem of knowledge, therefore, was reformulated by Peirce as the problem of how the process of inquiry, whereby doubt is transformed into belief – the process whereby beliefs are fixed – might operate, and whether any of the possible methods of inquiry lead people to arrive at anything that might be considered to be true knowledge. Peirce's answer was that one method, the method of science, was fundamental, but to explain it he first considered three other methods: the method of tenacity; the method of authority; and the *a priori* method.

In order to elucidate the significant features of what he considers the fundamental method of inquiry, he considers three other methods whereby beliefs may be fixed. The first and simplest of these is the method of 'tenacity'.

> If the settlement of opinion is the sole object of inquiry, and if belief is of the nature of a habit, why should we not attain the desired end, by taking any answer to a question which we may fancy, and constantly reiterating it to ourselves, dwelling on all which may conduce to that belief, and learning to turn with contempt and hatred from anything which might disturb it? (Peirce, 1877, p. 115)

The problem with this method is that 'the social impulse' is against it – other people will think differently, raising doubt. In other words, beliefs must be fixed in the community, not simply for the individual. The second method is the method of 'authority'. Instead of an individual holding tenaciously to a belief, it is sustained by an institution which prevents or suppresses dissent. This, too, however, though more powerful than the method of tenacity, will be unsustainable.

Preferable to either of these methods is the *'a priori'* method whereby beliefs rest on fundamental propositions that are 'agreeable to reason'. The problem with this method is that it makes inquiry 'something similar to the development of taste; but taste, unfortunately, is always more or less a matter of fashion' (Peirce, 1877, p. 119).

> To satisfy our doubts, therefore, it is necessary that a method should be found by which our beliefs may be caused by nothing human, but by some external permanency – by something upon which our thinking has no effect. (Peirce, 1877, p. 120)

The only method that meets this criterion is 'the method of science'.

The method of science

Peirce summed up the essentials of the method of science in the following way:

There are real things, whose characters are entirely independent of our opinions about them; these realities affect our senses according to regular laws, and, though our sensations are as different as our relations to the objects, yet, by taking advantage of the laws of perception, we can ascertain by reasoning how things really are, and if any man, if he have sufficient experience and reason enough about it, will be led to the one true conclusion. (Peirce, 1877, p. 120)

There are three fundamental aspects of this definition: realism, knowability and what may be called 'the universal community of inquirers'.

Peirce gives four grounds for accepting the doctrine that there is a knowable reality (Peirce, 1877, p. 120).

1. The method of science never leads to the conclusion that there are not real things – there is a harmony between realism and the method of science.
2. It is a doctrine 'that every mind admits'. If we had doubts about the existence of real things, 'this doubt would not be a cause of dissatisfaction' and hence would not lead to inquiry – it is the belief that there is a fact of the matter that renders doubt unsatisfactory.
3. Everyone uses the scientific method about many things, as long as they know how to apply it.
4. The method of science 'has had the most wonderful triumphs in the way of settling opinion'.

In short, realism is consistent with the way we in practice behave, it is the only viable basis for conducting inquiry, and inquiries based on it have been extremely successful.

As the last sentence of the previous quotation from Peirce makes clear, he was optimistic that the method of science would lead to the discovery of the truth. Individuals' beliefs might be mistaken, but the community would move towards the truth. There were, however, important qualifications.

1. The community of inquirers is universal – 'any' man must be able to reach the truth under the right circumstances.
2. Inquiry may require experience, imagination and skill. It is not simply a matter of observing the obvious.

3. Reasoning may have to continue a long time – 'enough' may involve more than the lifetime of an individual.

Peirce's vision was one where inquiry starts with a question and a series of possible answers. Testing leads to the progressive elimination of answers and will lead to the true answer only if the true answer is in the list (hence imagination is required) and if our powers of reasoning are adequate (for example, do we test answers in the right order?). Truth emerges as the answer on which an unlimited community of inquirers will converge in the long run.

Several features of Peirce's doctrine of truth need emphasis.

1. It is based on a fallibilistic view of knowledge. There is no implication that people can *ever* have completely secure knowledge. There are no indubitable foundations.
2. The doctrine of realism is essential, for without it there would be no reason to expect the beliefs of any community of inquirers to converge on anything.
3. Truth, being the limit of the process of inquiry, is independent of the beliefs of individuals. There is nothing subjective or relativistic about it, even though our starting point is individual beliefs.
4. The expectation that beliefs will progress towards the truth is based on confidence in a method of inquiry. Truth is thus defined in relation to method. It is scientific methods that are fundamental.

6.3   RATIONALITY AND REALISM

Science as problem-solving

Laudan (1977) has argued that science is primarily a problem-solving activity.[3]

---

[3] There are significant differences between Laudan (1977) and (1984) – he presents part of the latter book as a criticism of his former work. Our concern here is not with Laudan's work as a whole, but with certain issues that he raises. Thus whilst attention

The Pragmatist Tradition 69

Thesis 1: The first and essential test for any theory is whether it provides acceptable answers to interesting questions: whether, in other words, it provides satisfactory solutions to important problems. (Laudan, 1977, p. 13)

Thesis 2: In appraising the merits of theories, it is more important to ask whether they constitute adequate solutions to significant problems than it is to ask whether they are 'true', 'corroborated', 'well-confirmed', or otherwise justifiable within the framework of contemporary epistemology. (Laudan, 1977, p. 14)[4]

The primary concern of science is not with facts or truth but with solving problems.[5] These fall into two main categories: empirical and conceptual problems.

1. *Empirical problems* are treated as problems about the world – they are substantive questions about objects in the domain of a science. The can be subdivided into three categories: (a) unsolved problems (not solved by *any* theory); (b) solved problems; (c) anomalous problems (not solved by a particular theory, but solved by one or more competing theories).
2. *Conceptual problems* involve relationships between theories, methodology and more general assumptions about the world. They include internal inconsistencies within theories; conceptual ambiguities; conflicts between scientific and methodological theories; tensions between different scientific theories (ranging from inconsistency to mutual implausibility); and conflicts between theories and the prevalent view of the world.

---

will be paid to some of the differences between these books, they are incidental to the main argument.

[4] Except for the phrase 'in other words', These quotations were both italicized in the original.

[5] Laudan is considered here because his ideas fit into the argument that is being developed in this chapter. It is not suggested that he should be described as a pragmatist (the books discussed are primarily a response to Kuhn, and secondarily to what he terms 'cognitive sociology', not to the pragmatist literature). Whether or not Laudan should be described as a pragmatist, his work has clear links with pragmatism: (1) The emphasis on problems fits with Peirce's emphasis on the importance of questions. (2) He argues that values are involved in the process of theory evaluation. (3) He regards the question of truth as secondary to that of problem-solving.

Several points need to be made about problems as Laudan conceives them; (1) problems and solutions are both context-specific; (2) solutions may be approximate; (3) for a wide variety of reasons, problems, whether empirical or conceptual, are not all equally important. For the present argument, the most important of these points is context-dependence. This arises for two reasons. The first is that changes in world view, or external developments, lead to changes in both the set of problems and the criteria used to determine what are acceptable solutions to those problems. The second is that the status of what appear to be unsolved problems is not always clear: empirical effects may not be genuine, or they may be irrelevant to a particular branch of science. For example, the fact that the moon seems larger when near the horizon may be a problem for astronomy, optics or psychology. An unsolved problem may emerge as such only *after* it is solved. These difficulties led Laudan to the conclusion that,

> The only reliable guide to the problems relevant to a particular theory is an examination of the problems which predecessor – and competing – theories in that domain (including the theory itself) have already solved. (Laudan, 1977, p. 21)[6]

Within this framework, progress involves the transformation of unsolved and anomalous problems into solved problems.

What distinguishes Laudan's view from many others is his emphasis on the interaction of empirical and conceptual problems. A theory may solve an empirical problem, perhaps explaining an anomaly, but in the process create new conceptual problems. Alternatively progress may arise, not through a theoretical development solving more empirical problems, but through its solving conceptual problems: it may resolve an inconsistency, or render a theory more consistent with another confidently-held theory or with the scientific community's world view. As a result, Laudan's definition of progress is not a simple one.

> [T]he overall problem-solving effectiveness of a theory is determined by assessing the number and importance of the empirical problems which the theory solves and deducting therefrom the number and importance of the anomalies and conceptual problems which the theory generates. . . . progress

---

6 This sentence is italicized in the original.

can occur if and only if the succession of scientific theories in any domain shows an increasing degree of problem solving effectiveness. Localizing the notion of progress to specific situations rather than large stretches of time, we can say that any time we modify a theory or replace it by another theory, that change is progressive if and only if the later version is a more effective problem solver (in the sense just defined) than its predecessor. (Laudan, 1977, p. 68)[7]

Though he uses the language of counting problems, this is clearly a way of talking about something that involves judgement and evaluation.

Values, methods and theories

In *Progress and its Problems*, Laudan focuses on what he terms 'research traditions', developed from Kuhn's 'paradigms' and Lakatos's 'research programmes'. They are defined in the following way:

a research tradition is a set of general assumptions about the entities and processes in a domain of study, and about appropriate methods to be used for investigating the problems and constructing the theories in that domain. (Laudan, 1977, p. 81)[8]

A research tradition provides guidelines in the form of an ontology (covering entities and processes) and methodological rules governing inquiry. These guidelines (1) determine what count as empirical problems, pseudo problems, and problems that are fall in another domain (foreign problems); (2) they rule out certain theories (for example, as incompatible with the tradition's ontology); (3) they have a heuristic role; and (4) they justify certain types of theory. A research tradition does not entail specific theories – indeed, theories developed within a research tradition may be mutually inconsistent – but provides the tools needed in order to solve problems. Theories may be developed within one research tradition, but be taken over by an alternative one.

Successful research traditions lead to the solution of problems. They can be appraised on two grounds: *adequacy* (the problem-

---

[7] Italicized in original.
[8] Italicized in original.

solving effectiveness of the latest theory) and *progressiveness* (rate of progress, in the sense defined above). Laudan argues that the former is relevant to decisions about which theory to accept (to treat as if it were true), but the latter to decisions about which theory to pursue, or to develop.

With *Science and Values* (1984) Laudan moved away from this still very Kuhnian perspective, abandoning, for a variety of reasons, his analysis of science in terms of research traditions. He retained, however, the notion that there was a hierarchical structure to scientific debates, with methodology, ontology and (now) the aims of science being bound up with scientific theories. However, where he had previously emphasized ontology, Laudan now saw the *aims* of science as fundamental. These aims are the basis for the methods employed, and methods in turn justify theories. The relationship, however, is not one-way. Methods are not developed prior to theories, but the two are developed simultaneously – methodology takes account of theories. Similarly, the aims of science evolve, for certain aims (for example, absolute truth) may be unrealizable.

This leads to the situation summed up in Figure 6.1. Aims justify methods, which in turn justify theories. At the same time, however, theories constrain methods, and methods available affect the realizability of different possible aims. Underlying all this, there has to be harmony between the aims of science and scientific theories.

If theories, methods and aims evolved in step with each other, it would be possible to analyse history in terms analogous to Kuhn's, picking out a series of paradigms, research traditions or related entities. Historical evidence, however, suggests a rather different picture, in which theories, methods and aims evolve in different ways, with the links being much looser than Kuhn and Lakatos suggest. For example, the early nineteenth century saw a marked shift in the aims of science with the recognition that all scientific theories were fallible, and that it made no sense to pursue the aim of achieving certain truth. Instead the aim of science became to construct theories that were plausible, probable or well-tested in some sense. Though this had important consequences for the scientific method, and ultimately for scientific theories, this change in aims was not associated with specific changes in either methods or theories. The notion that major scientific changes involve a move from one aims-methods-theories package to another is untenable, whether we view these packages as paradigms, research programmes or research traditions.

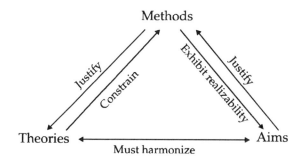

Figure 6.1: Laudan's 'reticulational' model of science

Source: Laudan (1984), p. 63.

Laudan is right to say that his new approach marks a significant shift away from his earlier, Kuhn-inspired, approach based on research traditions. Despite this, however, there are important common features, notably the emphasis on the interconnection of 'scientific' and methodological or philosophical issues.

Values and progress

Laudan consistently makes the point that appraisal of scientific theories is context-dependent. Yet he is emphatic that this does not lead to relativism. He is scathing about the 'epistemic relativism' found in the sociology of scientific knowledge literature, citing the work of Collins, Pickering and Pinch. Taking Collins as an example, he argues that,

> In each of the cases [controversies in theoretical physics] Collins has examined, he found that ingenious scientists can concoct a way to circumvent arguments and evidence against their pet theories. In effect Collins's claim is that the experimental evidence is always so ambiguous that virtually any theory can be maintained in the face of any evidence. As he puts it, 'the natural world in no way constrains what is believed to be'. Or, 'the natural world has a small or non-existent role in the construction of scientific knowledge'. Since, in Collins's view, the features of the world (as we come to learn about them from experiment and observation) do virtually nothing to

restrain our beliefs about the world, Collins has a ready explanation for the prolongation of scientific disagreement. But, as with Lakatos, Feyerabend and Kuhn, that explanatory virtue quickly becomes a liability because, having severed all significant causal links between the world and our beliefs about it, Collins cannot bring the world back into the picture as a factor driving scientists to eventual consensus. Although Collins says he is interested in the mechanisms of consensus formation in science (he asserts it is important to describe the 'mechanisms' which *limit* interpretive flexibility and thus allow controversies to come to an end), I predict he will find that, having written off the world as a constraint on our beliefs, he lacks the most relevant explanatory resources for tackling that problem. (Laudan, 1984, p. 21)

Like Peirce, Laudan is arguing that the existence of an external world which provides constraints on our theorizing is the only reason beliefs converge on anything. He clearly believes that Collins and others in the sociology of scientific knowledge tradition have, through endorsing what he calls 'cognitive egalitarianism' (Laudan, 1984, p. 30) gone too far.[9]

But problems, solutions and even the notion of progress are, for Laudan, context-dependent, and hence relativized. Even world views (1977) and the aims of science (1984) are endogenous, changing both in response to external factors and in response to developments within science. Given this, how does he himself avoid relativism? There are several answers.

1. He argues that problems can transcend different research traditions. Even if fundamental concepts (motion, force, mass) are understood differently, for example, problems (Why does a stone fall to the ground in a certain way?) may be the same in several traditions. The significance of these problems may be radically different, but that is another matter: there is a basis for comparison.
2. Though different weights may be attached to them, there are, in practice, shared understandings: concepts such as accuracy, scope and generality transcend individual research traditions.
3. In his later work he emphasizes the overlaps between theories, methods and aims. If all changed simultaneously, as in a Kuhnian

---

[9] It is worth noting that Laudan is equally critical of scientific realism which, he contends, cannot provide a viable set of aims for science (1984, pp. 136–7). For Laudan's critique of relativism, see Laudan (1990).

paradigm shift, there *might* be incommensurability, but this does not happen. There are always, at least locally, some common elements.

4. The most fundamental point, however, is that Laudan recognizes that we have to use *our own* values – our own view of the aims of science – in order to judge progress. If our values were different, then our judgement about progress might be different.

He sums it up in the following way.

> How, it might be asked, can we speak of science making progress if the very goals that constitute the axiology of science themselves shift? Such rhetorical questions seem difficult to answer. But the difficulties of reconciling the notion of scientific progress with the thesis of shifting goals are more apparent than real.
>
> Precisely because judgements of progress are, and always have been, parasitic on the specification of goals, we can continue to speak of progress just as we always have. Does a certain sequence of theories move scientists closer to realizing or achieving a certain goal state than they were before? Then progress (relative to that goal state) has occurred. If not, then not. The matter really is as simple as that. (Laudan, 1984, p. 65)

Laudan criticizes writers such as Kuhn, who 'seem to assume that progress must be judged relative to the goals of scientists who performed an action' (ibid.). He sees no reason why our judgements about progress should depend on acquiescence in the aims of those whose work we are seeking to assess. This attitude has the important merit of emphasizing that it is entirely reasonable for us to judge progress in respect to our own goals. To that extent, Laudan is right. There is, however, more to the story than this, for we also wish to understand the work of the scientists whose work we are studying. This requires us to see them as rational, seeking to achieve progress, which in turn requires us to examine their theories from the point of view of their own goals.

6.4   EXPERIMENTATION, REALISM AND ECONOMICS

Experimentation and realism

In the pragmatist tradition, Ian Hacking has argued that it is our ability to *do* things that gives us grounds for adopting a realist view of science. He argues that the crucial aspect of experimentation is not that it serves to test hypotheses, but that it shows that we can *do* certain things.

> Experimentation provides the strongest evidence for scientific realism. This is not because we test hypotheses about entities. It is because entities that in principle cannot be 'observed' are regularly manipulated to produce a new phenomena and to investigate other aspects of nature. They are tools, instruments, not for thinking but for doing. (Hacking, 1983, p. 262.)

This claim, that it is our ability to manipulate things and to use them to produce other phenomena that gives us grounds for believing they are real, is illustrated by his explanation of why we can regard electrons as real entities. A century ago, he claims, there were good grounds for being sceptical about any elementary particles:

> Anti-realism about electrons was very sensible when Bain wrote a century ago. . . . Things are different now. The 'direct' proof of electrons and the like is our ability to manipulate them using well-understood low-level causal properties. . . . Millikan's ability to determine the charge of an electron did something of great importance for the idea of electrons: more, I think, than the Lorenz theory of the electron. Determining the charge of something makes one believe in it far more than postulating it to explain something else. Millikan gets the charge on the electron: better still. Uhlenbeck and Gouldsmit in 1925 assign angular momentum to electrons, brilliantly solving a lot of problems. Electrons have spin, ever after. The clincher is when we can put a spin on an electrons, polarize them and get them thereby to scatter in slightly different proportions. (Hacking, 1983, p. 274)

Several points need to be drawn out from this discussion.

1. Hacking is suggesting a realism about entities, not about theories. Entities may not be observable, but can be shown to be causally

related to phenomena we can observe and things that we can do. Theories, in contrast, provide explanations. There is, he argues, no reason to be a realist about theories. Given that the realism of the entities with which economists are typically concerned (households, firms, prices, quantities) is not in dispute,[10] this argument is not directly relevant to economics. As will be explained, however, many of the issues involved are relevant.

2. Hacking's argument does not dispute the theory-ladenness of observation. Instead, it argues that it is irrelevant, because the theory on which observations depend is typically very different from the theories we are testing in our experiments. The working of a microscope, for example, is dependent on laws of optics. These laws will, however, typically be completely unrelated to the laws under investigation in experiments in which microscopes are used. In any case, the laws of optics have been used, and shown to work, in many circumstances unrelated to microscopes. It is, therefore, incorrect to argue that the theory-ladenness of observation necessarily implies that scientific theories cannot be tested against observations of the real world.

3. It is an argument for the epistemic value of measurement and applied work – of some of the activities Kuhn classified as normal science.

Though the examples Hacking uses are concerned with controlled experiments, this is not crucial to his argument. A controlled experiment is one where you show that you can produce certain results by manipulating nature so that those effects from what you wish to abstract are eliminated. An experiment can be repeated and replicated to confirm that the result was not accidental.[11] In so far as economic experiments can be undertaken, such arguments can clearly be carried over to economics.[12] Most economics, however, relies not on evidence from controlled experiments, but on historical evidence – on the 'natural experiments' provided by history. This type of evidence raises two main problems.

---

[10] There may be controversy about how the entities postulated in economic theories correspond to entities in the real world, but that is a different matter.

[11] See section 11.2 below.

[12] Whether or not economic experiments are as successful as natural-science experiments in establishing results is, of course, another matter.

1. The inability to control variables means that the economist has either to find examples when variables she wishes to hold constant were in fact constant, or to find a way of removing the influence of changes in 'interfering' variables.
2. Given that the economist is frequently an observer, not an instigator of policy changes, historical evidence has to be used to show that certain things were being 'done' in the economy analogous to the doing things that Hacking refers to in natural science experiments.

Intervening in the economy

To see the extent to which such arguments can be used in economics we need to consider carefully some of the differences between economics and physics. The most obvious contrast, mentioned above, is that there is little doubt as to the reality of the entities that form the subjects of economic theories. Households and firms may sometimes be hard to define precisely, but they clearly exist. So do prices, quantities, exchange rates, labour, production, consumption and so on. The issue of realism enters at a different level. Where doubt arises is over whether the behaviour of the entities described by economic theory bears any relationship to the behaviour of corresponding entities in the real world. For example, in most economic theories, a firm is defined by a cost function, market conditions and an objective (maximization of profits). Uncertainty arises in that it may not be clear whether the behaviour predicted by such a theory bears any relation to the behaviour of real-world firms. Similarly, with households the 'existence' of utility functions or well-ordered preferences is *equivalent to* the assertion that choices obey certain rules (such as the axioms of revealed preference).[13]

The major issue in economics is the reality of the causal mechanisms postulated by economists: monetary expansion through open-market operations raises prices through lowering interest rates and increasing the incentive to spend; minimum wages raise unemployment through reducing demand for labour and increasing supply; government spending raises the level of employment via the

---

[13] It might seem that realism would be more of an issue with phenomena such as perfect or monopolistic competition but here, too, realism of the phenomena is not the key issue, for they are almost universally accepted as ideal types.

multiplier effect on aggregate demand; and so on. In many cases, establishing that these causal mechanisms are operating involves establishing both the nature of the exogenous shock (an open market operation, the introduction of a minimum wage, an increase in government spending) and the links between this shock and the endogenous variables in which we are interested (the price level, unemployment, employment). 'Intervention' in the economy could be important for both of these. Of what, however, might such intervention consist?

One possibility is experimental economics. In principle experiments in economics can be viewed in the same way as experiments in natural science: experimenters are isolating a part of the world in order to show that when they do certain things they can produce certain phenomena. There are, however, important differences. (1) In economics the scope for experiment is, for obvious reasons, very limited. Certain aspects of individual behaviour (such as attitudes towards risk where relatively small sums of money are involved) can be investigated experimentally, but many important economic phenomena (from the impact of market structure to most of macroeconomics) cannot. (2) Because the subjects of economic experiments are aware that they are participating in an experiment, it is hard to be sure that their behaviour is not affected. It may not be possible to reproduce all relevant aspects of the contexts in which 'real-world' decisions (that is decisions made outside economists' laboratories) are made. If decisions depend on context-sensitive details, laboratory results may be misleading. There is thus considerable uncertainty about how accurately behaviour under experimental conditions mirrors normal behaviour.

Another form of intervention in the economy is government policy. Governments are continually seeking to intervene in the economy to achieve different objectives. If it could be shown that governments were able to use policy so as to achieve certain ends, this would be of great significance. It was in this vein that Nicholas Kaldor is reputed to have said, after the Conservatives defeated Labour in the 1970 general election, 'Now I shall find out whether my prediction that the effects of Selective Employment Tax are reversible is true'. There are, however, serious problems in using such evidence. The first is that other things are rarely constant, with the result that it is often hard to know what the impact of a policy was. Governments may even take steps to mitigate what for them are undesirable side-effects of their policies. The second is that it may not even be clear exactly what policy has been pursued.

These two points are well-illustrated by what is, at first sight, a very good example of an experiment in macroeconomic policy: the Thatcher government's attempt to reduce inflation after 1979. From the first quarter of 1979 to the first quarter of 1981, competitiveness (measured by relative unit labour costs) fell by an unprecedented 54 per cent, producing a massive fall in aggregate demand and a doubling of the unemployment rate. Yet there are doubts about how this should be interpreted. (1) It is not known how much of the appreciation of sterling was due to North Sea Oil coming on stream, and how much was the result of government policy. (2) There is dispute about what policy was pursued in 1979–80. Figures for some monetary aggregates suggest that the money supply was not being controlled effectively, whereas other evidence suggests that policy became very tight immediately the Conservatives came into office – that policy was even tighter than intended.[14] Thus there is dispute over both what 'experiment' was being performed and what its impact was. If we turn to the longer-term effects of the policy change (such as the effects on inflation or productivity) there is even greater uncertainty.

Intervention as described in the previous paragraph involves manipulation of exogenous variables in economic models (the money supply, government spending, tax rates). Another form is the design of institutions and rules. Kaldor's 'selective employment tax', mentioned above, designed to shift employment out of services into manufacturing, is one example. Others could be the introduction of schemes to encourage saving (tax-exempt savings accounts) or the design of financial market institutions to prevent speculative price movements without interfering with arbitrage and regular trade in such markets.

6.5   CONCLUSIONS

Pragmatism provides a way to think about truth and progress in science whilst avoiding the pitfalls of foundationalism and relativism. The key element in the work of both Peirce and Hacking

---

[14] See Buiter and Miller (1981) for a detailed discussion of this episode.

is realism – the doctrine that there is a world external to our thoughts, and that our interaction with that world constrains our beliefs. However, though it presumes an external world, we can never be sure that we know the truth about it. Truth is defined only in relation to method, with method in turn depending on the values we hold. Crucial to this argument is experimentation, or intervention in the world, for it is by undertaking experiments – by *doing* things – that scientists confront the real world. Given that most economics is non-experimental, this raises the question of what economists do that results in the real world constraining their beliefs.

7.   The Popperian tradition

7.1   A POPPERIAN RESPONSE TO POST-MODERNISM

Rorty's argument is that knowledge needs to be justified; and that since such justification cannot be provided by the metaphor of a mirror, it has to be sought in the consensus of a particular community. Rorty is, in other words, committed to the notion that knowledge must be justified, and he merely seeks to replace one form of justification with another. In view of the importance of this point it is worth quoting Munz.

> He [Rorty] thinks all knowledge is only worthy of that name if it can be 'justified'. He has shown over and over again that it cannot be justified as representational. But since it has to be justified, Rorty sees only one alternative. If knowing does not have an essence (Rorty, 1980, p. 389) then we have the 'right to believe' what 'current standards' recommend. If words are not transparent to the real (*ibid.* p. 368) then we must 'deconstruct' them and accept that they acquire privileges from the men who use them. In short, Rorty gives us a choice between justificationism and relativism which latter amounts to holding that proposition to be justified which has the consensus of a given community. So the real choice, according to Rorty, is between straight justificationism and relative justificationism. Rorty never considers the possibility that there is a genuine third possibility – the possibility that we consider as knowledge a proposition which is *not* justified, neither by the fact that it 'represents' nor by the fact that it has found the acclaim of a speech community. (Munz, 1984, pp. 207–8)

Whether or not it is vulnerable to other criticisms (see, for example, Caldwell, 1991; Hausman, 1992) an alternative to both the positions considered by Rorty is a Popperian view, according to which all knowledge is hypothetical. For Popper, as much as for Rorty or Fish, there are no givens:

The empirical basis of objective science has thus nothing 'absolute' about it. Science does not rest upon solid bedrock. The bold structure of its theories rises, as it were, above a swamp. It is like a building erected on piles. The piles are driven down from above into the swamp, but not down to any natural or 'given' base; and if we stop driving the piles deeper, it is not because we have reached firm ground. We simply stop when we are satisfied that the piles are firm enough to carry the structure, at least for the time being. (Popper, 1959, p. 111)

[T]he experiences which are 'given to me' such as the experience of seeing something (or, with Descartes, the experience of doubting) seem to offer themselves as the natural starting points. Subjectivists uncritically assumed that upon the basis of these 'data' the edifice of knowledge – scientific knowledge – can be erected. But this assumption is incorrect. Nothing can be built on these 'data', even if we assume that they themselves exist. But they do not exist: there are no uninterpreted '*data*'; there is nothing simply 'given' to us uninterpreted; nothing to be taken as a basis. *All* our knowledge is interpretation in the light of our expectations, our theories, and is therefore *hypothetical* in some way or other. (Popper, 1983, p. 102)

These arguments apply not simply to individuals' experiences (and subjectivism) but equally well to communities' shared experiences (and theories which see knowledge as pertaining to discourse communities).

The fact that Rorty's arguments (and the comparable arguments of Fish) are effective only against 'foundationalist' epistemologies could explain why, despite his claim to be showing the futility of all 'Methodology', McCloskey's and Weintraub's explicit arguments take positivism as their target.[1] Popperian falsificationism is important not because it is claimed to provide a 'recipe' for scientific success (more on this later) but because it provides an alternative to foundationalist epistemology.[2][3]

---

[1] McCloskey describes the official rhetoric, to which he is objecting, as 'an amalgam of logical positivism, behaviourism, operationalism, and the hypothetico-deductive model of science' (McCloskey, 1983, p. 484). Similarly Weintraub characterizes 'Methodology' as foundationalist, being based on 'Philosophers' attempts to justify knowledge claims' (1989, p. 266). It is also significant that his brief summary of the history of philosophy ends with logical positivism.

[2] McCloskey (forthcoming, Chapter 1) clearly recognizes that Popper's *Logic of Scientific Discovery* (1959) constituted the 'knell' of logical positivism. Yet he does not explore the implications of much economic methodology, including writings of both

7.2   THE LOGIC OF SCIENTIFIC DISCOVERY

The critique of induction

Popper's starting point in *The Logic of Scientific Discovery* (1959) is the problem of induction. What we observe is expressed in *singular* statements – statements about specific events at specific places and specific times. Thus the observation that when British Airways announced it was negotiating with two other airlines over the future of US Air, its share price rose by 10 per cent, or the observation that when the balance of payments statistics were published in July 1995, Sterling appreciated 5 Pfennigs against the Deutschmark, are singular statements. Scientific statements, on the other hand, are *universal* statements – statements that whenever certain conditions are satisfied, certain circumstances will occur. An example of a universal statement is the claim that unanticipated increases in the money supply will be followed by transitory increases in output. The problem of induction concerns the conditions under which universal statements can be derived from singular statements.

Popper's radical solution to the problem of induction was to argue that it could not, and need not be solved: 'the various difficulties of inductive logic sketched here are insurmountable' (Popper, 1959, p. 29). There is, he argued, no way in which, on the basis of singular statements, we can ever know that a universal statement is true. However many observations we make, we can never be sure that the next will not show our universal statement (or theory) to be false. The reason why this does not matter is that, though universal statements cannot be proven on the basis of singular statements, they can be shown to be false.[4] One contradictory observation, if it is accepted, is sufficient to dispose of a theory. This led Popper to advocate what he termed the deductive testing of theories, or the empirical method.

'methodologists' and working economists, having been influenced by Popper. We have simply the intriguing statement that 'Karl Popper has played a role on both modernist and antimodernist sides' (1986, p. 12). Similarly, Rorty (1991, p. 23) refers to Popper's work as being based on a pragmatist view of truth, but containing 'lingering positivist elements'.

[3] This point has also been made by Hands (1993), Chapter 12.

[4] The converse of this proposition is that existential statements (for example, there exist monopolistic markets) cannot be falsified, only verified.

The empirical method

Deductive testing involves four stages (Popper, 1959, pp. 32–3).

1. Logical comparison of the conclusions of a theory – testing the theory for internal consistency.
2. Logical analysis of the theory to decide whether it is empirical (falsifiable) or tautological.
3. Comparison with other theories to see whether it would constitute a scientific advance if it were to survive our tests.
4. Testing the theory by way of empirical applications of the conclusions drawn from it.

The purpose of testing is to find out how far the new consequences of the theory (those consequences not derivable from current theory or, even better, contradicted by current theory) are consistent with the results of practical applications and experiments. When their conclusions are confronted with evidence, theories are either corroborated or falsified. However, corroboration does not show that the theory is true – merely that it (1) has withstood detailed and severe tests; and (2) has not been superseded by another theory.

A consequence of this changed perspective is that Popper adopted a new demarcation criterion. Rather than distinguish between true and false theories, Popper emphasized the distinction between falsifiable and non-falsifiable statements. Empirical statements are falsifiable in the sense that there is a set of observations with which they are inconsistent – that would cause the theory to be abandoned.

> I do not demand that every scientific statement must *have in fact been tested* before it is accepted. I only demand that every such statement must be *capable* of being tested; or in other words, I refuse to accept the view that there are statements in science which we have, resignedly, to accept as true merely because it does not seem possible, for logical reasons, to test them. (Popper, 1959, p. 48)

Notice that Popper does not reject statements that cannot, as a practical matter, be tested, provided there is no logical reason why they cannot, in principle, be tested. Analogously to Popper's definition of empirical statements, he defines an empirical theory as one that 'allows us to deduce, roughly speaking, more *empirical* statements than we can deduce from the initial conditions alone' (Popper, 1959, p. 85).

If this were all there were to testing theories, the matter would be very straightforward. An empirical method would have been derived simply by means of logic. Things are, however more complicated, for two reasons.

1. Faced with an apparent falsification it is always possible to introduce an *ad hoc* auxiliary hypothesis, or an *ad hoc* change in a definition.
2. The availability of singular statements that can serve as premises in falsifying theories.

Popper's response to this is to bring in a number of methodological rules, or conventions, about scientific inquiry. The main such rules are the following.

1. 'The game of science is, in principle, without end' (Popper, 1959, p. 53) – there never arises a time when scientific theories become immune from testing.
2. Theories that have been corroborated are not allowed to drop out without 'good reason' – that is unless one of its implications is falsified, or another, better, theory is advanced.
3. Theories are not saved from falsification by 'conventionalist stratagems' such as the *ad hoc* changing of auxiliary assumptions or the *ad hoc* alteration of definitions (Popper, 1959, p. 81).

This, of course, begs the question of what counts as an *ad hoc* modification to a theory. Popper's answer is that modifications to a theory should be viewed as creating new theories. These new theories should be judged by the criteria already laid down – by whether they constitute an advance of knowledge. *Ad hoc* assumptions are ones where the resulting new theories do not advance knowledge, for they are less falsifiable than the original theory.[5]

---

[5] The evolution of concept of *ad hoc*ness within the Popperian tradition is discussed in Hands (1993), Chapter 7.

What about the argument that there are no logical grounds for having confidence in the singular 'basic' statements that are used to test theories? Popper argues that though such statements are objective in the sense of being inter-subjectively testable – the phenomena concerned are reproducible – they are in no sense absolute. They are the result of a decision analogous to the verdict of a jury.[6]

> Their acceptance is part of the application of a theoretical system; and it is only this application which makes any further applications of the theoretical system possible. (Popper, 1959, p. 111)

Decisions to accept or reject theories rest, ultimately, on conventions concerning methodological rules and the empirical basis.

The growth of knowledge

Popper's emphasis is on the *quest* for knowledge. He concludes *The Logic of Scientific Discovery* with the following words.[7]

> [I]t is not his *possession* of knowledge, of irrefutable truth, that makes the man of science, but his persistent and recklessly critical *quest* for truth. ... Science never pursues the illusory aim of making its answers final, or even probable. Its advance is, rather, towards an infinite yet attainable aim: that of ever discovering new, deeper, and more general problems, and of subjecting our ever tentative answers to ever renewed and ever more rigorous tests. (Popper, 1959, p. 281)

His belief is that rigorous testing, in the sense of exposing systems to falsification, *in every conceivable way*, will lead to progress: the aim of science is to select the fittest theory by exposing all theories to 'the fiercest struggle for survival' (Popper, 1959, p. 42).[8] The methodological rules Popper proposes are designed to maximize the

---

6 Popper contrasts the judgement of a judge, based on reasoning from other statements, with the verdict of a jury, which can be challenged only on the grounds that proper procedures were not followed. (1959, p. 110).

7 These words are the final ones of the original text. In later editions he expanded the book with an Addendum and various Appendices.

8 Boland (1994) has argued that the emphasis on unremitting criticism is the key Popperian characteristic.

exposure of theories to criticism. We may not be able to know that our theories are true, but we can ensure that knowledge grows.

But if science depends on the acceptance of certain conventions, what grounds can we have for believing that these conventions are the optimal ones? It is not possible to prove them to be correct using logical analysis.[9] Popper's answer is that the criteria by which his conventions are judged are that (1) they can be applied without inconsistencies arising; (2) they help us; and (3) they are really needed.[10]

7.3   THE METHODOLOGY OF SCIENTIFIC RESEARCH PROGRAMMES

Lakatos's methodology of scientific research programmes (MSRP) lies squarely in the Popperian tradition. Though he presents it as a compromise between the Popperian attempt to provide a rational account of scientific growth and Kuhn's tendency towards 'irrationalism' (1970, p. 8), it can be seen as involving only a small shift from the position outlined in the previous section. In particular, the MSRP is, like Popperian falsificationism, immune to Rorty's anti-foundationalist critique: it is non-foundationalist, locating rationality in the growth of knowledge rather than in foundations. Yet Lakatos adds a new twist to the Popperian theory of progress. To see these points, consider the way in which Lakatos develops his MSRP through a critique of falsificationism. Throughout this critique, two themes are dominant.

1. Saving science from scepticism is inextricably linked with establishing science as an empirical activity.
2. The empirical nature of science is to be found in scientific progress, not in empirical foundations.

Thus Lakatos writes:

---

[9] C.f. Peirce's claim that by logical analysis of the question, it was possible to derive conclusions about method.

[10] These are the criteria Popper uses to reject the principle of induction (Popper, 1959, pp. 52–3).

If *all* scientific statements are fallible theories, one can criticize them only for inconsistency. But then, in what sense, if any, is science empirical? If scientific theories are neither provable, nor probabilifiable, nor disprovable, then the sceptics seem to be finally right: science is no more than vain speculation and there is no such thing as progress in scientific knowledge. Can we still oppose scepticism? *Can we save scientific criticism from fallibilism?* (Lakatos, 1970, p. 20)

This paragraph clearly illustrates the links Lakatos sees between empiricism, scepticism and progress.

Lakatos's critique of falsificationism

Falsificationism is criticized in three stages: dogmatic falsificationism, naive methodological falsificationism, and sophisticated methodological falsificationism. Of these, dogmatic falsificationism is the most straightforward. It is the version of falsificationism that sees falsification as a straightforward, clear-cut activity that leads to the rejection of scientific theories. This fails, Lakatos argues, because it is based on three assumptions, each of which is false.

1. There is a sharp distinction between what is observational and what is not.
2. Observations 'prove' that observational statements are true or false.
3. Scientific theories are logically inconsistent with some finite set of observational statements.

Given these assumptions, it would be possible to argue that theories could be decisively falsified. However, the first assumption is refuted by the history of science, which shows that the distinction between theoretical and factual propositions is far from clear-cut. The second involves a logical fallacy: propositions can be derived only from other propositions, not from observations. The third fails because many important scientific theories 'fail to forbid any observable state of affairs' (Lakatos, 1970, p. 16), essentially because all statements about observable states of the world contain *ceteris paribus* clauses.

Naive methodological falsificationism responds to this by arguing that certain singular statements are, *by convention*, taken as unfalsifiable – on the grounds that 'there exists at the time a "relevant technique" such that "anyone who has learned it" will be able to *decide* that the statement is "acceptable"' (Lakatos, 1970, p. 22). The theories on which such statements are based are, again by taking a decision, regarded as unproblematic background knowledge. On the basis of such evidence, decisions are then taken to reject theories that are inconsistent with such evidence. Because the evidence may turn out to be mistaken, however, rejection is not the same as disproof. The absence of firm foundations means that theories cannot conclusively be disproved.

Why, then, if conventions may be mistaken and mistaken theories rejected, should scientists behave in this way? Lakatos's answer is that the risk of making mistakes is the price we pay for progress, for without an alternative method of criticism, scientists are inevitably driven towards irrationalism. The methodological falsificationist insists that the choice is between 'some sort of methodological falsificationism and irrationalism' (Lakatos, 1970, p. 29). Methodological falsificationism is, for Lakatos, unavoidable because he is committed to the notion of progress and it is the only way in which the concept of progress can be saved. He argues, however, that it is not necessary to make quite so many seemingly arbitrary methodological decisions – that there is a more sophisticated version of methodological falsificationism.

Sophisticated methodological falsificationism

For the sophisticated methodological falsificationist, acceptable theories have excess empirical content compared with their predecessors – they lead to the discovery of novel facts. More formally, a theory T is falsified only if there arises another theory, T' which has the following three characteristics.

1. T' predicts facts that were improbable or even forbidden given T.
2. T' explains the previous successes of T.
3. Some of the excess content of T' is corroborated.

Rather than aim, as does naive methodological falsificationism, at falsification at any price, sophisticated methodological falsificationism imposes standards on the adjustments by which theories can be saved. If a theory T can be modified to obtain T', where *T'* satisfies these three conditions, the modification is allowed. It constitutes a progressive problemshift (theoretically progressive if the first two conditions are met; empirically progressive if all three are). If modifications to a theory fail to meet these criteria, the problemshift is degenerating, or pseudoscientific, and should be rejected.

Several points are worth making about Lakatos's sophisticated methodological falsificationism.

1. The appraisal criterion applies only to *sequences of theories*, not to individual theories in isolation.
2. Scientific, empirical, knowledge is defined explicitly in terms of growth. Falsification becomes synonymous with the emergence of a better theory.

> Our empirical criterion for a series of theories is that it should produce new facts. *The idea of growth and the concept of empirical character are soldered into one.* (Lakatos, 1970, p. 35; original emphasis)

3. Where Popper had introduced the prediction of novel facts as one amongst many criteria by which theories should be judged, Lakatos elevated it into the *sole* criterion.

> for the sort of Popperian empiricism I advocate, the only relevant evidence is the evidence anticipated by a theory, and *empiricalness (or scientific character) and theoretical progress are inseparably connected.* (Lakatos, 1970, p. 38)

Though prediction of novel facts has a long history as an appraisal criterion, going back to Leibnitz and Whewell, it is only within the Popperian tradition, where acceptance and truth are separated, that it comes into its own.

Research programmes

Once we reach this point, where it is *sequences* of theories that have to be appraised, it is but a short step to consider research programmes, defined by Lakatos as sets of methodological rules: some rules (positive heuristics) tell us what to do, and others (negative heuristics) tell us what not to do. These two types of rule have very different functions.

1. The *negative heuristic* ensures the integrity of the research programme, through directing researchers not to question its hard-core assumptions. This hard core is treated as irrefutable, by a methodological decision of the scientists working in the programme. Anomalies are solved by modifications not to the hard core, but to the protective belt of auxiliary assumptions, observational hypotheses and initial conditions.
2. The *positive heuristic* sets out an agenda for research, telling the scientist how to proceed. It predicts anomalies (refutations) and provides the means whereby they can be dealt with.

These heuristics account for a number of otherwise inexplicable features of science: the continuity of science and the relative autonomy of theoretical work. Theories are always confronted with numerous anomalies (Lakatos uses the phrase 'ocean of anomalies') and the heuristics provide a strategy by which they are dealt with.

One reason why anomalies always exist is that scientists work with 'models' – simplified representations of the world that scientists know are inadequate. In deciding to use a model, the scientist *creates* anomalies in the knowledge that, if the model is successful, there is a strategy by which the anomalies can be eliminated. 'Actual' counter-examples (the available data) are ignored in favour of eliminating counter-examples produced by the theory. Lakatos goes so far as to claim that 'if the positive heuristic is clearly spelt out, the difficulties of the programme are mathematical rather than empirical' (Lakatos, 1970, p. 51). This is very clearly illustrated by the example of the Newtonian analysis of the solar system, which followed the following strategy (Lakatos, 1970, p. 50).

1. Work out the motion of a fixed, point-like, sun and a single point-like, planet.
2. Replace this with a model where sun and planet revolve around their common centre of gravity.
3. Introduce more planets, but ignoring inter-planetary interactions.
4. Replace the assumption that sun and planets were mass-points with the assumption that they were mass-balls.

5. Introduce spinning planets, wobbles, perturbations, bulging planets and so on.

The positive heuristic of Newton's research programme could be summed up as a metaphysical principle: 'the planets are essentially gravitating spinning-tops of roughly spherical shape' (Lakatos, 1970, p. 51).

What is being described here is the process whereby an acceptable theory is developed. Because Newton was working with inadequate models (such as one assuming planets were point masses), the rectification of known inadequacies took precedence over dealing with anomalies whose theoretical significance was not understood. Refutations are less important than verifications of the programme's predictions. Research programmes (hard cores) are to be supported as long as they are progressive – as long as they lead to the successful prediction of novel facts. They are to be abandoned when they degenerate – when they cease to predict novel facts, or when predictions are repeatedly shown to be inconsistent with the facts.[11]

The methodology of historical research programmes

One of the objections to Popper's falsificationism is that the methodological rules Popper puts forward are in a sense left hanging in the air. He argues that if science is to progress, such rules are necessary, otherwise theories would never be falsified, but he cannot show that other different rules would not fulfil the same task, possibly more effectively. He does not apply his own demarcation criterion, that scientific theories should be falsifiable, to his own theory. Lakatos's response to this problem is to propose a criterion by which the methodology of scientific research programmes can be judged – his methodology of *historical* research programmes.

Lakatos's methodology of historical research programmes is based on the assumption that a theory of scientific rationality should be consistent with the views of the relevant scientific community. This is a realistic criterion to employ, for whilst there may be no explicit

---

[11] This criterion may be softened by arguing that abandoning a programme should take place only when it has degenerated beyond repair – when there is no hope that it will ever become progressive again. This would allow scientists to continue with a degenerating programme as long as there was the prospect of its becoming progressive at a later date.

agreement on what constitutes good science in general, there is considerable agreement on whether specific scientific achievements were successful or not.

> While there has been no *general* agreement concerning a theory of scientific rationality, there has been considerable agreement concerning whether a particular single step in the game was scientific or crankish, or whether a particular gambit was played correctly or not. (Lakatos, 1971, p. 124)

Lakatos then argues that any theory of science should be applied to itself. If we are Popperian, for example, we should reject falsificationism if it is falsified by the evidence of how the relevant scientific community judges particular achievements: 'a rationality theory – or demarcation criterion – is to be rejected if it is inconsistent with an accepted "basic value judgement" of the scientific élite' (Lakatos, 1971, p. 124). To give an example, Popper requires that scientists be prepared to state in advance the conditions under which they would be prepared to give up their basic assumptions. But Newtonian scientists would never have been able to agree on the types of evidence that would cause them to abandon Newton's laws of motion and gravitation. Given that Newtonian science has undoubtedly been extremely successful, this falsifies this particular Popperian methodological rule.

Turning to his own methodology, Lakatos argues that it should be accepted if it can be shown to constitute a progressive historical research programme – if it predicts novel, previously unexpected, historical facts that are corroborated by historical research.

> Thus progress in the theory of scientific rationality is marked by discoveries of novel historical facts, by the reconstruction of a growing bulk of value-impregnated history as rational. (Lakatos, 1971, p. 133)

He saw his methodology as constituting a progressive problemshift relative to those of Kuhn and Feyerabend, for where they saw 'irrational change', he predicted that the historian would be able to see rational change. The methodology of scientific research programmes could reconstruct more of the actual history of science as rational. It qualifies as science according to its own criteria.

The method Lakatos advocated for achieving this was his method of rational reconstructions. The historian should write the history of science as though it had developed in accordance with the methodology of scientific research programmes, and then compare this 'rational reconstruction', or 'internal' history, with the historical record. If it were found necessary to rely continuously on 'external' factors (factors that were not part of the methodology)[12] in order to explain what actually happened, this would be evidence against the methodology of scientific research programmes. If, on the other hand, the rational reconstruction were in substantial agreement with the historical account, this would be corroborating evidence for the methodology.

7.4 CONCLUSIONS

Popper and Lakatos, like Peirce, locate scientific rationality in method, seeking to lay down a series of rules that will ensure that knowledge grows. The empirical character of science is located in the growth of knowledge, not in the availability of secure foundations. This is particularly true of Lakatos, who makes the prediction of novel facts the key to scientific progress. Popper's falsificationism, with its scepticism about all knowledge, and its insistence on methodological rules which maximize the exposure of theories to criticism, might seem to maximize the growth of knowledge. This, however, is not the case, for the Popperian methodology is too critical to be workable. The Lakatosian 'softening' of Popper, with its recognition that, as Kuhn recognized, it may be rational for scientists to adhere to a hard core of assumptions that is not regarded as open to criticism, is much more workable.[13]

Though Lakatos's methodology of scientific research programmes will not be used explicitly, several aspects of this methodology inform the chapters that follow.

---

[12] Note that this is an unconventional use of the term 'external'.

[13] Note that to say this is not to claim that research programmes can be identified by their hard cores, which remain unchanged as long as the research programme continues. For reasons given by Laudan (see above, section 6.3), and other reasons (Backhouse, 1992e, p. 31; 1994c, pp. 186–7), it may be appropriate to define research programmes more broadly.

1. The relative autonomy of theory is important. In considering progress, it is necessary to pay attention to theoretical and empirical progress, and to the relationship between them.
2. The prediction of novel facts may have been overemphasized by Lakatos when he made it the *sole* criterion for progress, but it is nonetheless extremely important.
3. Lakatos's methodology of historical research programmes points in the direction of an empirical approach to economic methodology based on the idea that, even though consensus on what constitutes successful research strategies may be difficult to achieve, there may be consensus on examples of successful scientific developments.

8. The concept of progress

8.1 WHAT IS PROGRESS?

Before turning to the more specific issues of theoretical and empirical progress in economics, it is helpful to recap on some of the possible definitions of progress that have emerged in previous chapters.

DEFINITION 1: Increased agreement

Increased agreement could be seen as constituting progress. If we were to define truth as what a particular community believed, increased consensus could mean that truth was more clearly defined. One reason for such a view might be certain values concerning the role of shared beliefs. If, for example, we were to follow William James in seeing truth as what it is good to believe, and if we believed that shared beliefs were valuable to a community, it would follow that movement towards a consensus would be valuable in itself, and would thus constitute progress. Increased consensus, however, is more commonly seen as progressive, not for its own sake, but because it is believed that the process whereby consensus is achieved will tend to eliminate error and lead scientists towards the truth in some other sense. Thus Peirce, for example, defined truth as the limit of a process of scientific inquiry because of his faith in the powers of scientific method (see page 68). However, although increased consensus is a definition of progress that should be discussed, it is not usually valued as an end in itself.[1]

---

[1] In economics, there is the further objection that to accept increased consensus as a definition of truth would be to evade some of the criticisms that have been levelled against economics – namely the charge that the discipline has been led astray by the pursuit of certain values.

DEFINITION 2: Closer approximation to the truth

Realism involves the assumption that there is an independent reality about which we can learn. Progress, therefore, can be seen in terms of discovering the truth about the world in the sense of improving the correspondence between theories and reality. This is the every-day, common-sense view of scientific progress. There are, however, some potential difficulties with such a view.

1. Judgements about progress can be made only in relation to our current beliefs about what reality is like, not in relation to any ultimate truth. If these beliefs change, then so too will our evaluation of progress.[2] However, though our definition of progress may thus become local, this is not necessarily a major problem. Peirce, for example, showed that truth, though unknown, could serve as a regulatory ideal – it was the beliefs on which a universal community of inquirers, following the method of science, would eventually agree. However, care must be taken not to define progress simply in terms of truth, otherwise the argument becomes circular. Progress, even if we are prepared to talk about it as movement towards truth, in some sense, still needs to be justified in terms of method.
2. There may be no unique representation of the world on which science can converge. Scientific theories draw on concepts and ideas that are influenced by culture and the very language we use. We should not simply assume that the categories we use necessarily correspond, whether more or less accurately, to natural categories, inherent in reality. If there are many ways in which the world can be divided into categories, each defensible with a given theoretical framework, it is possible that beliefs may not converge on any unique truth.

This would seem to be especially true in economics, and more generally in social science, where the phenomena frequently have to be considered from a variety of seemingly unrelated perspectives. Economics has even been defined as dealing simply with one aspect of behaviour (c.f. Robbins, 1933). Realism may be a defensible

---

2 This is the problem Kuhn raised in the context of paradigm change (see Chapter 5 above).

option, but it does not have to go along with a correspondence theory of truth.

DEFINITION 3: Increasingly reliable knowledge

The pragmatist way of viewing progress has the merit of dispensing with the metaphysical problem of the relation between truth and reality. Truth is defined in terms of what works: knowledge rests in the ability to answer questions and solve problems. Progress in this sense has to do with enabling us to *do* things.

DEFINITION 4: Improved explanatory power

Scientific theories are about explaining phenomena – about saying *why* things happen as they do – not simply about prediction or control. This has led some economists (for example, Hahn) to emphasize the virtues of explanation. However, whilst the importance of being able to explain phenomena is hard to deny, it poses a serious problem: what constitutes the best explanation depends very much on the standards we apply. It could, for example, be argued that the test of explanatory power is the ability to predict successfully. Without any explanation of these standards, defining progress in terms of increased explanatory power does not get us very far.

DEFINITION 5: Irreversible change

The above four definitions interpret progress as improvement – as moving forwards towards some desirable end. An alternative perspective is to see progress simply as irreversible change. This is the definition used by Bliss, one of the few economists to have asked what is meant my progress in the subject.

> What is meant [by a *'progressive tendency'*] is that the subject cannot turn back on itself and retrace its past. It is driven on by an ordered principle, something like the principle of entropy. (Bliss, 1986, p. 365)

The premise (highly disputable) on which this rests is that past ideas are not forgotten. Though Bliss goes on to adopt a realist view, asserting that in science there is an ultimate truth that scientists are seeking to attain, this is separable from his definition of progress.

8.2   WHAT IS THEORETICAL PROGRESS?

DEFINITION TP1: Increased generality
DEFINITION TP2: Increased scope

The domain of a theory is defined by its assumptions. Typically, additional assumptions narrow the domain of a theory. Thus if assumptions can be removed or replaced by weaker ones (ones that exclude fewer possible states of the world) the theory is more general. The converse of increased generality is decreased content, for unless they are redundant, the relaxation of assumptions will mean that there are some results that can no longer be proved. For example, suppose a theory T_2 assumes a production function $F(K, L)$ (with the standard properties) and T_1 assumes $AK^\alpha L^{1-\alpha}$, T_2 will apply to all situations where T_1 applies, and to others besides. But some theorems that could be proved in T_1 (constancy of relative shares under perfect competition) cannot be proved in T_2. Increased generality, therefore, does not *necessarily* constitute progress.

The reason for this is that economic theories typically contain many assumptions concerning which we have no direct evidence and even assumptions that are *a priori* unlikely. Thus replacement of a production function $AK^\alpha L^{1-\alpha}$ with $F(K, L)$ is considered progress because we normally have no reason to believe that the Cobb-Douglas is correct. On the other hand, it is not progress for a Belgian economist with a model of a small open economy to replace it with one in which size and openness are unspecified, even though this would be more general.

A useful distinction here is between the *generality* and the *scope* of a theory. A theory has greater scope if it applies to a wider range of *identifiable* situations. Making more general assumptions constitutes an increase in scope only if it means that the theory is applicable to a wider range of identifiable situations. Thus if we knew that some economies were characterized by Cobb-Douglas production functions, and others by CES or Leontief production functions, moving to $F(K, L)$ would represent an increase in scope. But given that we do not know this, it does not. In contrast, in so far as there are markets that can be identified as non-competitive, a model of oligopoly (such as Cournot's) that includes perfect competition as a limiting case, applies to more situations than a model of perfect competition, and hence has wider scope. This is not simply a matter of whether or not the assumptions of a theory are realistic. Workability is crucial. Assumptions such as whether there is a finite number or a continuum of agents, may, even though one is clearly more realistic than the other, be irrelevant to the scope of a theory. Thus Debreu's example (1986, p. 1267) of the removal of differentiability assumptions may not involve an increase in scope.

It can also be argued that one theory has wider scope than another even if the one theory is not a special case of the other. Thus the theory of utility maximization has wider scope than the Keynesian theory of consumption, even if the latter cannot be derived from the former.[3]

Increased scope clearly represents progress if there are situations that need to be analysed that fall within the range of the new theory but which were outside that of the old theory. Is it a cost that certain theorems (for example ones specific to perfect competition) will be lost? The answer depends on whether it is possible to retain the old theory alongside the new. In the former case, there is progress. In the latter case it is unclear – further criteria are needed.

DEFINITION TP3: Increased precision

This can be interpreted in at least two ways. The first is as the opposite of generality. A precise theory has greater empirical content than a general one. The second is as reduction in vagueness (we may not know exactly what a theory implies – what its content is).

DEFINITION TP4: Increased rigour

This is similar to reduction in vagueness, but it applies to the methods by which a theory is established. *Ceteris paribus*, it is debatable whether this, in itself, constitutes progress. Debreu, for example, has argued that 'the effort toward rigor substitutes correct

---

[3] The term 'Keynesian consumption function' is used to refer to the notion that there is a 'fundamental psychological law' governing consumption behaviour. Even if life-cycle theories can be used to derive non-proportional short-run consumption functions, they remain partially incommensurable theories.

reasonings and results for incorrect ones' and 'usually leads to a deeper understanding of the problems to which is applied' (Debreu, 1959, p. x). For him, increased rigour does not constitute progress, but assists progress.

DEFINITION TP5: Elimination of error

This refers not to error in the sense of not conforming to reality, but in the sense of clear mistakes. If someone records a result incorrectly, makes a keyboard or a transcription error, the elimination of such an error clearly represents progress.[4]

DEFINITION TP6: Elimination of inconsistency

The elimination of inconsistency might seem to be covered by TP4, for it could be argued that inconsistencies are errors. There are, however, cases where one might consciously make assumptions that are, at one level, inconsistent. For example, much macroeconomics, from the 1940s to the 1960s, simultaneously assumed both perfect competition and non-clearing markets, or at least a non-clearing labour market. Given that perfect competition implies market clearing, this is an inconsistency, but it is not an error, for there may be good reasons for constructing a theory in this way. It may be believed that, though demand and supply for labour both depend on the real wage in a way that can be modelled in terms of optimizing, price-taking agents, movements in prices depend on other factors that are too little understood to be modelled explicitly. If the inconsistency can be removed without incurring other costs, progress has occurred.[5]

DEFINITION TP7: Increased simplicity (or beauty)

Simplicity is motivated in part by aesthetics – the search for elegance. One of its merits is 'the quest for the most direct link between the assumptions and the conclusions of a theorem' (Debreu, 1986, p. 1267). More direct proofs are more transparent, so errors are

---

[4] This corresponds to what Cartwright (1991) and Collins (1991) have called 'checking'. Though econometricians often prefer the term 'replication', this is misleading.

[5] In general, economic models are not formal axiomatic systems where axioms are all independent of each other.

easier to spot. Simplicity can also be justified as a characteristic of progress using the argument that, though the world may be complex, knowledge is dependent on our capacity to understand, which requires simplicity.

DEFINITION TP8: Prediction of novel facts

A theory that predicts novel facts has more content than one that does not. These predictions can then be tested, providing a direct link between theoretical and empirical progress.

8.3 WHAT IS EMPIRICAL PROGRESS?

Definitions of empirical progress

Five main definitions of empirical progress emerge from Chapters 6 to 7. Having been discussed in more detail already, they need be summarized here only briefly.

DEFINITION EP1: Increases in the number and quality of empirical generalizations

Empirical generalizations (for example, the absence of clear contra-cyclical movement in real wages, or the short-run non proportionality of consumption and income) are important as constraints on theorizing, because they may be important in deriving answers to questions relevant to economic policy, and because they may be important in their own right. On their own, empirical generalizations are of limited use, for they provide no understanding of *why* certain phenomena are observed. In addition, it is frequently not clear whether, and if so under what circumstances, they will break down. The classic example is the pre-Friedman/Phelps Phillips curve, which at one time appeared, to many economists, to be a well-established empirical generalization, but which broke down when circumstances changed (or even, perhaps, because its discovery caused a change in the behaviour of economic agents, thereby causing it to break down). Another is the stability of M1 velocity, which broke down with the effects of financial deregulation.

Empirical generalizations in economics may be more complicated than in the natural sciences (the law of gravity, Hooke's law, conservation of momentum) because they involve more complicated *ceteris paribus* clauses. Other empirical generalizations, however, are simple correlations, with no *ceteris paribus* clauses (the long run constancy of the share of wages in national income). These are frequently not numerical laws but 'stylized facts': generalizations that do not hold exactly, and which are typically not established by any formal statistical procedure.

DEFINITION   EP2:   Increased   predictive   success/increased
     corroboration

As with empirical generalizations, increased predictive success may be important for two reasons: for its own sake (the predictions may be important to policy makers) or because it constitutes a test of theories. This is the Popperian condition for empirical progress – theories are corroborated through surviving severe tests.[6]

DEFINITION EP3: Successful prediction of novel facts

This is the Lakatosian criterion for the progressiveness of a research programme.[7] Novelty can be defined in a variety of ways.[8]

DEFINITION EP4: Improved problem-solving ability

This is the pragmatist criterion. It is important to note that it makes empirical progress depend on more than simply *knowing* – knowledge is judged by its ability to help us *do* things that could not be done without it.

Establishing facts and testing theories

A further distinction can be drawn between two categories relating to progress: establishing facts about the world[9] and testing theories.

---

[6] See page 85 above.

[7] See page 90 above.

[8] See page 114 below.

[9] Note that this does not imply anything, one way or the other, about whether these facts should be seen as 'discovered' or 'constructed'.

Empirical generalizations and predictions, though they may derive their significance from theories, and though the processes whereby facts are selected and established may be irretrievably theory-laden, are atheoretical in the sense that they offer no explanations. Testing theories, in contrast, is concerned with testing explanations of economic phenomena.

8.4   TRUTH AND PROGRESS

The claim that any discipline, whether economics or any other, can provide true knowledge in the sense of knowledge that rests on completely secure, indubitable foundations is clearly unwarranted. There are no external standards – no God's eye view from which we can judge theories to be true or false in an absolute sense. It may even be the case, as Rorty has argued so forcefully, that truth is an uninteresting concept, with which we can dispense.

It is, however, unjustified to conclude from this that there are no standards by which theories can or should be judged. Economists are looking for theories and methods of analysis that enable them to say significant things about the economic world: (1) to explain economic phenomena in a convincing way, (2) to predict as accurately as possible and (3) to provide decision-makers with advice that will assist them in the task of achieving their objectives. In short, they are searching for theories that work. These objectives may seem very general, but they are nonetheless sufficiently precise to rule out certain options. Economics, if it is to meet these criteria (all of them, not simply the first) must be empirically based.[10] To make such a claim is not to fall victim to 'positivist' dogma – such objectives are as consistent with pragmatism as with any form of positivism.

Though we may not be able to say whether economic knowledge is true, either because the concept of truth cannot be tied down sufficiently tightly, or simply because the world is too complicated

---

[10] This does not rule out part of the subject being concerned with issues arising out of, say, political philosophy (c.f. the discussion of Rosenberg in section 9.2 below). But to undertake welfare economics it is, as Walras (1874/1954) recognized when he sought to analyse a 'realistic utopia', any design for society must reflect real-world constraints.

for such a goal to be feasible, we can ask whether economics is being pursued in a way that is likely to lead to progress (defined relative to the objectives of the subject). Both the pragmatist and the Popperian traditions offer useful pointers as to how such progress might be conceived. We could even go so far as to think of truth, in a sense, as the limit of such a process of inquiry.

This far, the argument is very general and might apply to almost any discipline. To go further, however, we need to explore the nature of economics in more detail – to consider the structure of the discipline and the way various practices contribute towards, or detract from the progress of the subject.

9. Is economics an empirical science?

9.1 INTRODUCTION

Previous chapters have explored the nature of truth and progress in economic knowledge at a fairly abstract, philosophical, level. Subsequent chapters will consider some more concrete issues relating to theoretical and empirical progress in economics. Before turning to such issues, however, it is necessary to address the question of whether economics should be regarded as an empirical science, in the sense of either being based on well-established empirical generalizations or producing reasonably reliable predictions, at all.

9.2 ECONOMICS AS A NORMATIVE ENTERPRISE

Whether or not such a goal is attainable, or even desirable, it has been argued that economics is in practice not an empirical science, and that there are good reasons for this. Such a case has recently been argued by Rosenberg.

> Much of the mystery surrounding the actual development of economic theory – its shifts in formalism, its insulation from empirical assessment, its interest in proving purely formal, abstract possibilities, its unchanged character over a period of centuries, the controversies over its cognitive status – can be comprehended and properly appreciated if we give up on the notion that economics any longer has the aims or makes the claims of an empirical science of human behavior. Rather we should view it as a branch of mathematics, one devoted to examining the formal properties of a set of assumptions about the transitivity of abstract relations: axioms that implicitly define a technical

notion of 'rationality', just as geometry examines the formal properties of abstract points and lines. (Rosenberg, 1992, p. 247)

Apart from arguing, completely convincingly, that such an interpretation makes sense of much of the historical record, Rosenberg supports this claim by arguing that economists have remained committed to an approach to modelling individual behaviour that is inconsistent with a desire to improve the discipline's predictive power. Economists are committed to modelling behaviour in terms of beliefs and desires, or expectations and preferences. The problem this creates is that beliefs and desires are not identifiable independently of each other or of other beliefs and desires. They are thus unmeasurable. If economists were concerned with generating improved predictions, Rosenberg argues, they would have followed the example set by psychology, and moved away from such a view of individual behaviour. Given that they have not, he concludes that economists must have other aims.

But if the axioms underlying economic theories and models are not empirically founded, and if its goal is not empirical, why should economists be interested in such mathematics? Rosenberg suggests that the normative element in economics provides the answer. Economics provides a surprising answer to the question of what an economy controlled by a very large number of different agents, each motivated by their own self interest, will look like, namely that there may be order, not chaos. It thus provides an answer to a fundamental question of contractarian political philosophy – 'the preferability for society of decentralized market mechanisms over centralized planning ones' (Rosenberg, 1992, p. 219). Economics, then, should be seen, not as an empirical science, but as a branch of contractarian political philosophy. Economics is not empirical, but normative.

A related view was expressed many years ago by Frank Knight in response to Hutchison's *The Significance and Basic Postulates of Economic Theory* (1938). He argued that economic propositions relate actions to human purposes or motives. Because human motives can never be inferred from observations of behaviour, economic propositions could never be verified by any empirical procedure.

The formal principles of economic theory can never carry anyone very far toward the prediction or technical control of the corresponding economic behavior. (Knight, 1940, p. 30)

He thus objected to Hutchison's drawing a sharp distinction between 'propositions which can be tested' and 'vague conceptions of common sense'.

The testable facts are not really economic, for positive process is not of the economizing character. This inability to test may or may not be regarded as 'too bad'; anyhow, it is the truth. (Knight, 1941, p. 752, emphasis in original)

Though Knight adopted a different (Austrian) starting point in that he saw the basic postulates of economics as being known by experience, he reached the same conclusion: that economics is not an empirical science.

9.3   THE ROLE OF PREDICTION IN ECONOMICS

Pragmatic scepticism concerning prediction

Many economists have been very sceptical about the existence of economic laws and the ability of economists to make successful predictions. Hahn, for example, greatly plays down the importance of prediction, which he sees as an unattainable goal, in favour of 'explanation'.

Of course Popperians, and American Popperians in particular, ask for predictions. My own view is that they will for a very long time yet be beyond us except in very special cases. Of course all theories contain predictions, but testing these has not yet been a conspicuous success. I do not find that depressing. If I were not confined to one page I would go on to sing the praises of 'understanding'. (Hahn, 1992a, p. 5)

I want to emphasize the word 'understanding' and that it is not directly related to positivist prediction. For instance, we understand the cause of earthquakes but cannot at the moment predict them. (Hahn, 1984, p. 10)

Rosenberg has argued that scepticism about the ability of economists to predict successfully is even more widespread. The evidence he adduces is that a failure to improve the quality of predictions is implied by the stance of economists who *defend* the predictive power of economics:

> I try to show that their methodological position would be pointless except against the background of failure to improve the predictive power of economic theory. (Rosenberg, 1992, p. 57)

His main example is Friedman. If the accuracy of economic predictions had improved over time, Friedman would never have had to defend economics against the charge that its assumptions were unrealistic. In addition, restricting the domain of economic theories to what it is intended to explain, where this excludes the behaviour of individuals, is a sign of weakness not of strength. Generic predictions – 'predictions of the existence of a phenomenon, process or entity as opposed to specific predictions about its detailed character' (Rosenberg, 1992, p. 69) – are simply not enough.

Even stronger evidence for the inadequacy of economics' predictive power is the existence of the methodological doubts that periodically strike the profession. If economists believed that the predictive power of economics was increasing, such methodological crises would never occur.

The market argument that prediction is impossible

McCloskey takes the arguments against prediction a stage further, claiming that 'PREDICTION IS NOT POSSIBLE IN ECONOMICS' (McCloskey, 1986, p. 15, capitalization in original).[1] His main argument is a version of what he calls 'the American question', namely 'If you're so smart, why aren't you rich?'.[2] If prediction were possible, then economists would become rich by selling their predictions, whereas in practice one does not observe economists being conspicuously wealthy.

This argument is vulnerable on many counts. It is, of course possible to point to successful economists who make fortunes by selling predictions (Otto Eckstein, for example). More significant, however, is competition between economists: if economic

---

[1] He has since modified this to the much weaker claim that *profitable* prediction is impossible. The argument deserves to be rebutted nonetheless.

[2] See page 10, footnote 1.

knowledge is widely available, competition should ensure that economists, on average, make no more than normal earnings. It is not even clear that all predictions can be used to make money. Predicting the movements in the stock market or foreign exchange rates would clearly permit economists to make money, but not all predictions are of that type. Forecasting movement in unemployment, or the effects of raising the level of VAT on domestic fuel are valuable, but provide less easy routes to wealth. Thus whilst the market argument against the possibility of prediction can serve as a salutary warning, it does not establish that prediction is in general impossible.

Critical realism

Perhaps the most forthright critique of the possibility of prediction in economics is provided by Lawson (1994)[3] and other proponents of 'critical realism'. Critical realism is premised on the assumption that it is necessary to distinguish between three domains of reality: the 'empirical' (experience and impression), the 'actual' (events and states of affairs) and the 'non-actual' or 'deep' (structures, mechanisms, powers and tendencies) (Lawson, 1994, p. 262). The last two of these, it is claimed, are 'out of phase' with each other, which means that deep structures cannot be read directly from events. The existence of deep structures or mechanisms does not necessarily lead to event regularities. The main reason for this, in the social sphere, is that because it depends on human agency, social structure cannot be treated as fixed. Human actions transform the social structure.

Event regularities, or constant conjunctions of events, are, Lawson claims, 'rare even in natural science and more so in the social realm' (Lawson, 1994, p. 276). The response of natural scientists to this is controlled experiment: to isolate, or close off, part of the world in such a way that the underlying mechanisms are revealed. In the social realm, however, this is not possible. Economies are 'open' systems, with numerous forces operating, with the result that none are directly visible. This openness is inevitable in a system where human agency plays a role, and it means that event regularities will simply not be there to be found. Establishing empirical regularities

---

[3] Lawson's views are expounded in numerous other places, but this one is chosen as containing perhaps the most concise statement of his position.

and making predictions are thus pointless exercises. The reason econometrics has failed is that it is pursuing a chimera.

The problem with this perspective is that if deep structures are never revealed in event-regularities, we can never know they are there – they will be invisible. If they are totally invisible, leaving no traces at the level of events, we can never test hypotheses about them. In order to have any implications for the world we observe, therefore, they must have *some* systematic effects. These will, of course, be mixed up with the effects of other 'disturbing' causes, and it may be very difficult to disentangle different causes. This, however, is sufficient to undermine the argument that, *a priori*, there can be no event regularities in an open system. Whether or not there are event regularities is an empirical question, to be settled by observation. Critical realism is saying no more than that there are disturbing causes that cannot be eliminated by controlled experiment – it adds nothing to what Mill said a century and a half ago.

If the absence of event regularities cannot be established on purely *a priori* grounds, it is possible to fall back on the argument that, despite decades of research, none have so far been discovered. Whilst it is clear that econometrics has failed to live up to the enormous expectations once held for it, it is far from clear that no event regularities have been discovered.

1. For short periods, regular patterns can be found. The fact that econometric equations may not be valid for all time does not mean that they cannot be found to hold for periods of time that are sufficiently long to be useful.
2. There are empirical generalizations that persist over long periods, but which are less precisely defined – stylized facts, or historical generalizations. For example, it is fairly clearly established that real wages do not move contra-cyclically; that where there is capital mobility, different countries' interest rates move together and that investment is more volatile than consumption.

In so far as Lawson's claim that economics should be concerned with 'identifying and elaborating the structures and mechanisms, etc., that underlie the phenomena of experience and govern them' (1994, p. 276) is asserting that economics should be concerned with explanation, not simply with prediction, it is reasonable.[4] This is, however, as far as his argument should be taken. 'Recording events and their constant conjunctions' is not, as he implies, an alternative to providing an explanation, but a necessary aspect of testing explanations. Critical realism appears to have implications for economic theorizing only because Lawson (and other proponents) make a number of controversial assertions about what constitutes an adequate economic theory that are unrelated to the critical realist ontology.

Prediction as the goal of economic inquiry

Though Rosenberg argues that economics as it now exists cannot be understood as an empirical science, he argues that such a goal could be attained, just as it has been in psychology. He pours scorn on McCloskey's claim that important scientific theories make no predictions. Whether or not the theory of evolution makes predictions, Rosenberg points out, is a highly contentious issue in biology. More important, there are many other theories in biology that clearly do make predictions, as do theories in physics. Scientists attach enormous weight to the predictive power of their theories.

> the best and most prized of scientific theories are in fact those with the greatest predictive power. Indeed, the history of physical science, if it shows anything, shows that scientists are prepared to sacrifice almost anything to increase the predictive power of their theories, and that they are willing to swallow all manner of intellectual discomforts in order to acquire it. Perhaps the best example of this willingness to sacrifice explanatory power, mathematical rationality, and even intelligibility on the altar of predictive power is quantum electrodynamics. (Rosenberg, 1992, p. 49)

Economists need to be able to predict, not simply to emulate natural scientists (though the example of the natural sciences should create scepticism about the claim that explanation can be divorced completely from prediction) but because predictions are necessary if they are to fulfil the role of providing policy advice. Predictions may

---

[4] Kincaid (1996) has made the point that causal explanations do not *require* mechanisms to be specified in detail. Natural selection, for example, may provide a convincing causal explanation, even if we do not know the precise mechanism through which it takes place.

be hedged with qualifications, they may be expressed in terms of probabilities rather than being deterministic, they may sometimes be very imprecise, possibly even qualitative, and there may be things that simply cannot be predicted; but none of this affects the importance of prediction. If economics is to be of use to policy makers, it must lead to an improvement in our ability to predict.[5] It may be that, for reasons such as those offered by the economists discussed earlier in this section, prediction is very difficult in economics, but no one has argued convincingly that it is impossible. As long as it is possible, it is important that improving the discipline's predictive power as much as possible remain a prominent aim. In other words, it is important that economics exhibits empirical progress, at least in this sense. This leads on to the question of how empirical progress occurs, and the relationship between empirical progress and the various practices of economists.

9.4   THE PREDICTION OF NOVEL FACTS

Novel facts

The prediction of novel facts has a long history as an appraisal criterion,[6] but novelty has been understood in a variety of ways. At least six definitions are possible.[7]

1. Strictly temporal novelty: the fact was unknown when the theory was proposed.
2. Heuristic novelty: the fact was not used in constructing the theory.
3. Novelty with respect to background theory (Musgrave): the fact was not predicted by the best existing predecessor to the theory.
4. Novelty with respect to background theory (Watkins): a fact about which the old theory says nothing at all.
5. Temporal novelty for the individual:[8] the fact must be unknown to the person who constructed the theory at the time the theory is constructed.

---

[5] See Hutchison (1977), Chapter 2; (1992), Chapter 10.

[6] See Backhouse (1997b).

[7] The first five of these are taken from Hands (1991, pp. 96–9).

6. Novelty with respect to design: facts the theory was not designed to explain.

Economists and novel facts

Specialists on economic methodology have argued strongly against Lakatos's emphasis on the prediction of novel facts as the main criterion by which economic theories should be judged. Hands, for example, is scathing about what he has called 'novel fact fetishism':

> Why would we want to accept the position that the sole necessary condition for scientific progress is predicting novel facts not used in the construction of the theory? Surely humankind's greatest scientific accomplishments have amounted to more than this. . . . Even if we can find a few novel facts here and there in the history of economics, and even if those novel facts seem to provide an occasional 'clincher', the history of great economics is so much more than a list of these novel facts. (Hands, 1990, p. 78)

This statement would be echoed by many other economic methodologists. Hausman, for example, in comparing his position with Lakatos's, adopts the position that 'Novel predictions are not the only relevant evidence' (1992, p. 223).

Despite this, many *economists* endorse the prediction of novel facts as an appraisal criterion. One of the most common defences of economic theories based on abstract assumptions such as utility maximization is that they 'work'. What is usually meant by this is that such theories predict novel facts, usually in the sense of facts not used in the construction of the theory. It is common for a theorist to take a standard model, add some new twist (asymmetric information, transactions costs) and to show that the model can now explain some phenomenon previously thought incompatible with the standard assumptions. This is heuristic novelty.

It has been suggested that the appeal of Lakatosian methodology to economists arises because of its permissiveness: it relieves economists of the injunction to seek to falsify theories, whilst at the same time Lakatos's concept of a research programme provides a justification for the development of theory being driven largely by internal factors, by the heuristics of the programme. It was in this

---

[8] Hands (1991, p. 99) refers to this as "Novelty$_k$".

vein that Rosenberg criticized Weintraub (1985) for offering 'Lakatosian consolations to economists' (1986). If this explanation were correct, however, we would expect the most vociferous advocates of Lakatosian ideas within economics to be theorists. This is not what we find. The most ardent supporters of the prediction of novel facts as the criterion by which to judge economic theories are economists committed to rigorous empirical testing of economic theories.

Friedman has, from his writing on positive economics and the consumption function (Friedman 1953, 1957) right through to his recent defence of his work on money demand (Friedman and Schwartz, 1991) consistently argued that prediction of novel facts is the only criterion by which theories should be judged.

> The ultimate goal of a positive science is the development of a 'theory' or 'hypothesis' that yields valid and meaningful (i.e., not truistic) predictions about phenomena not yet observed. (Friedman, 1953, p. 7)

> A persuasive test of their [Hendry and Ericsson's] results must be based on data not used in the derivation of their equations. That might mean using their equations to predict some kind of phenomena for other countries, or for a future or earlier period for the United Kingdom, or deriving testable implications for other variables. . . Similarly, that is the *only* kind of evidence that we would regard as persuasive with respect to the validity of our own results. (Friedman and Schwartz, 1991, p. 47; emphasis added)

The first of these is temporal novelty, the second is heuristic novelty. Similar statements occur in Friedman's other writings, such as his work on the consumption function.

Another example is David Hendry. Though he disagrees profoundly with Friedman on economic theory and on the way in which empirical research in economics should be conducted (see Chapter 12), Hendry accepts the key role played by predicting novel facts, going so far to make it the basis for what he calls, using explicitly Lakatosian terminology, a 'progressive research strategy'.[9]

Why do these empirically-orientated economists place such emphasis on the prediction of novel facts, and how should we regard the different meanings of the term? Anticipating some arguments put forward in Chapter 11, one possible answer can be

---

[9] See below, section 12.3.

found in the notion of 'reproducing' a result, and considering how this might be implemented in a non-experimental science.

Reproduction of results and the prediction of novel facts

Replication involves producing an experimental result using what is, in essentials, the same experiment. The same set of causal laws is believed to be at work. In contrast, reproduction of a result involves deriving the result using a different experiment, relying on a different set of causal laws. The crucial aspect of this is having *independent* corroboration. The prediction of novel facts is also about providing such corroboration, but works the other way round: instead of proceeding from a variety of experiments to the same phenomenon, we start with a phenomenon and use our knowledge of it to predict what will happen in new situations. The more our predictions turn out to be correct, the greater is our confidence in the phenomenon.

As an illustration, suppose that the theory in which we are interested is the claim that monetary expansion causes inflation: $\Delta M \rightarrow \Delta P$, where ΔM denotes an increase in the money supply and ΔP a rise in the price level and the arrow denotes a causal law. For convenience, call this the quantity theory. This could be tested experimentally by conducting open market purchases of government securities and testing the hypothesis that $OMO \rightarrow (\Delta M, \Delta P)$ – that an open-market purchase of securities (OMO) regularly leads to rises in the money supply (M) and the price level (P). Note that this is more than a correlation between OMO and (ΔM, ΔP), the crucial feature of the test being that it is an experiment, where the Bank of England intervenes in the economy. The direction of causation is known. This tests the combination of two causal laws: $OMO \rightarrow \Delta M$ and $\Delta M \rightarrow \Delta P$. Replication involves establishing that this relationship is robust – that the relationship $OMO \rightarrow (\Delta M, \Delta P)$ is true whoever is Governor of the Bank of England, or that it is true whether it is the Bank of England or the Deutsche Bundesbank that undertakes the open market operations. However, even if we have established that $OMO \rightarrow (\Delta M, \Delta P)$ holds, we have not tested the quantity theory, for it may be that the true sequence is not $OMO \rightarrow \Delta M \rightarrow \Delta P$ but $OMO \rightarrow \Delta r \rightarrow \Delta C \rightarrow (\Delta M, \Delta P)$, where Δr is the rise in the rate of interest rate and ΔC the consequent rise in firms' costs. Reproduction of the result involves establishing the quantity theory by finding a new experiment in which the quantity theory is combined with a different causal law. For example, the experiment might be to raise the money supply by running a government deficit. Our new experiment is $Deficit \rightarrow (\Delta M, \Delta P)$. Again, this needs to be replicated. If this experiment works too, it strengthens the case for the quantity theory, for interest rates will be lower, making it difficult to hold that the connection between ΔM and ΔP arises because rising interest rates raise both prices and the money supply.

Prediction of novel facts, on the other hand, involves starting from the quantity theory and deriving from it a variety of implications. In the above example, the logic would be that we start with the prediction,

$$(\Delta M \rightarrow \Delta P) \cap (OMO \rightarrow \Delta M) \Rightarrow (OMO \rightarrow \Delta P).$$

In other words, if an increase in the money supply causes inflation, and an open market operation leads to an increase in the money supply, it follows that an open market operation leads to inflation. This might, for example, be the evidence that the quantity theory had been developed to explain. Prediction of a novel fact involves deriving some other prediction, such as,

$$(\Delta M \rightarrow \Delta P) \cap (Deficit \rightarrow \Delta M) \Rightarrow (Deficit \rightarrow \Delta P),$$

where the prediction $Deficit \rightarrow \Delta P$ satisfies one or more of the criteria for novelty listed on page 114 above. The similarity between this argument and the one involved in reproducing a result is clear. In deriving the novel fact, the quantity theory, $\Delta M \rightarrow \Delta P$, has been combined with another law, $Deficit \rightarrow \Delta M$, independent of the law $OMO \rightarrow \Delta M$ used to derive the original prediction.

In economics, the prediction of novel facts is particularly important for three related reasons.

1. The limitations on what we can do – our inability to perform the experiments that we would like to perform – means that the scope for independent corroboration of the assumptions made in economic theories is limited. It means that it is very hard to test relationships such as $OMO \rightarrow (\Delta M, \Delta P)$: we have to be content with testing the correlations between OMO, ΔM and ΔP. It is harder to establish which is are the exogenous variables.

Causation has to be inferred by testing a long series of series of predictions, each of which, taken on its own, provides only weak support for the theory. It is important, therefore, to generate a wide range of predictions from a theory.

2. Statistical hypothesis tests are used extensively in the construction of econometric models. They are used as design criteria, which means that they cannot also be used as tests of the models, for they will inevitably be satisfied.[10] It is necessary to find some criterion, not used in constructing a model, by which to test it.

3. In economics, theory is comparatively over-developed relative to empirical evidence. This is not to say that there is a paucity of economic data – far from it. What is lacking is well-established empirical generalizations that can act as constraints on theorizing. Because there are so few constraints, and because most theorizing is based on a theory which in its most general form lacks content in that forbids no state of the world, theorists can produce theories to explain almost any phenomenon. It follows that the most significant predictions are of phenomena that the theory was not intended to explain.

On the other hand, whilst the prediction of novel facts is important, theorists are *not* concerned to derive all the predictions that can be derived from their theories, because many of these would not be corroborated. It is trivial to generate predictions that are clearly false from all economic models.

Given these considerations, which of these types of novel fact are most important? The weakness of empirical constraints on theorizing means that background theory novelty (3 and 4) is of little epistemic value, though it may be evidence for the ingenuity or even brilliance of the theorist. Heuristic novelty (2) is significantly stronger, but where a fact is known to the theorist, even if it is not listed in the theory's assumptions, it is difficult to be sure that it played no role in the construction of the theory: knowledge of it may have caused the theorist to develop the theory in one direction rather than another. Novelty with respect to design (6) is similar, though again there is often ambiguity about precisely what a theory was designed for. Temporal novelty for the individual (5) is much stronger, though

---

[10] This point is considered in more detail in section 12.3.

leaves open the problem that theories can be viewed as being produced by communities as much as by individuals, leading to the same problems as occur with heuristic novelty. Temporal novelty (1) is subject to none of these problems and has the greatest epistemic value.

This ranking of types of novelty is inconsistent with a strict separation of the contexts of discovery and justification. Background theory novelty is a criterion that can easily be accommodated within the Popperian framework: in the hands of, for example, Hamminga (1991) it becomes something closely related to falsification. Valuing genuine temporal novelty, defined relative to an individual or a community, above other forms of novelty, on the other hand, is to argue that the context of discovery does have an epistemic value, an un-Popperian conclusion.

10. Theoretical progress in economics

10.1 THREE APPROACHES TO THEORETICAL PROGRESS IN ECONOMICS

The refinement of economic models

Theoretical progress would seem to provide an easy way into the nature of progress in economics. Economic theories would appear, over the past half-century or more, to have exhibited at least three clear-cut symptoms of progress.

1. Increased rigour.
2. An increasingly wide range of implications, in two senses: an increase in the range of problems addressed, and an increase in the range of predictions concerning these problems.
3. Increasingly general assumptions (for example, models now routinely deal with uncertainty, limited information, oligopoly, bargaining and other aspects of the world that were previously neglected).

This is the 'refinement' of economic theory as understood by, for example, Hahn (1984, p. 111). It undoubtedly captures something of what has happened in economics, but it fails to get to the heart of what has happened. It gives no account of *how* theory progresses, or of changes that have taken place in the nature of economic theory.

The imperatives of formal mathematical analysis

A clear statement of this view of progress in economic theory has been provided by Debreu. He argues that the mathematization of economics has led to theory being scrutinized more efficiently for logical errors, the result being greater rigour, and that

> the greater logical solidity of more recent analysis has contributed to the rapid contemporary construction of economic theory. It has enabled researchers to build on the work of their predecessors and to accelerate the cumulative process in which they are participating. (Debreu, 1991, p. 3)

Progress in economics, according to this view, is driven by the imperatives imposed by mathematical analysis. Referring to the insight that convexity in the commodity space can be achieved by aggregation over a set of insignificant agents, he writes,

> An economist who experiences such an insight belongs to the group of applied mathematicians, whose values he espouses. ... [Mathematics] ceaselessly asks for weaker assumptions, for stronger conclusions, for greater generality. In taking a mathematical form, economic theory is driven to submit to those demands. ... Mathematics also dictates the imperative of simplicity. It relentlessly searches for short, transparent proofs and for the theoretical frameworks in which they will be inserted. (Debreu, 1991, p. 4)

He emphasizes the autonomy of the mathematical imperative.

> As a formal model of an economy acquires a mathematical life of its own, it becomes the object of an inexorable process in which rigor, generality and simplicity are relentlessly pursued. (Debreu, 1986, p. 1265)

Note the choice of words: 'ceaselessly', 'driven to submit', 'dictates', 'inexorable', 'relentlessly'. There is no room for compromise.

Given that it is a route towards both greater generality and greater simplicity, economists have followed the route towards greater abstraction. For example, Arrow's reinterpretation of the concept of a commodity to specify the state of the world in which it is available (a more abstract concept of a commodity) permits both increased generality and increased simplicity.

Theory as a sequence of increasingly realistic models

One of the most widely read accounts of how theory evolves was provided by Koopmans.

[We should] look on economic theory as a sequence of conceptional *models* that seek to express in simplified form different aspects of an always more complicated reality. At first these aspects are formalized as much as possible in isolation, then in combinations of increasing realism. . . . The study of the simpler models is protected from the reproach of unreality by the consideration that these models may be prototypes of more realistic, but also more complicated, subsequent models. (Koopmans, 1957, pp. 142–3)

This conception of economic theories has, rightly, been strongly criticized. Not only does theory frequently remain unrealistic, but models become, in some ways, *more*, not less, unrealistic. More fundamental, this process presumes that we can know what more realistic models would look like, for this is what drives the process of theorizing. Crucially, however, it ignores the process whereby theories evolve out of other theories in response to theoretical criticism.

Increasing the plausibility of a theory

Taking as his evidence the development of the Ohlin-Samuelson research programme in the theory of international trade, Hamminga (1983, pp. 67–9) has discerned four ways in which economic theory has developed.

1. Field extension (where field comprises certain assumptions of the theory – *l* countries, *m* goods, *n* countries).
2. Weakening of conditions (finding less restrictive conditions for the curvature of production and utility functions, or the range of possible factor endowments).
3. Derivation of conditions for conditions (instead of making the assumption that countries do not specialize, provide restrictions on production functions to ensure that they do not).
4. Derivation of alternative conditions (that are neither stronger nor weaker than the previous ones).

He suggests that the strategy underlying these developments is one of seeking to increase as far as possible the plausibility of the economically-interesting theorems produced by the research programme. 'Economically-interesting theorems' are theorems that are of interest to the community of economists by virtue of the problems they are trying to solve and the explanatory ideals with which they are working. 'Plausibility' is defined loosely as the probability of a theory being true (Hamminga, 1983, pp. 70–1). More formally, it is the plausibility of

$$W_a \in C(T)$$

where W_a denotes the 'actual' world, and $C(T)$ the class of all possible worlds for which theorem T is true.[1] Plausibility can, *ceteris paribus*, be increased by increasing the class of possible worlds.

Following the heuristics of a Lakatosian research programme

One way to make sense of developments in economic theory is to view them as being driven by the hard core of a Lakatosian research programme. The programme that arguably fits economics best is what has been called the neo-Walrasian programme (Weintraub, 1985), driven by the following heuristics.[2]

1. Construct fully specified, consistent models, simplifying where necessary in order to be able to do this, and draw only those conclusions which can be proved to be implied by the models.
2. Specify the model-specific meanings of equilibrium and disequilibrium and analyse the model in terms of these.
3. Construct theories in which agents optimize subject to constraints.
4. Specify the rules governing the interaction of agents (in terms of game theory, make the game explicit).
5. Construct theories in which agents have a well-defined set of information about relevant phenomena.

Much abstract economic theory, such as the models that form the subject of general equilibrium analysis, can, Weintraub has argued, be explained as a series of instantiations of the hard core of this research programme. Through the analysis of such models the research programme has become more clearly defined – its hard core has 'hardened'.

---

[1] I have simplified Hamminga's algebra here.

[2] This list is taken from Backhouse (1995, pp. 159–60). Weintraub's heuristics can be seen as a limiting case of this.

This Lakatosian perspective, however, presumes that the justification for the research programme is its success in predicting novel facts: theoretical progress is defined in very narrow terms. Though economics can be defended as having made progress according to this criterion (Weintraub, 1988; Backhouse, 1995, pp. 167–9) it seems hard to reconcile with economists' general attitude towards theory and the use of empirical evidence to test theories.

As with Hamminga's story, this fits what has happened in much recent economic theory quite well, and it is intuitively more acceptable than Koopmans's story, but there is still much that is missing.

10.2 INFORMAL MATHEMATICS

Lakatos's *Proofs and Refutations*

Modern economic theory is mathematical.[3] Even where theories *could* be expressed without recourse to mathematics, they are normally expressed and developed using mathematical models.[4] This suggests that one way to understand the evolution of economic theory is, as Rosenberg has suggested,[5] to seek to understand it as mathematics. One barrier to this has been thinking of mathematics in purely formalist terms, which rule out any logic underlying the way the subject has progressed. But this is a problem in mathematics too. Thus Lakatos has written,

> in formalist philosophy of mathematics there is no proper place for methodology qua logic of discovery. According to formalists, mathematics is identical with formalised mathematics. But what can one *discover* in a formalised theory? Two sorts of things. *First*, one can discover the solution to problems which a suitably programmed Turing machine could solve in finite time (such as: is a certain alleged proof a proof or not?). . . . *Secondly*, one can discover the solutions to problems . . . where one can be guided only by the 'method' of 'unregimented insight and good fortune'. (Lakatos, 1967, pp. 3–4)

---

[3] It has been described as a branch of pure mathematics, distinguished only by its origins.

[4] There are notable exceptions, most of these are commonly regarded as lying outside the mainstream of the discipline.

[5] See page 107 above.

His alternative is to see mathematics as *informal*.

> Now this bleak alternative between the rationalism of a machine and the irrationalism of blind guessing does not hold for live mathematics: an investigation of *informal* mathematics will yield a rich situational logic for mathematicians, a situational logic which is neither mechanical nor irrational. (Lakatos, 1967, p. 4)

Lakatos's investigation of informal mathematics provides a way to view economic theory.

Lakatos's subject, in *Proofs and Refutations* (1967) is the history of Euler's theorem relating the number of faces, edges and vertices of a polyhedron ($V - E + F = 2$). Proofs are proposed and then refuted using counter-examples. For example, suppose we define a polyhedron as a solid whose surface consists of polygonal faces. If we do this, we can construct the 'polyhedron' shown in Figure 10.1, for which $V - E + F = 3$. We then have, given our definition of a polyhedron, a counter-example to Euler's theorem.

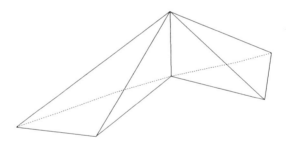

Figure 10.1: A counter-example to Euler's theorem

Source: Lakatos (1967), p. 15

Lakatos then analysed the all-important issue of how mathematicians responded to such counter-examples.[6] For example, two simple, but unproductive, strategies are to abandon the theorem as false, or to deem the alleged counter-example to be a 'monster' – inadmissible as a counter-example. More productive, in the sense of leading to progress, are concept-stretching and theoretical

---

[6] Two attempts to apply Lakatos's discussion of this issue to economics are Fisher (1986) and Vint (1994).

adjustment. Take concept-stretching first. A polyhedron might be defined as:

1. A solid bounded by a finite number of faces.
2. A surface of connected faces.
3. A connected system of edges.
4. A system of vertices, faces and edges linked by an incidence matrix.

For a simple polyhedron (think of a cube) all four definitions are equivalent, whereas for more complex shapes they may diverge. It is possible to respond to a counter-example, therefore, by 'stretching' the concept of a polyhedron so as to think of the problem in a new way. Thus moving from understanding a polyhedron as a solid to understanding it as a surface involves stretching the concept of a polyhedron so as to think of it in a new way.

Such a response to the counter-example shown in Figure 8.1 is generally more fruitful than simply abandoning either the theorem or the counter-example. Theoretical adjustment is similar, but involves changes to the theorem or the proof. For example, instead of claiming that the theorem applies to all polyhedra, it might be applied to all simply-connected polyhedra. If such adjustments merely serve to rule out counter-examples they will amount to monster-barring, reducing the content of the theory; but if the modification results in new ways of thinking about the problem, it may increase the content of the theory: what was a counter-example becomes corroborating evidence for the theory.

An important aspect of the process as Lakatos describes it is the *analytification* of the theorem. At first, Euler's theorem was a hypothesis about polyhedra – an everyday, seemingly well-understood, concept. It turned out, however, that the initial statements of the theorem had to be revised in response to counter-examples. The end result was a logically-watertight theorem, expressed in terms of vector algebra. The price of increased rigour, however, was that the concepts involved in the theory became separated from the phenomena they were intended to describe. This leads to the problem of 'translation' – is the translation of the new (precise, proof-generated) meaning of 'polyhedron' into the old meaning (vague, but applying to a known phenomenon) true? Uncertainty is not completely eliminated. It is just moved outside the theorem. There are several ways in which this problem can be handled.

1. Accept that elements of the old, vague concept may get lost in translation.
2. Regard the translation as infallible.
3. Scrap the old definition.

The first method involves admitting that the search for certainty has failed. Formalism may lead to certainty concerning theorems within the formal system, but their relevance to anything else is uncertain. The second method simply evades the issue. The last method involves abandoning the original problem to which the new, certain theorem is meant to provide the solution.

The mathematics described in the previous section is informal in the sense that:

1. It involves theorems concerning phenomena that are not precisely defined even though, prior to analysis, their meaning may seem clear;
2. Mathematicians have an 'intuitive' idea of what certain concepts mean, even when definitions are refined as the theorem is revised in response to counter-examples and proof-analysis.

This intuitive notion of what imprecise definitions are seeking to define plays a vital regulatory role in the development of a theory. It guides the selection of counter-examples and the response to counter-examples that are discovered.

Economic theory as informal mathematics

This 'informal' mathematics, I suggest, provides a good explanation of the nature of theoretical progress within economics. As an example, consider the development of the so-called 'invisible hand' theorem. Oversimplifying the story, we might pick out four stages:

1. Smith's theorem that by pursuing their own self-interest, individuals frequently promote the interests of society more effectively than when they intend to promote it (Smith, 1776, II, p. 456).

2. Walras's theorem that under 'free competition' consumers will obtain the greatest satisfaction of their wants consistent with the requirements of commutative justice.
3. The Bergson–Samuelson derivation of the necessary conditions for a welfare optimum in the sense of a situation where it was impossible to make one person better off without making someone else worse off.
4. The Arrow–Debreu theorems that any competitive equilibrium is Pareto-efficient, and that any Pareto-efficient equilibrium can be achieved as a competitive equilibrium.

One interpretation of this is as a refinement of Smith's original theorem. Thus Hahn writes,

> When the claim is made – and the claim is as old as Adam Smith – that a myriad of self-seeking agents left to themselves will lead to a coherent and efficient disposition of economic resources, Arrow and Debreu show what the world would have to look like if the claim is to be true. (Hahn, 1984, p. 136)

He sees Smith's 'basic theory' as having been 'much refined' (Hahn, 1984, p. 111).[7] In terms of the strategies for dealing with the problem of translation listed on page 128, Hahn is opting for the third: scrapping the old definition. He interprets Smith's theorem as a primitive version of the Arrow–Debreu theorem – Smith's original definition has been lost.

When we look at the sequence of theorems, on the other hand, we find that not only has the theorem become more precise, but its meaning has changed significantly. The concepts of competition, markets, agents, social welfare and equilibrium all underwent substantial change between Smith and Arrow–Debreu. Underlying all these were 'intuitive' ideas of what these concepts meant in the real world. Smith's theorem involved imprecise, but readily understood concepts. With Arrow–Debreu the concepts have become completely precise, but there are immense problems of translation involved in relating theoretical concepts to equivalent real-world ones. The concept of competition in Arrow-Debreu, for example, bears little relation to Smith's, to the everyday notion of

---

7 This view is very similar to that of Debreu (1991).

competition, or even to observable markets.[8] The invisible hand theorem has been analytified.

Other examples can be found almost anywhere we care to look. Robinson's reformulation of the theory of imperfect competition can be seen as analytifying Marshall's theory of the firm. The theory became more rigorous but, instead of a theory dealing with heterogeneous firms, irreversibilities and evolutionary change, the result was a theory of static equilibrium in markets where all firms were identical.[9] Baumol and Tobin did the same to Keynes's demand for money function. In all such cases the meaning of concepts changed as the theorems became more precise, with the result that a gap emerged between theory, where concepts were defined precisely, and discourse about the real world where concepts were more loosely defined.

In Lakatos's story of the Descartes–Euler theorem concerning polyhedra, he could assume an intuitive idea of what a polyhedron was. In economics, on the other hand, the subject matter of our theories is much less directly known,[10] and it changes over time. We could, therefore, see theories as evolving, along the lines Lakatos suggests for mathematics, in response to intuitive ideas concerning the meaning of economic concepts which are themselves changing in response to empirical evidence. The role of empirical evidence, therefore, could be seen as shaping and guiding economists intuitions, affecting the concepts that are found within economic theories only indirectly. Testing hypotheses, making predictions, and the like are clearly important in this process, but it is not a simple process of testing the models that form the subject-matter of economic theory.

---

[8] See Backhouse (1990).

[9] See Backhouse (1985).

[10] Note that this is solely a comparative statement. It does not state that the concept of a polyhedron is directly known.

10.3 THEORETICAL AND EMPIRICAL PROGRESS

With the possible exception of Debreu's,[11] all the views of theoretical progress discussed in the previous two sections make theoretical progress contingent on the relationship of economic theory to empirical evidence. In the simplest stories (Debreu, Hahn, Koopmans), there is assumed to be a well-established, even if changing, stock of economic phenomena to be explained. Examples include: the allocation of resources through the price mechanism; the existence of uncertainty and limited information; oligopoly; contracts, with particular terms and characteristics; and so on. Progress involves two things.

1. Providing more rigorous explanations of these phenomena, relating them to precisely-defined sets of axioms. If we are prepared to accept the axioms, such progress results in our becoming more confident that we have a satisfactory explanation of the phenomena. For example Debreu (1986, p. 1268) argues that only through rigorous specification of the Walrasian model could its explanatory power be fully appraised.
2. Extending theories to encompass, *either as axioms or as implications,* more phenomena. Here, the agenda – specifying the phenomena that require incorporation in the theory, and the order in which they are to be dealt with – is not specified beyond the fact that it involves (notably for Koopmans) relaxing assumptions believed to be unrealistic. Presumably the unstated agenda is dictated by a mixture of external and internal factors: some phenomena are high on the agenda because of their political importance, or because they are related to problems on which it is embarrassing for economists to be silent; others are dictated by their amenability to explanation using currently-available techniques.

Of these two aspects of progress, Debreu emphasizes the latter, Koopmans the former. Whether they are regarded as complementary

---

[11] I cite Debreu as a *possible* exception on the grounds that, after putting forward the views quoted above, he goes on to entertain Leontief's critique of economics as being adversely affected by the structure of incentives in the profession (see Chapter 13). It is not clear, however, how far he endorses this view which appears to run against his clearly enthusiastic belief in the progress that has resulted from the mathematization of economics.

or competing aims depends on the relationship between generality and realism.

1. In that generality and simplicity involve the removal of simplifying assumptions that are false as descriptions of the world, the move towards greater generality makes theories *more* realistic.
2. Generality and simplicity produced at the expense of increased abstraction make theory *less* realistic in the sense that fewer details of the world are reflected in the theory. Increasing the generality of a theory may not increase the theory's scope (in the sense defined on page 100). It may even leave the scope of the theory more ambiguous.
3. Though this is not emphasized by Debreu, the mathematization and the increasing generality of economic theories are often purchased by means of *unrealistic* assumptions.

Debreu cites Arrow's extension of the concept of a commodity to include the time and state of the world in which it is available as an example of an innovation that led to progress. It is important to note that the assumption that there exist markets for all dated, state-contingent commodities is unrealistic in the sense of being false (as virtually everyone who uses such models admits). It is made simply for analytical convenience. This development is incompatible with Koopmans's definition of progress as a sequence of increasingly realistic models. It may, of course, represent progress in other senses, but that is a different matter.[12]

This conflict between generality and realisticness is precisely the conflict that Lakatos identified when he argued that rigour is achieved at the cost of a theorem being 'analytified'. Ambiguity remains, but it is transferred from the proof (which becomes more rigorous) to the assumptions (whose connection with empirical phenomena becomes more problematic). From this perspective, increased rigour is important not because it increases the certainty of our knowledge, but for other reasons.

1. Testing logical claims that may be flawed.

---

[12] If economics is essentially normative (Rosenberg, 1992; see also Chapter 9) progress has to be defined differently.

2. Exploring alternative definitions of vague concepts.
3. Reformulating problems in alternative ways that may prove fruitful in leading to further extensions of the theory.

Taking as an example the Arrow–Debreu extension of the concept of a commodity as dated and state-contingent, it is arguable that this leads to new ways of thinking about problems that *may* turn out to be fruitful. Debreu, for example, writes that 'greater abstraction brought Walrasian theory closer to concrete applications' (Debreu, 1986, p. 1268). It is tempting to say that this is part of what general-equilibrium theorists mean when they say that the Arrow-Debreu model can be used as a benchmark. The model, it is argued, shows that the invisible hand theorem fails because the set of markets is incomplete. However, this does not imply the much stronger claim that has been made my some theorists (Hahn, Debreu) that the Arrow–Debreu model shows the conditions that *must* hold if the invisible hand is to work. It may be that, given current knowledge, the Arrow–Debreu assumptions are necessary *if we are to be able to prove rigorously* that the invisible hand works, but that is not the same thing. Our inability to prove something rigorously does not mean that it cannot be true. It is like claiming that because our keys are not within the area illuminated by a street lamp, they cannot be anywhere on the sidewalk (even this may be too generous, as it implies the area lit by the street lamp includes part of the sidewalk).

What all these accounts have in common is the assumption that there exist economic phenomena, the existence and characteristics of which are sufficiently unproblematic to serve as a benchmark by which theories can be judged. Their truth serves as an external standard by which to judge progress.

Hamminga's story of theoretical progress as increasing plausibility is an improvement on the ones discussed earlier in some important respects.

1. It illuminates the concept of increased generality.
2. It does not depend on any assumption that there are economic data that we know with certainty and which can be used to judge the realisticness of theories.
3. The emphasis is on plausibility, not truth.

The problem is that Hamminga's definition of plausibility is explained only in terms of the probability of a theory being true: that the real world is one of the possible worlds described by the theory. The reason why this explanation of plausibility does not settle anything is that nothing is said about how this probability (inevitably a Bayesian, subjective, probability) is determined. Whilst this may be a useable criterion in cases where unrealistic assumptions are relaxed or removed without introducing any other changes (as when the number of goods in a trade model is increased) it will in most cases be very difficult to apply. In short, whilst Hamminga's approach to the problem of progress may work within a very narrowly-defined research programme, such as that Heckscher-Ohlin trade theory, it does not provide a general solution to the problem of testing for theoretical progress in economics.

It follows from this that if economists claim, as they generally do, that the goal of theorizing is to explain what is going on in the real world, the existence of theoretical progress is dependent on a stock of sufficiently reliable facts that can guide and constrain economic theorizing. Given a starting point where the stock of such facts is it is generally accepted, inadequate, theoretical progress requires that this stock is increased and improved. In short, theoretical progress requires empirical progress.[13]

---

[13] If the goals of the subject were different, of course, theoretical progress could be understood independently of empirical progress.

11. Econometrics and the establishment of economic facts

11.1 ECONOMETRICS AND MODERN ECONOMICS

In the early decades of the twentieth century, many economists were confident that the accumulation of statistical data would result in the transformation of economics. Though he was far from alone in holding such views, this was very clearly expressed by Wesley Clair Mitchell in his Presidential Address to the American Economic Association. In view of improvements in quantitative data and in methods for analysing those data, he reached the conclusion that,

> it seems unlikely that the quantitative workers will retain a keen interest in imaginary individuals coming to imaginary markets with ready made scales of bid and offer prices. Their theories will probably be theories about the relationships among the variables that measure objective processes. (Mitchell, 1925, p. 26)

The decades since Mitchell's address have seen the quantification of economics that he predicted, but the subject has developed in ways very different from those he envisaged.

1. Theory has become stronger than ever. Far from losing interest in imaginary individuals, theories based on imaginary ('representative') individuals have come to dominate academic economics.
2. Academic empirical economics[1] has become dominated by econometrics, where econometrics is understood as involving modelling economic data as generated by a probability

---

[1] Both adjectives are important.

distribution, with the task of the econometrician being to provide a representation of that probability distribution.[2]

However, despite the immense effort, undreamed-of increases in computing power, and the development of vastly more sophisticated statistical techniques, econometrics has failed to produce the quantitative laws that many economists, at one time, believed it would.

One explanation for this failure is that economic phenomena are inherently unpredictable and that the entire project of quantifying economics is necessarily doomed to failure (see Section 9.3 above). Yet even if precise predictions are impossible, it might be expected that econometrics would play a key role in establishing empirical generalizations and in persuading economists to accept or reject theories. This, according to many critics, simply has not happened. Though econometrics *has* played a role in the development of economics, its influence on the way economists have conceived economic phenomena has been, for the most part, a minor one.[3] Why?

11.2   CHECKING, REPLICATING AND REPRODUCING A RESULT

Checking

The characteristic of checking is that it can be carried out according to established, agreed procedures. If, in a scientific experiment, someone has made an arithmetic error, measured a voltage incorrectly or failed to keep the temperature of solution constant, there is no dispute as to what has happened or about what should be done about it. Checking, whether by the experimenter or by another scientist, verifies that the experiment has been conducted correctly. The only thing it establishes is the competence of the experimenter. Because there have to be agreed procedures, checking is possible only with those parts of an experiment that are not in dispute: with

---

[2] The change that led to this situation has been termed 'The probabilistic revolution', the key contribution being Haavelmo (1944). See Morgan (1990).

[3] See, for example, Backhouse (1995), Chapters 8–10; Blaug (1992).

the application of settled and agreed techniques. Checking is extremely important to science, but it is of little philosophical interest.

Replication

Replication involves repeating an experiment in order to test, not the competence of the experimenter, but the existence of some phenomenon. It takes place where the outcome of an experiment is not known – where the result is in dispute. It establishes *that there is a phenomenon to be explained*.[4] As such, it is fundamental to scientific progress.[5] Replication and checking both involve repeating experiments, but there are two important differences between them.

1. Replication concerns a genuinely contested result. This means that there are no independent tests of whether or not an experiment has been performed correctly: because the result is contested, the precise requirements for a successful test are unknown. The correctness of the experimental procedure cannot be established independently of the outcome of the experiment.
2. When an experiment is replicated, it is *not* repeated exactly: the new experiment should be identical in all relevant respects (temperature, the mix of chemicals used) but unlike the one being replicated in respects that are believed to be irrelevant (the location of the laboratory, the team doing the work). Thus if an experiment were repeated by the same team, working in the same laboratory, this would not count as replication.

The first of these problems, the unavailability, where results are contested, of independent tests of whether an experiment has been performed correctly, has been labelled, by Collins (1985, 1991; Collins and Pinch, 1993) 'the experimenter's regress'. This is the problem that you cannot be confident about the results of an experiment unless you know that it is set up properly, but you cannot know it is set up properly unless you know whether the results are correct. As Collins puts it,

---

[4] This definition is taken from Cartwright (1991).

[5] See O'Brien (1992), pp. 97–100 for some illustrations of this.

You want to know if *x* exists; to find out if *x* exists, you build a good *x*-detector; to check if the *x*-detector is good, you try it out on observing *x*; but to know whether it is a good *x*-detector should see *x* or not-*x*, you have to know whether *x* exists; to know this you have to have a good *x*-detector, and so on. (Collins, 1991, p. 131.)

Simply repeating an experiment gets nowhere towards cutting through this problem – the relevant community of scientists has to be persuaded that other scientists, working in different laboratories, using different pieces of apparatus, can produce the results. Because there are no rules governing what will be taken as persuasive evidence, Collins defines replication sociologically: 'Replication is the establishment of a new and contested result by agreement over what counts as a correctly performed set of experiments' (Collins, 1991, p. 132). It is the outcome of a process of negotiation within the scientific community.

This definition of replication as the establishment of a consensus is compatible with the earlier definition in terms of establishing the existence of phenomena to be explained, though somewhat weaker. Establishing the existence of phenomena to be explained presumes that there are phenomena to be explained – in other words, a form of realism. Collins's sociological definition does not imply this. The difference between these two perspectives arises, as Cartwright makes clear, from her being a realist about what she terms 'phenomenological laws' — empirical regularities. She argues (Cartwright, 1983) that these phenomenological laws are true of the objects in reality.[6] Collins, in contrast, is not a realist, even in this limited sense: he is content to remain at the level of analysing scientists' beliefs, without asking whether or not these beliefs are true, and how these beliefs get established. In this chapter, the term replication will be used in the sense in which Cartwright defines it. From Collins's perspective, some of the distinctions I draw may seem to be somewhat insubstantial.

---

[6] She goes on to argue a claim with which I will not be concerned here, that 'theoretical' or 'fundamental' laws, namely the laws which scientists use to provide explanations of observed phenomena, are true only of objects in models: they are not true of objects in reality. This is the sense in which Cartwright is to only a limited extent a realist. This realism about phenomena but not about theories also characterizes the position of Hacking (1983) (see section 6.4 above).

The two differences between replication and checking listed above are linked – the existence of differences between the original experiment and its replication. Because the results are contested, it is not possible to specify *ex ante* an exhaustive list of the relevant requirements for a successful experiment. This is something that emerges only after replication has successfully been accomplished. Clearly, it has to be possible for a different scientific team to produce the result, but just how different the circumstances need to be is often a matter of dispute: if a different team of scientists can produce the results, but using, say, the same particle accelerator, this may or may not count as replication, depending on what the points at issue are.

An important implication of this definition of replication is that what counts as checking and what counts as replication changes over time with shifts in the boundary between what is and what is not considered open to dispute. Typically, as new phenomena and methods for investigating them become understood, activities that were previously considered replication become no more than checking.

Reproduction[7]

Whilst replication establishing that there is a phenomenon to be explained, through other experimenters managing to produce the same results in the same way as did the original experimenters, it does not establish that our theoretical explanation of why the experiment produces those results is correct. To show that our explanations of the phenomena we observe are correct we need to reproduce the results in a different way. Reproduction involves getting the same result by performing a *different* experiment, not by repeating (even with minor variations) the same experiment. As with the distinction between checking and replication, the distinction between replication and reproduction is fluid: it is not possible to lay down simple rules for what counts as replication and what counts as reproduction. This depends on the context, and on what experimenters can agree upon.

---

[7] For a more detailed discussion, see section 9.4 above.

11.3   ECONOMETRICS AND EXPERIMENTAL SCIENCE

Experimental science

The terminology described above deals with experimental science. In so far as economics is experimental, arguments about checking, replication and reproduction can be carried straight across. However, most econometrics is non-experimental, which means that before we start talking about replication in econometrics, it is necessary to distinguish carefully between what is going on in econometrics and in experimental science. Though it has to be used very carefully, the clearest way to sort this out is with a diagram.

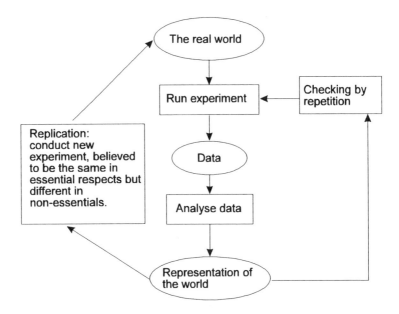

Figure 11.1: Experiment

Figure 11.1 provides a schematic representation of what is going on in an experimental science. It is simplified, but adequate for the points that need to be made. The starting point is what is labelled 'the real world'. The task of scientists is to construct a representation of the world.[8] They do this by conducting an experiment, or 'intervening' in the world, thus generating data that can be used as the basis for a representation of the world. When the same experiment is repeated under exactly the same circumstances, a new set of data is generated, which enables the original data to be checked – the right hand loop in Figure 11.1.

Replication involves the creation of a new, slightly different experiment, indicated in Figure 11.1 by saying that we go back to the real world, generating a new set of data. If the second experiment confirms the representation of the world that was constructed on the basis of the first experiment, the latter has been successfully replicated.[9] If the new experiment is not consistent with the view of the world that resulted from the first experiment, there is a discrepancy to be resolved in some way, probably involving further attempts to replicate. A representation of the world is established when successful replication occurs. It is a crucial feature of this process that it involves an interaction between the scientists and the real world.

Econometrics

This somewhat oversimplified diagram becomes a useful reference point when we compare it with Figure 11.2, which depicts what goes on in most econometrics. I am going to define as 'econometrics' what happens below the horizontal line which divides the figure. For the moment ignore everything above the line, including the arrow marked (b) in Figure 11.2. The nature of the data generation process will be considered later on.

---

[8] This account is influenced by Hacking (1983). See above, section 6.4.

[9] Representations of the world include descriptions of the causal processes operating. Our concern here, however, is simply with representation at the level of describing the phenomena.

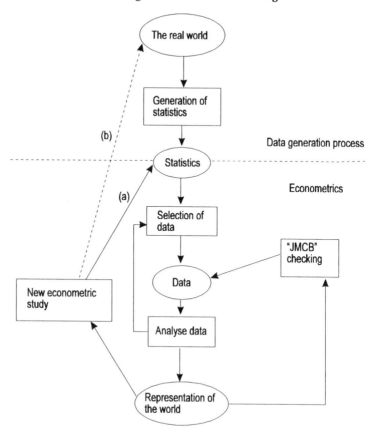

Figure 11.2: Econometrics

This diagram can be used to make several comments about what econometricians do.

1. *Econometric theory*, as traditionally understood (the construction of estimators, the analysis of their properties, and so on) is concerned with data analysis.
2. Recent developments, associated, for example, with Leamer and Hendry go beyond this, to consider the principles which should

determine how the econometrician selects data.[10] Call this *econometric strategy*.

3. Work such as that undertaken in the *Journal of Money, Credit and Banking* (*JMCB*) study (Dewald *et al.*, 1986), which is what econometricians frequently (perhaps normally) have in mind when they refer to replicating results, involves nothing more than *checking the data analysis*. It simply verifies that the calculations were made correctly: it does not even attempt to verify that best-practice techniques had been used. There is no attempt to explore the issues raised in debates over econometric strategy or even econometric theory.

4. Finally we have the all-important category of what is, in Figure 11.2, *new econometric studies*. To count as new, a study has to involve some significant difference from the old studies, in the same way that replication in natural science experiments involves more than an exact repetition of an old experiment. What counts as significant difference? This can be answered in a number of ways. A Popperian answer would be that a significant difference is one that is believed to increase the set of potential falsifiers: the greater the likelihood of a result being refuted, the more significant is corroborating evidence. A sociological perspective, such as that of Collins, would instead emphasize that hard-and-fast rules cannot be laid down: that what counts as a significant difference can only be settled by negotiation within the relevant scientific community. In either case, what counts as significantly different will depend on the context – on the current state of knowledge and the problems that need to be tackled. This needs to be considered in more detail.

---

[10] See, for example, the survey by Pagan (1987) and the collection in Granger (1990). The statement in the text is an oversimplification of what the debates surveyed by Pagan are about, but it is sufficient for the current argument.

11.4 REPLICATION IN ECONOMETRICS

Replicating econometric techniques

The boundary between checking and other activities is, as was mentioned above, fluid. This is well-illustrated by considering the question of whether repeating another economists' work, but using a different computer or different computer software, constitutes checking or replication. It might be argued that when computer technology was in its infancy, repeating someone's regression on a different computer, using different hardware and different numerical algorithms, constituted replication. It was concerned with verifying that regression results were describing properties of the data, not simply artefacts of the computing equipment and methods being used. It is thus possible, that given the period covered by the *JMCB* study (the early 1980s), when these problems arose, such work *did* constitute replication. On the other hand, in the days when regressions were performed using hand calculators, or log tables, it would have been simply checking, because such methods were completely understood. Similarly, today, now that computer technology is well understood, it is also checking. It has been suggested that the extreme difficulty experienced by Dewald *et al.* in replicating economists' results is a phenomenon confined to this period: that fewer mistakes were made both in the days of hand calculators, and today.[11] Another possible factor is that in the early days of econometrics, students were taught to watch for errors and to check their results, something that may nowadays be less common.

The category 'replicating econometric techniques' is also the place to consider another type of activity that economists commonly describe as replication: studies based on essentially the same data set, but which estimate different equations. Citing estimates of the elasticity of hours with respect to the wage rate reported in a survey by Pencavel (1986), Cartwright (1991) argues that such activity does not constitute replication. Her argument is simple: estimation of different functional forms does not provide independent evidence for a result, for the estimated equations are alternatives to each

---

[11] I owe this point to David Hendry. Hendry and Morgan (1995) show that much of the early work on econometrics can be 'replicated' using modern computing technology.

other. If one is true, the others must be false. Thus if one economist obtains a negative elasticity using a linear model, whilst another obtains a negative elasticity using a log-linear model, or using a different list of conditioning variables, at least one of the results must be wrong. Cartwright draws the conclusion that no replication is involved. As regards replication of the results, she is entirely correct. Such activity does nothing to assure us that there is an economic phenomenon to be explained that is independent of the techniques used to derive the result. Economists would, therefore, do better not to describe such activity as replication. The most that can be said is that there is replication in respect of the econometric techniques, where 'econometric techniques' is understood somewhat broadly as including model selection. It shows that a negative elasticity is obtained irrespective of the model specification used. This may be a useful activity, but its significance is strictly limited. For this reason it will be ignored in the discussion which follows.[12]

Types of economic data

Before we can comment on what, if anything, in this scheme constitutes replication, we must pay attention to the data-generation process. Consider three possibilities.

1. Experimental data.
2. Cross-section data on individual persons, households or firms derived from sample surveys.
3. Aggregate time series data.[13]

(1) *Experimental data.* With experimental data we have a situation that is, potentially, like the situation in natural science. If an experiment is repeated exactly (by the same team, in the same circumstances, using the same equipment and methods) we

---

[12] Cartwright's argument that the studies surveyed in Pencavel (1986) should not be regarded as replicating the conclusion of a negative labour supply elasticity is correct insofar as the studies use the same data set. However, given that the dates of the studies range from 1973 to 1984, is likely that the data sets are not identical and that an element of replication is involved. This raises the issues discussed below.

[13] These three categories are not exhaustive (there are, for example, econometric studies which analyse samples of countries and cohort studies, which fall into none of these categories) but they are sufficient to raise the important points.

represent it by the arrow labelled (a) in Figure 11.2. It is generating a data set that is, barring errors, exactly the same as that generated in the original study. It does not count as a returning to the real world to generate a new data set, except in the limited, albeit important, sense of reducing sampling errors. On the other hand, if the experiment is altered in an appropriate way, varying things that are believed to be inessential (such as the identity of the experimenter, the location, and so on) it counts as returning to the real world, performing a new experiment, thereby generating a new data set – path (b) in Figure 11.2.[14]

(2) *Cross-section survey data.* Cross section survey data can, in some respects, be considered like experimental data. The survey that generates the data can be regarded as a form of experiment. The situation is, however, more complicated. If new studies take the same data set (say the 1973 Family Expenditure Survey) then they are following route (a) in Figure 11.2: there is no interaction with the real world, merely with one set of statistics. On the other hand, if a new study uses a different data set, then we can in principle regard it as going back to the real world. There are, however, complications. If the survey involves going back to the same population (the same 'world'), but extracts the data in a similar but appropriately different way (using the same principles, but using a different randomization process, using different individuals to ask questions, and so on) we are going back to the world and generating a new data set.

Problems arise in economics, however, which do not arise in natural science, because we cannot be sure that we are going back to the same 'world'. By this I mean going back to a world that works in the same way (is characterized by the same phenomenological laws) as the world on which previous studies were carried out. If we carry out a certain study in England and in France, or another in South Birmingham in 1980 and in 1990, we do not know whether we should expect to obtain the same results. There may be cultural

---

[14] Do Monte Carlo studies constitute experimental evidence? Insofar as it is the econometric techniques themselves that are disputed, and need to be replicated, the answer would appear to be yes. When it comes to exploring the real world, however, Monte Carlo studies are best regarded as an (experimental) branch of mathematics. They help us better to understand the properties of our models. What such studies reveal about models may reveal things about the models' congruence with empirical evidence, but this is not in itself replication.

differences (such as the French having a higher preference to hold savings in gold than do the English) or habits may have changed over time (the influence of Thatcherism). Following Collins, we might term this problem *the econometrician's regress*. To confirm that we are measuring an economic phenomenon correctly we have to show that it occurs in more than one data set drawn from the same population; to know whether our data sets are drawn from the same population we need to show whether they exhibit the same phenomenon; to establish whether they exhibit the same phenomenon we have to be able to measure it correctly, and so on. This problem does, of course, occur in experimental sciences, but its significance is incomparably greater in (non-experimental) economics.

(3) *Aggregate time-series data*. The problem of the econometrician's regress arises with a vengeance when studies use aggregate time-series data, typically compiled by government agencies. If we wish, for example, to establish whether there is a negative relationship between inflation and unemployment in the UK in the 1990s, for example, it is inherently impossible to get the world to throw up a second data set by taking another sample. We are dealing with something of which there is only one sample.[15] To find other samples we have to go to different time periods, or different countries, whereupon the problem of the econometrician's regress arises. A further problem is thrown up by the fact that the way in which statistics are compiled is beyond the control of the econometrician. Even if the econometrician is able to show that the data generation process has certain properties, it is often difficult, if not impossible, to show that these are properties of the real economy, rather than being simply artefacts of the process by which government agencies compile their statistics. For example, estimating depreciation rates from published capital stock figures could, at best, get back to the statisticians' assumptions about asset lifetimes.

---

[15] It has been argued that because something can happen only once, conventional measures of statistical significance are invalidated. I am not making this claim.

Methods of replication

When Collins and Cartwright talk about replication in natural science they are (though Collins would not accept that this is a useful way to talk about it) referring to activities which, because scientists are doing things in the real world, confirm all the stages linking the real world and representations of the world. The significance of replication, therefore, is that it assures us that our representations do indeed represent reality. In econometrics, on the other hand, the activities commonly labelled replication, are typically doing much less than this. Consider some of the possibilities.

(1) *Applying the same econometric techniques to the same data set*. This is perhaps the most common use of the term replication in econometrics, but for the most part it is no more than checking, for the procedures that are being repeated are well-understood and agreed.[16] Work of the type involved in the *JMCB* survey should, as Collins has pointed out, be regarded as checking, not replication.

(2) *Applying different econometric techniques to the same data set*. This could be regarded as checking the econometric strategy pursued. For example, it an econometrician might start from a list of variables that she believes ought to be in a consumption function and, perhaps following a Bayesian methodology, derive a consumption function. Another econometrician might instead adopt a general-to-particular strategy, estimating a consumption function on the same data set. If the result was an identical equation, this might, given that econometric strategy is not an area on which there is consensus, be regarded as replicating the original result.[17] Although such activity

---

[16] I am using the phrase 'the same econometric techniques' to cover not simply estimation methods (OLS, 2SLS and so on) but procedures for including and eliminating variables, significance levels, responses to insignificant coefficients, and so on. Where different strategies are being employed, it counts, for the purposes of this argument, as a different econometric technique.

[17] Care has to be taken here. It would often be considered a successful replication if, using a different functional form, or a different list of explanatory variables, a second investigator produced the same value for a coefficient such as the marginal propensity to consume. Such an inference would not, however, necessarily be justified, for if the list of other explanatory variables or the functional form is

may involve replication, however, it is replicating only a part of the link between the real world and its representation. It confirms only that a particular data set exhibits certain properties, not that these properties are true of the world.

(3) *Applying the same econometric techniques to a new data set drawn from the same population.* If (i) the new data set is derived by experiment or sample survey from a population which is clearly the same as the one on which the old study is performed, (ii) the econometric techniques employed are well-understood, and known to be reliable, and (iii) the new study is similar to, and different from, the old one in appropriate ways, then we can speak of replication in the sense that the term is used in natural science. All the links between the real world and the representation of the world will have been confirmed. If the econometric techniques employed are controversial and open to dispute, however, all that will have been replicated is the data-generation process. We will know that the results are not an artefact of the data-generation process, though they may be an artefact of the econometric procedures. In this case, replication will require that the results are confirmed using alternative econometric procedures.

An interesting problem is posed by studies which refer to the same economic unit and the same time-period, but use more up-to-date statistics. What is being tested here is whether the original results were an artefact of the process whereby the statistics were generated. This is replication, but involving only a part of the process linking the real world to its representation. The importance of such replication will depend on the likelihood of the earlier study's results having been caused a quirk of the process whereby the statistics were generated.

(4) *Analysing a new data set, drawn from a different population.* This category is added for completeness, as it cannot, for obvious reasons, be regarded as replication. For reasons explained above, however, it is often difficult to establish whether or not two data sets can be regarded as drawn from a population that exhibits the same relevant regularities as the original one. For most econometric analysis which uses aggregate data, therefore, it will be a difficult, controversial

---

different, so too is the interpretation of the coefficient on a variable. On the other hand, it may show that estimates are not sensitive to auxiliary assumptions.

decision as to whether to regard a new study as falling into category (3) or category (4). In one case it replication is possible, in the other it is not.

11.5   ECONOMETRICS AND THE ESTABLISHMENT OF ECONOMIC FACTS

Does sufficient checking occur?

It is widely claimed that an insufficient amount of checking of published econometric results takes place. Dewald, Thursby and Anderson (1986) created alarm by finding that they could 'replicate' (the word is placed in quotation marks because it is not being used in the sense defined above) only 2 per cent of the results in their sample. Levy and Feigenbaum (1993), reporting on a different experiment, reached similar conclusions.   They argued, like Mirowski and Sklivas (1991), that the incentives facing economists, as both authors of articles and editors of journals, discouraged replication. Like others before them (for example Mayer, 1980) they assumed that checking is desirable, and they suggested institutional changes that would make checking more widespread: requiring authors to submit data when articles are submitted; changing editorial policies concerning the publication of such work, and so on.

In response to these arguments, Collins (1991) points out that even outside economics only a small proportion (around 10 per cent) of scientific articles is ever cited. The 90 per cent of articles that are never cited are the price that is paid for the 10 per cent (or perhaps only 1 per cent) of articles that are important. Most results are, therefore, not checked, simply because they do not matter enough for anyone to check them. Where results do matter, Collins suggests, they will be checked.[18]

It is arguable, however, that this fails to get to the heart of the matter – the possibility that, in economics, econometric results are not checked because they are not persuasive in the way that experiments in natural science are. This needs to be explored further.

---

[18] Even this is generally not true in economics, for checking someone else's results is normally a time-consuming activity.

The precision of econometric estimates

Mirowski (1995, 1994) has drawn a sharp contrast between the precision with which physical constants are measured and the precision of what he claims to be analogous constants in economics. The device he uses for this is the Birge ratio. Denoting the estimate reported by each experimenter as X_i, with reported variance σ_i^2, and n is number of experiments, the Birge ratio, B, is given by,

$$B = \frac{1}{n-1} \sum_{i=1}^{n} \left(\frac{X_i - \overline{X}}{\sigma_i} \right)^2 ,$$

where $\overline{X}$ is the group mean, weighted inversely by the variances.[19] This ratio is a measure of the degree of agreement between experimenters. If it were equal to unity, this would imply that the variance across experiments was exactly what would be expected on the basis of reported variances. If it were less than unity, it would imply that experimenters were overestimating the uncertainty surrounding their results. The typical case, however, is that Birge ratios exceed unity: the differences across experiments are higher than they should be if the reported variances were correct. Looking at it the other way round, Birge ratios above unity can be read as implying that experimenters are underestimating the uncertainty attached to their estimates: that they are being overconfident in their results. In practice, ratios exceeding unity are to be expected, not simply because scientists have an incentive to be overconfident, but because reported standard errors report only sampling errors, whereas in practice there are additional reasons for results to differ.

Mirowski correctly observes that Birge ratios should be considered simply as a comparative device, 'indicating rough orders of magnitude of quantitative disagreement' (1994, p. 582). He then compares Birge ratios for physical constants, psychological measurements and coefficients in some economic studies, showing, as Table 11.1 makes very clear, that whilst psychology has achieved a level of agreement comparable to that of physics, economics clearly has not.[20]

---

[19] Henrion and Fischhoff (1986), p. 792.

[20] Note that achieving a similar level of agreement does not imply that psychological and physical knowledge are equally certain.

Mirowski uses these results to argue that economics has not evolved the social structures necessary to reconcile divergent results.

> The primary reason that both physics and psychology display distinctly lower Birge ratios than does economics is that *they have institutionally acknowledged that fact:* at some juncture in the twentieth century, both have managed to institute structures of meta-analysis both to foster and to enforce the reconciliation of error attributions on the part of individual experimentalists. Physicists have their particle data-groups, and psychologists have a special journal and the subdiscipline of meta-analysis. The empirical economists have nothing comparable. (Mirowski, 1994, p. 584).

Economics, he conjectures, has not pursued the same route as physics and psychology because of economists' belief in free markets.[21] They regard free markets as an effective mechanism for arbitrage between economists, and oppose the establishment of an agency to do this.[22] Whereas physicists can look up a recommended value for the speed of light, there is in economics no institution that publishes, for example, recommended values for the elasticity of demand for money.

Before going any further, it is important to make three points. The first is that Birge ratios can be very sensitive to individual observations where these diverge sharply from the others. This is a reason why, in the calculations of Birge ratios for physical constants, 'outliers' were ignored. Removing the clearest examples of outliers results in drastic reductions in the ratios for the money demand elasticities: dropping Laidler's estimate causes the Birge ratio for US money demand to fall from 4.24 to 2.9; dropping three estimates causes the ratio for UK money demand to fall from 17.1 to 6.1.[23]

---

[21] It should be pointed out that psychology is not homogeneous, Mirowski's points applying only to part of the discipline.

[22] Mirowski claims that attempts to set up such an agency have been blocked, but he cites no examples to support this claim.

[23] The estimates of the elasticity of US money demand are: −0.022, −0.017, −0.012, −0.009, −0.019, −0.01, −0.01, −0.168 (Laidler), 0.022. Laidler's estimate is nearly 8 times the nearest estimate, whereas if we leave Laidler's estimate out, the highest is only 2.5 times the lowest. The estimates of the elasticity of UK money demand are: −0.032, −0.708, −0.018, +0.195, −0.066, −0.019, −0.147. Identifying outliers here is clearly more difficult, but the second, fourth and final estimates appear to be out of line with the rest, and eliminating them gives the figure in the text. The extreme sensitivity of the

Table 11.1: Selected Birge Ratios

Physical constants		B	n
Speed of light	1875–1958	1.42	27
Gravitational	1798–1983	1.38	14
Muon lifetime	1957–80	3.28	10
Charged pion mass	1957–80	2.23	10
Psychological measurements			
Sex/spatial perception		1.64	62
Sex/verbal ability		4.09	11
Open ed./reading		5.87	19
Open ex./self-concept		1.39	18
Economic parameters			
US money demand interest elasticity	1971–88	4.24	9
UK money demand interest elasticity	1971–91	17.10	7
Purchasing power parity, 1920s FF/$	1973–88	3.04	6
US import income elasticity	1974–90	27.09	14
US import price elasticity	1974–90	4.86	10
US export income elasticity	1963–90	24.37	13
US export price elasticity	1963–90	4.33	9
Employment-output elasticity, US manufacturing	1967–74	10.50	6
Male labour supply	1971–76	15.11	7
Welfare spell length and race	1986–92	1.94	5

Source: Mirowski (1994), tables 1–3, pp. 582–3. Birge ratios for economic parameters have been recalculated from Mirowski's data using a variance-weighted mean, not the unweighted mean used incorrectly by Mirowski.[24]

The differences between physics and economics are still clear, but not quite so dramatic.[25] In addition, there remains the problem that

---

measure to errant observations is shown by the fact that dropping the second and fourth, but including the final one, gives a ratio of 23.4.

[24] Using an unweighted mean, Mirowski obtains values of 49.7, 73.4, 3.14, 29.87, 5.49, 24.9, 4.89, 22.7, 1.26 and 2.23 for the Birge ratios on economic parameters.

[25] A technical argument for calculating the statistic without outliers concerns the shape of the χ^2 distribution (the Birge ratio has a χ^2 distribution with n–1 degrees of freedom).

identifying outliers in the economic estimates is frequently much harder than with the physical constants: there is so little agreement that it is hard to establish which estimates are outliers and which are not.

The second point is that, irrespective of whether we base it on standard errors reported by experimenters, or on standard errors calculated from different experimenters' results, the precision with which physical constants are estimated vastly exceeds that with which economic parameters are estimated. In tables listing the precision of various auxiliary and fundamental physical constants, the scales run from 10^{-10} to 10^{-6}, and 10^{-7} and 10^{-4} respectively.[26] Econometric estimates would be a *long* way off such scales.

The third point (which applies to other sciences too, though the way the effect operates need not be the same) is that the studies reported in journals are neither a comprehensive, nor a random sample of all studies undertaken. The process of refereeing and editorial decision-making biases published results in favour of ones that are thought 'interesting'. Thus 'significant' results are more likely to be published than 'insignificant' ones. More critically, it has been suggested that the nature of the bias may change over time: in the early stages of research into a topic, only positive (statistically significant) results are considered interesting, whereas once the literature matures and certain results are accepted, negative results become interesting (Goldfarb, 1995). 'Interesting' results are ones that challenge the generally accepted view in a way that economists find plausible. The implication of this is that the process of drawing conclusions from a range of published studies is complex: it involves more than simply aggregating the results and applying a statistical test.

Why has the establishment of agreement in econometrics not been institutionalized?

Mirowski attributes the failure of economics to develop a mechanism for arbitrating between estimates to economists' belief in free markets. There are, however, possibly much deeper reasons.

A fundamental problem with estimating Birge ratios, or for that matter any other measure of disagreement, is that different estimates

---

[26] Petley (1985), Figures 9.4 and 9.5, pp. 307–8.

of, say, the interest elasticity of money demand may not all be measuring the same thing. Elasticities of demand are estimated using equations that model demand for money as a function of interest rates and a list of other variables. If this list of other variables differs between equations, the properties of the probability distribution will be different: the mean and variance of the interest elasticity of demand will be different.[27] For estimates to be comparable, the list of conditioning variables must be the same. This, of course, just pushes the problem back a stage – why is there no agreement on what has to be held constant when, say, the interest elasticity of demand for money is estimated. That, however, is a problem for economic theory.

A further problem concerns the nature of the concepts that underlie parameters such as these. Elasticities of demand for exports and imports – for large aggregates – are problematic, especially when estimated from highly colinear time-series statistics. Purchasing power parity involves great theoretical and empirical conceptual problems relating to the inclusion of non-traded goods. Interest elasticities of the demand for money become difficult to interpret when changes in financial system and relative amounts of assets held alter both the characteristics and relative amounts held of different financial assets.

These issues are linked to the issue of replication. The various estimates of physical and psychological constants cited by Mirowski are the result of different experimenters replicating experiments, and in some cases developing new experiments that will determine constants with greater accuracy. When econometricians, on the other hand, estimate US money demand, they will typically be analysing a common body of data. If they use the same model specification and the same data, they will, barring mistakes, arrive at exactly the same conclusions. Typically, however, data and model selection procedures will differ between economists. The result is that there is no replication, except of the econometric techniques broadly interpreted. This is very different from the situation in physics and psychology. In so far as new data are used (later studies should use more up-to date data) there is the issue of establishing that the world has not changed (this is also a potential problem in psychology). There is much less agreement in economics on how to proceed.

---

[27] This point is the focus of the literature on exogeneity.

One example is interesting as an exception to Mirowski's assumption that mechanisms to enforce agreement do not exist. This is the Macroeconomic Modelling Bureau (at Warwick University). This Bureau has the task of bringing together all the information necessary to run the major UK forecasting models, and for undertaking comparative studies of model properties. It does not produce a consensus, but it takes the analysis a significant step in that direction. The key ingredients would seem to be the political importance of forecasting models, the size of the financial commitments involved, and the power of the Research Council to require grant recipients to provide the required information to the Bureau.

The nature of economic theory and the role of economic constants

Why is there not greater agreement on the list of conditioning variables, making it possible for economists to agree on what they should be trying to estimate? The answer would appear to lie in the nature of economic theory, which is unable to settle the matter. Economic theory, it is widely admitted, has very little, if anything, to say on lags or the properties of the error term. It is frequently not possible to specify with any certainty which variables should be in an equation. One reason for this is that economic theory is not based on the existence of certain numerical constants, but on 'underlying' factors such as preferences and technology. Where theorizing has been based on the existence of constants (for example, post Keynesian arguments based on a propensity to consume out of profits; Okun's Law) economists have been generally been sceptical, preferring such variables to be modelled explicitly. Even where empirical evidence supports the existence of such constants, economists are, in the absence of any theoretical justification, frequently sceptical about whether such regularities will survive should there be a change elsewhere in the economic system.

Given the nature of economic theory, it is quite reasonable for economists, even if they are sceptical about the merits of free markets as an arbitrage mechanism, to see no role for institutions to establish agreement on the numbers. The prior question of whether such constants are there to be found, let alone what they are and the domain to which they apply, has not yet been settled.[28] In one sense (this qualification is important), economists are not interested in institutions to establish parameter values because these parameters do not matter to economic theory.[29] This, however, leads into the question of testing theories, to which we now turn.

---

[28] Economists' lack of concern with establishing constants fits well, however, with Rosenberg's argument about economists not being interested in prediction, discussed in section 9.2.

[29] This discussed further in section 13.3 below.

12. Econometrics and testing economic theories

12.1 ECONOMIC THEORIES AND ECONOMIC MODELS

Replication establishes that there are some real-world phenomena to be explained – that apparent regularities are not just artefacts of some particular data set. It does not, however, provide any explanation of *why* the phenomena occur. For this we need a theory. Here a problem immediately arises – the relationship between economic theories, economic models and econometric models.[1] Even when they think of themselves as theorizing, the activity in which economists are typically engaged is modelling. For example, in *The Theory of Value* (1959), Debreu expounds the *theory* of value by analysing a *model* of general competitive equilibrium. Similarly, Solow's book on growth *theory* (Solow, 1970) analyses a sequence of *models* of economic growth. These examples are typical. Economists may defend theories, and it is theories which provide explanations, yet they analyse theoretical models and test empirical or econometric models. It is necessary, therefore, to distinguish more carefully between these three concepts.

1. *Economic theories* can be thought of as generalizations, or sets of generalizations, concerning the causal. mechanisms underlying

---

[1] The terminology adopted here is similar to that used by Hausman (1991, Chapter 5). The terms 'theory' and 'model' are sometimes used differently. Economists, for example, typically reserve the term 'theory' for what is here termed 'theoretical models'. However, though there are advantages in using terms in the way defined in the text, nothing hinges on the precise labels used.

economic phenomena.[2] In most modern economics, heterodox economics apart, theories relate economic phenomena to individual constrained optimization and rules governing the interaction of economic agents. Thus the theory of general competitive equilibrium explains prices and quantities traded in terms of profit-maximizing firms, consumers choosing the most preferred bundles from those available within their budget constraints, and perfectly competitive markets.

2. *Theoretical models* are specific examples of economic theories. They are formulated sufficiently precisely for it to be possible to prove, logically, the results that need to be proved. In addition to the basic assumptions required by the theory, a range of auxiliary assumptions will have to be made: functional forms (possibly still very general) and assumptions that define which variables are to be included and which are not. Thus we might refer to neoclassical growth theory, meaning theories in which long-run growth is explained as the equilibrium growth path of a competitive economy. This theory is embodied in models, such as the one-sector model with exogenous population growth and technical progress; two sector models; models with endogenous technical progress; models of monetary growth; and so on. These are theoretical models.

3. *Empirical (or econometric) models* are even more specific. Functional forms are specified in detail, variables are defined in terms of observable, measurable variables, and coefficients are quantified, using statistical inference or other techniques. Given data on exogenous variables, empirical models can be used to make quantitative predictions, and their consistency with empirical evidence can be investigated.[3] The difference between theories and empirical models is that, though both make claims about the

---

[2] This definition is more specific than some found in the literature on science in general. For example, the definition offered by one authority is the following:

> The task of a theory is to present a generalized description of the phenomena within [its] intended scope which will enable one to answer a variety of questions about the phenomena and their underlying mechanisms; these questions typically include requests for predictions, explanations, and descriptions of the phenomena. (Suppe, 1977, p. 223)

[3] At this stage, this sentence is being left slightly vague. It will be discussed further as the chapter progresses.

world, theories are generalizations about causal mechanisms, whereas empirical models are mathematical relationships between observable variables.

These distinctions are important for several reasons. Whilst econometrics deals with empirical models it is theories that encapsulate economists' beliefs about the world. Models contain many assumptions to which economists are not committed, but which are made in order to make problems manageable. Few economists, for example, would argue that any national economy produces a homogeneous product, or that agents have identical preferences. But theories can typically not be tested formally. Indeed, the link between theories and testing is doubly loose, for the relationship between data, models and theory is as shown in Figure 12.1. Auxiliary hypotheses, for which there will frequently be no real justification other than analytical convenience, are introduced in the transition from theory to theoretical model, and in the transition from theoretical to empirical model. Note that the arrows in Figure 12.1 are drawn pointing in both directions. Theories both inform and are informed by economists' experience in constructing theoretical models. Weintraub (1985), for example, has argued that the models that are the subject of general equilibrium analysis served to articulate and define general equilibrium theory.[4] Theoretical models in turn inform and are informed by empirical models. The choice of auxiliary assumptions, which affects the nature of the model, is made in order that the model will achieve what the economist is trying to do with it. The nature of the empirical model will not only depend on the data (coefficients may be estimated from data) but will also influence the economist's choice of data.

---

[4] Though he used different terminology, an economist who has emphasized the distinction between theory and model is Friedman. In defending the quantity theory of money he has defended it as a 'framework' for monetary analysis, not a specific theory. In our terminology, he argued that it was a theory, not a model. If specific models were shown to be wrong, whether by logical analysis or by empirical testing, this did not invalidate the theory itself (the framework, as he called it), for alternative models could be constructed.

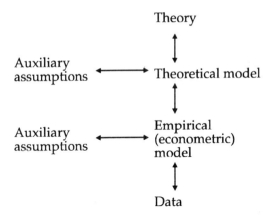

Figure 12.1: Theories, models and data

Thus if a model is tested and shown to be false, it is still easy to claim that the theory on which it is based has not been refuted.[5]

12.2 ECONOMETRICS AND TESTING

The standard view

The standard view of econometrics, stemming from Haavelmo (1944) and the work of the Cowles Commission,[6] is to regard economic processes as joint probability distributions across all relevant variables, with observed data being treated as samples from these distributions. This assumption makes it possible to test hypotheses by calculating the probability of observing the actual data if the hypothesis were true. Though the econometrician cannot take random samples, he or she can analyse the samples thrown up by nature. It is this perspective that provides the basis for applying statistical techniques such as correlation and regression. Without it such techniques could be used, but only as measurement techniques: models cannot be tested using formal statistical inference.

---

[5] This is the Duhem-Quine problem: that predictions depend on a set of assumptions, and that when a prediction fails, it may be any of the assumptions that are at fault.

[6] See Morgan (1990), Chapter 8.

Within this framework, econometric research was seen as comprising three stages:

1. Formulate a mathematical model.
2. Collect data that is believed to correspond to the variables in the theory.
3. Use statistical significance tests to determine whether the theory could (subject to confidence intervals determined in advance) have generated the observed data.

Econometrics is viewed as concerned primarily with testing theories, and secondly with measuring coefficients. But the role of evidence in suggesting new theories is minimized.

This is described as the 'standard' view because, at least till the 1980s, it came to be accepted as the way econometric research had to be undertaken. This was, however, not always so. Prior to Haavelmo, the emphasis was on measuring and on the use of empirical evidence to suggest new theories. Statistical tools (least squares regression, correlation) were used as descriptive statistics. Haavelmo's argument against such methods was that they relied for their justification on an underlying probability model. If this model were denied, as many economists claimed it should be, there was no basis for using such methods.

The merit of the standard view is that it appeared to provide a way for econometrics to progress: some theories would fail and would be rejected. In addition, test statistics made it possible to make a rational comparison of alternative theories by exploring how well each of them fitted the data. Why, then, was this approach not more successful?

The use of significance tests

A widely-held view about why the standard view failed to lead to greater progress is that economists have misused significance tests, in a variety of ways. Economists are trained to construct regression equations in such a way that coefficients are significant at a given level, normally 5 per cent. In practice this involves running a series of regressions until one is found where, for each variable in the equation, the t ratio (the ratio of the coefficient to its standard error) is greater than 2, all other variables having been dropped.[7] Such an approach has a number of problems.[8]

1. Statistical and economic significance are frequently confused. If t ratios are sufficiently large, coefficients are said to be 'significant'. All this means is that there is a small probability that the non-zero value of the coefficient is due to sampling error. This says nothing about the economic significance of the coefficient – for this it may be more important to consider its magnitude, a question that requires broader analysis of the economic problem in which the coefficient is to be used. A coefficient may be statistically significant (sampling error is very small) even though it is so small as to be economically insignificant.

2. Failure to show that a coefficient is significantly different from zero is not the same as showing that it is zero. For example, suppose we are testing the hypothesis that a coefficient is not zero, and the t statistic is 0.7 – much less than the critical value of 2 (assuming a 5 per cent significance level). On the conventional criterion we would reject the hypothesis on the grounds that the coefficient is not significantly different from zero, and would be likely to drop the corresponding variable from our equation. On the other hand, the probability of obtaining a t value of 0.7 simply by sampling error is less than 50 per cent. In other words, it is more likely that the coefficient is positive than that it is zero or negative.

3. A coefficient may be statistically insignificant for two reasons. The reason on which economists frequently focus is that the coefficient is close to zero. The other possibility, however, is that the number of observations may be so small that the sampling error is large. In setting confidence intervals, therefore, account should be taken of sample size.

4. The most important problem, however, is that a series of equations is examined, with only the successful one being reported. The list of variables to be included, functional forms, and how variables are measured are chosen so as to get the best-fitting equation. Such procedures clearly increase the chance that

---

[7] The same arguments apply to other statistical tests. Reference is made only to t tests merely to simplify the exposition.

[8] This section draws on Darnell and Evans (1990), pp. 33–7; Mayer (1993), Chapter 10; Mayer (1995); McCloskey (1983); McCloskey and Ziliak (1996).

an economist will find an equation that fits the data well over and above that suggested by the formal test statistics.

The underlying problem here is that statistical tests are being used in two ways. They are used as design criteria, guiding the economist's choice of model, and they are used as tests of hypotheses. These, however, are incompatible.

Given the limited guidance provided by economic theory, economists have no choice but to search the data for suitable models. The issue is how they do this, and what criteria they employ in responding to the data and in evaluating their results. It is necessary to pay attention to modelling strategies, not simply tests of individual hypotheses, something for which the Neyman–Pearson methodology, which underlies the standard view, provides no guidance.

12.3   ECONOMETRICS AS DESIGNING A MODEL

Econometrics and laboratory experiments[9]

Many economists have seen econometrics as analogous to laboratory experimentation. The difference is that where the laboratory scientist can conduct controlled experiments, eliminating certain effects by keeping relevant variables constant, the econometrician has to use the experiments thrown up by society.[10] Control takes the form of estimating the effects of 'interfering' variables, so that they can be eliminated. Thus if we wish to estimate the interest-elasticity of money demand, we control for variations in other variables by estimating their effects, so that any remaining variation in money demand is attributable either to variations in the interest rate or to the error term.

This analogy is, however, imperfect. An experiment relates the variable of interest, y_t to some control variable, x_t (which may be a vector of variables), but the experimental procedure is not precise so a random error, v_t is involved.

---

[9]   This exposition follows Hendry (1995a), pp. 27–9.

[10] This discussion obviously excludes experimental economics.

$$y_t = f(x_t) + v_t,$$

where $f(.)$ is the relationship between the two variables. v_t is an independent cause of changes in y_t. The situation in econometrics is rather different. The econometrician estimates the equation,

$$y_t = g(z_t) + \varepsilon_t.$$

Superficially, this is the same as the previous equation. What underlies it, however, is very different.[11]

With the first equation it is clear that causation runs from right to left. The errors are due to imperfections in the experimental technique – they represent random drawings from nature. In contrast, $\{\varepsilon_t\}$ is not a series of random drawings from nature, but a derived process. It is what is left over after removing the variation in y_t that can be accounted for by variation in z_t. What the equation does is to decompose y_t into two components: a part that can be explained in terms of z_t and a part that cannot. ε_t includes all errors in the model, whether they arise from errors in selecting z_t or in the specification of $g(\cdot)$.[12] In short, if causation is to run from right to left, the equation should be written in the form

$$\varepsilon_t = y_t - g(z_t).$$

In addition, whether or not y_t depends on $g(z_t)$, it is possible that more than one process $\{\varepsilon_t\}$ can be fitted to the data. Thus even if an equation is a good statistical fit, it cannot be assumed either that the estimated relationship is unique or that it represents the process that determines y_t.

The key issue here is that the correct model is unknown. If we knew which variables appeared in the model, and if we knew enough about the correct specification of the equation, we could

---

[11] The discussion will refer to time series models. Many, though not all, the points made carry over to other types of econometric work.

[12] In drawing this contrast, it should be admitted that with some experiments in natural sciences, the situation may look more like that facing economists.

regard econometric work as testing the model, but typically we do not.[13] What, then, are econometricians doing?[14]

Models as reductions of the data generating process

One answer to this question is that they are searching for reductions of the data generating process (DGP). The starting point is the assumption that the DGP can be represented by a joint probability distribution over all relevant variables. However, in its most general form (a function that assigns a probability[15] to every conceivable state of the world) this is so general as to be useless. It tells us nothing about the structure of the world. What is required is a simplification of the DGP that tells us something about what is going on. Specifically, we wish to reduce the general DGP described above to a model in which a set of endogenous variables is a related to a list of lagged endogenous variables, a list of exogenous variables and a set of parameters.[16] This can be done in four ways.

1. Eliminating variables that do not matter for those variables in which we are interested;
2. Conditioning endogenous variables on exogenous variables;

---

[13] The difference between these two conceptions of stochastic equations can have direct, practical implications. Take, for example, the problem of how to respond to serially-correlated error terms. If the 'experimental' model is appropriate, it may make sense to fit a more complicated model of the error term, but if we take the view that the second interpretation of the equation is correct, it makes far more sense to presume that the serial correlation results from omitted variables or mis-specification (Hendry and Mizon, 1978).

[14] For other answers to this question, see Morgan (1988) and Goldfarb (1995).

[15] Or, where variables are continuous, a probability density.

[16] Formally, this can be described by:

$$\prod_{t=1}^{T} D(x_t | X_{t-1}; \theta),$$

where x_t is a vector of observations on all relevant variables in period t, $X_{t-1} = (x_1, \ldots, x_{t-1})'$ and θ is a vector of parameters of the joint density function, $D(.)$. The aim is to reduce this DGP to a model such as,

$$\prod_{t=1}^{T} D(y_t | Y_{t-1}; Z_t; \phi)$$

where y_t is a vector of endogenous variables, Y_{t-1} is past values of y_t, and Z_t is a vector of exogenous variables, with ϕ a vector of known parameters. (This exposition follows Gilbert, 1986.)

3. Searching for simple representations;
4. Replacing unknown parameters with estimated values.

An econometric model, therefore should be seen as a reduction or simplified representation of the DGP. This leads on to the questions of the criteria that are to be used in undertaking this reduction, and how one appraises the resulting models.

Data congruency and progressive research strategies

The most general criterion to be satisfied by an econometric model is that it be consistent with *all* available information. This information can be divided into a number of categories. The first type of information is that provided by the data, the term data-admissible being used to describe models that are consistent with all information contained in the data. Hendry (1993) has operationalized this criterion by dividing the information contained in the data into three categories, each of which has a different statistical implication.[17]

1. Past data – innovation errors should be homoscedastic (have constant variance).
2. Present data – conditioning variables should be weakly exogenous for parameters of interest.[18]
3. Future data - parameters of interest should be constant over time and invariant across regimes.

These are all criteria that can be tested against empirical evidence. A model that meets all these criteria is defined as being *congruent with the data* or *data-admissible*.

There are, however, other important sources of information, and models should take account of these, just as much as information contained in the data.

4. Theory information – relationships should be consistent with economic theory. Typically, Hendry assumes that theory indicates long-run equilibrium relationships.

---

[17] This list is a paraphrase, with many phrases quoted, from Hendry (1993), p. 19. For a more formal statement of these criteria, see Hendry and Richard (1982), pp. 311–23.

[18] A variable x is weakly exogenous with respect to parameter β if the distribution of x contains no information about β. For a more formal definition, see page 173.

5. Measurement information – models should be data-congruent when accurate observations are used.
6. Rival model information – 'results which encompass the findings of other empirical models of the same phenomena and explain additional phenomena' (Hendry, 1993, p. 19). Even if rival models are inadequate (why else would a new study be undertaken?) they contain information.

Hendry defined a congruent model as one that satisfies all these conditions. The task of the econometrician is to search for congruent models. Because there are clear-cut, operational criteria for all these conditions, this is a feasible task. It is important to note that this is not the same as searching for true models, for congruence need not correspond with truth (even if this can be defined). Congruence is, however, a *necessary* condition for a model to be true.

This view of models as reductions of the DGP means that the error term cannot be regarded as an autonomous process, analogous to the error term in controlled experiments. The error term can be regarded as autonomous only when the reduction of the DGP can be achieved with no loss of information. In this case the error term is the same as the error term in the original DGP. In view of the nature of economic phenomena, it is reasonable to work on the assumption that this is never satisfied: models are always approximations, involving some loss of information. Different reductions result in different error terms.[19]

Reduction of the DGP is achieved through calculating various diagnostic statistics and modifying models in response to what they reveal.[20] The significance of this is that test statistics, based on the available data set, are being used as *design criteria*. This applies to parameter-stability and out-of-sample tests as much as to any other test. The implication of this is that, because models are designed so as to meet these criteria, the fact that they do meet them cannot be used as a test of a model. If a model is to be tested, it needs to be

---

[19] This is the point made in section 11.5 in response to Mirowski's arguments concerning high Birge ratios in economics. Different models involve different reductions of the DGP, and hence involve different error processes. There can thus be no presumption that the variances of two different models will be similar.

[20] Hendry has argued that the appropriate procedure is to start with general models and then simplify: general to particular.

confronted with new information, not used in the construction of the model. It must predict novel facts.

Hendry's final criterion, that models encompass the results of existing models as well as explaining additional phenomena is perhaps the most interesting of the criteria he lays down for congruence. His reason for specifying this as a criterion is that it results in a *progressive research strategy*, where the term progressive is understood in a Lakatosian sense. If the results obtained by previous investigators can be explained, and some new results are obtained as well, there are grounds for arguing that a model is an improvement over previous models. Hendry's methodology, therefore, rests on the notion of progress.

12.4 TESTING THEORIES USING INFORMAL METHODS

The importance of 'natural experiments'

Friedman has emphasized the prediction of novel facts[21] as the only criterion by which theories are to be judged. However, he takes this in a very different direction from Hendry. The main feature of Friedman's approach is his emphasis on what he terms natural experiments – the experiments thrown up by history. His attitude here is very clearly revealed in the concluding chapter of *A Monetary History of the United States, 1967–1962* (Friedman and Schwartz, 1963). In that chapter, which provides a summary of the book's arguments, Friedman and Schwartz make several clear statements about method.

1. In the absence of controlled experiment we have to look at historical episodes where the phenomena in which we are interested can be found, but in a variety of different circumstances.

   The varied character of U.S. monetary history renders this century of economic history renders this century of experience particularly valuable to the student of economic change. He cannot control the experiment, but he

---

[21] See page 116 above.

can observe monetary experience under sufficiently disparate conditions to sort out what it common from what is adventitious and to acquire considerable confidence that what is common can be counted on to hold under still other circumstances. (Friedman and Schwartz, 1963, p. 676)

2. Sometimes history throws up 'natural experiments' where the disturbing causes are so clear cut as to be unmistakable, and where the consequences are sufficiently dramatic to be identifiable. These are specific historical events, but they are made possible by the existence of certain institutions. In US monetary history, the Federal Reserve System, established in 1914, is of particular significance.

The establishment of the Federal Reserve System provides the student of money a closer substitute for the controlled experiment to determine the direction of influence than the social scientist can generally obtain. ... [T]he establishment of the System gave a small body of individuals the power, which they exercised from time to time, to alter the course of events in significant and identifiable ways through a deliberate process – a sequence parallel with the conduct of a controlled experiment. (Friedman and Schwartz, 1963, p. 668)

The analogy between the actions of the Federal Reserve Board and the scientific experimenter is explicit. Friedman and Schwartz recognize that the Federal Reserve Board will frequently be responding to the prevailing climate of opinion (including available information on the economy), but argue that this does not invalidate the analogy: natural scientists too respond to the contemporary climate of opinion in deciding what experiments to carry out, and how to interpret the results of these experiments.

In either case, such dependence on the existing state of knowledge does not alter the scientific independence from the prior or contemporary course of events of the changes introduced into the controlled variables. What it means is simply that later students may reinterpret the results of the experiments in light of the changed body of knowledge and draw conclusions that are different from those drawn by the original experimenters (Friedman and Schwartz, 1963, p. 688).

This analogy is, however, possibly misleading. Two issues Friedman and Schwartz do not discuss are: (a) whether the problem of reflexivity, caused by economists' being part of the system they are analysing, causes fundamental problems with this analogy (c.f. Hands, 1994); (b) whether even partial endogeneity of the money supply calls into question some of their ordinary least squares regressions.

3. In order to determine causation, a variety of qualitative evidence must be used. The economist always knows more than the bare numbers, and should make use of this information. Correlation, by itself, tells us nothing about causation:

> The close relation between changes in the stock of money and changes in other economic variables, alone, tells nothing about the origin of either or the direction of influence. ... A great merit of the examination of a wide range of qualitative evidence, so essential in a monetary history, is that it provides a basis for discriminating between these possible explanations of the observed statistical covariation. We can go beyond the numbers alone and, at least on some occasions, discern the antecedent circumstances whence arose the particular movements that become so anonymous when we feed the statistics into the computer. (Friedman and Schwartz, 1963, p. 686)

4. Friedman frequently argues in terms of what might be called the 'natural units' thrown up by history – business cycle expansions and contractions – rather than arbitrary calendar time periods. He emphatically does not regard, for example, quarterly data as containing four times the information contained in an equivalent set of annual data.

Thus where most econometricians would regard phase-averaging as losing information and, possibly, introducing spurious correlations into the data, Friedman argues that the business cycle provides the natural units in which data should be measured. Given that calendar years or quarters are, in a sense arbitrary, why should we model economic series by assuming that a random drawing is made from nature each year?

Friedman's eclectic approach

In contrast with Hendry, and most econometricians, Friedman does not regard the task of statistical analysis as being to produce a single equation encompassing all other models. Rather, he adopts an eclectic approach. This is clearly summed up in Friedman and Schwartz (1991), referring to Hendry and Ericsson's critique (1991) of *Monetary Trends in the United States and the United Kingdom* (Friedman and Schwartz, 1982).

> To examine a wide variety of evidence, quantitative and nonquantitative, bearing on the question under study; test results from one body of evidence on other bodies, using econometric techniques as one tool in this process, and build up a collection of simple hypotheses that may or may not be readily viewed as components of a broader all-embracing hypothesis; and finally, test hypotheses on bodies of data other than those from which they were derived. Both ways – and no doubt others as well – have their use. None, we believe, can be relied on exclusively. (Friedman and Schwartz, 1991, p. 39)

Where Hendry and Ericsson respond to the problem of the real world being too complex to be fully comprehended by arguing that models must be viewed as reductions of a DGP, Friedman and Schwartz respond by arguing that one cannot rely on a single model (equation). It is necessary, they argue, to explore a wide range of equations and to use these alongside other information.

Friedman and Schwartz emphasize the importance of being familiar with the data, and in particular with the way in which the data are constructed. Such knowledge, they argue, may give information about the error term. For example, they point out that for data early in the sample, interpolation was frequently used in the construction of monetary aggregates, whereas for more recent years this was not the case. Because data are at the beginning of their sample are smoother than more recent data, a heteroscedastic error term (one where the variance is lower at the beginning of the period than at the end) is to be expected. In addition, Friedman and Schwartz emphasize the importance of allowing for errors in variables: (1) variables do not correspond exactly to the economic concepts; (2) measurement errors are often significant.

The roles of statistics and economic theory

Comparing Hendry's approach with Friedman's highlights a number of issues concerning the roles of statistical analysis and economic theory in econometrics. The first concerns the emphasis on testing theories, versus finding a good representation of the data.

Hendry sees the task of econometrics as being, in the first instance, the construction of a congruent model. Such a model does not, in itself, constitute a test of any economic theory, for theories are typically not expressed in a form that renders them amenable to such testing. Friedman, in contrast, starts with the stated aim of testing the quantity theory of money, through looking at a range of evidence.[22] In recognising that the theory itself is untestable (it is the theoretical framework to which he is committed, not any specific model) he refuses to attach much importance to tests of individual models.[23]

Following the tradition set by Haavelmo, Hendry starts from the presumption that the economy should be modelled as a DGP, where this is understood as a joint probability distribution. In explaining Hendry's method, Gilbert goes so far as to claim that the joint density function described on page 166 above is 'uncontroversial' (Gilbert, 1986, p. 281). In so far as he is claiming that the economic process *can* be represented in this way, he is right. This, however, is a long way from saying that it is useful to regard it as the *only* way to think about the world. Friedman's approach, which may involve having one model to explain long-run trends, and another theory to explain short-run cyclical phenomena, could be read as questioning this assumption.

Friedman and Hendry agree that theory and other information have to be used in constructing economic models. Hendry, however, tends to place less emphasis on such information than does Friedman. Like Friedman, he regards the main contribution of theory as being to suggest long-run relationships between variables. Friedman, however, uses theory and historical information to establish things that Hendry seeks to establish statistically. The clearest example is exogeneity, which they treat in completely different ways. For Hendry, exogeneity is a statistical property of the data. The relevant criterion that the independent variables in a regression must satisfy is 'weak exogeneity', which is a condition on the covariation of parameters of probability distributions.[24] The

---

[22] Mayer (1993) sees this as the main difference between Hendry and Friedman.

[23] See Backhouse (1995), Chapter 11.

[24] Simplifying the problem, suppose that there is a joint density function over the variables in which we are interested, y_t, and some explanatory variables, z_t. Past values of the variables will typically be involved, but these are omitted for simplicity.

significance of this criterion is that it means a variable can be taken as exogenous without losing any information relevant to parameters in which we are interested. In contrast, for Friedman, exogeneity is understood in terms of causal relations.

> In our view, exogeneity is not an invariant statistical characteristic of variables. Everything depends on the purpose. In economic analysis it may be appropriate to regard a variable as exogenous for some purposes and endogenous for others. A simple example is the quantity of money. For the United States after World War I, we believe it is appropriate to regard the money stock as exogenous (i.e. determined by the monetary authorities) in an economic analysis of long-run money demand. We do not believe it would be equally appropriate to do so for week-to-week or month-to-month movements for which, in HE's words, 'the money stock appears to be endogenously determined by the decisions of the private sector'. For the period before World War I, . . ., it is not appropriate to regard the money stock as exogenous even for money demand analysis . . . (Friedman and Schwartz, 1991, p. 42)

Friedman is viewing the data as produced by something analogous to a controlled experiment. In the same way as the actions of the experimenter, who takes actions that affect her subject matter, enable us to say that certain things are exogenous, so knowledge about the economy and in particular the way in which decisions were taken, enables the economist to make assertions about causality and exogeneity.

This difference in attitudes towards exogeneity is linked to differences, discussed above, in attitudes towards probabilistic modelling of the economy. Friedman has a much broader view of the range of non-statistical information available to the economist, which means that he finds the approach of viewing the economy as a single DGP less attractive than do most econometricians. The nature of modern economic theory and Haavelmo's probabilistic revolution have between them more or less forced econometricians to explain phenomena as either functional relations between variables, or

---

This joint density, D_X can be factorized into the product of a conditional and a marginal density function:

$$D_X(y_t, z_t) = D_{Y|Z}(y_t|z_t)D_Z(z_t).$$

z_t is weakly exogenous for the parameters of interest if these parameters depend solely on the parameters of $D_{Y|Z}$ and if there is no covariation between the parameters of $D_{Y|Z}$ and D_Z. This is a simplified version of Hendry, 1993, p. 14.

stochastic error terms. Friedman asserts that there are phenomena that are best explained historically, using knowledge about institutions and other non-quantitative information.

It is important to point out that the dividing line between these two approaches is not always clear cut. For example, Friedman argues, for various reasons, that Federal Reserve board decisions can be regarded as exogenous. Yet Federal Reserve policy may be identifiable from minutes of Board meetings, and turned into statistical series which can then be analysed using econometric techniques (Romer and Romer, 1989). New sources of data may render 'historical' evidence amenable to statistical testing.

The importance of informal empirical work

It has been argued that informal empirical work, of the type undertaken by Friedman, has been far more influential than formal econometrics. Stanley Fischer,[25] when asked to name the key works that have had a major impact on post-war macroeconomics, picked out Friedman and Schwartz's *Monetary History of the United States*, describing it as 'extraordinarily important'. A similar, more wide-ranging claim has been made by Summers, who has combined it with a critique of econometrics. His starting point is the failure of formal econometrics to have a major impact.

> This paper argues that formal empirical work which, to use Sargent's phrase, tries to 'take models seriously econometrically' has had almost no influence on serious thinking about substantive as opposed to methodological questions. Instead the only empirical work that has influenced thinking about substantive questions has been based on methodological principles directly opposed to those that have become fashionable in recent years. Successful empirical research has been characterized by attempts to gauge the strength of associations rather than to estimate structural parameters, verbal characterizations of how causal relations might operate rather than explicit mathematical models, and the skilful use of carefully chosen natural experiments rather than sophisticated statistical technique to achieve identification. (Summers, 1991, pp. 129–30)

---

[25] Quoted in Snowdon, Vane and Wynarczyk (1994), p. 33.

The links between theory and empirical models are too loose for 'refutations' to weaken theories, whilst positive results are rarely replicated on other data sets.

The strengths of pragmatic, informal empirical work, on the other hand, are that:

1. It deals with stylized facts, not parameter estimates.
2. It produces regularities of a kind that theory can explain (wealth entering the consumption function; the Phillips curve).
3. No single test is seen as decisive (Friedman used 16 different types of evidence to support the permanent income theory of consumption).[26]

The emphasis is on robust results – results that are not sensitive to mis-specification of the underlying model or to errors in the data. It is because he wants to find results that do not depend on specific model specifications that Friedman estimates not one but many money demand functions (whether he is successful in this is another matter altogether[27]). As Hendry and Ericsson (1991) make very clear, such a procedure opens the doors to data mining, and is vulnerable to the charge that if enough regressions are run, and if rigorous testing procedures are not employed, corroborating a theory is comparatively easy. Though Hendry's 'general-to-particular' methodology invites similar criticism, his defence lies in the use of a much more rigorous set of (statistical) design criteria than Friedman and Schwartz employ.

---

[26] Summers (1991), p. 140.

[27] It can be argued that Friedman's (1982) estimation of a variety of money demand functions can do no more than establish that certain of his results are independent of certain details concerning model specification. It cannot replicate the result that the US or UK economy is characterized by a money demand function of the form that Friedman claims. The similarity of US and UK money demand functions could constitute replication, provided that one had confidence that the results of work on one country did not influence the outcome of research on the other. The absence of formal testing procedures in Friedman's work makes it much harder to be confident that this is the case.

12.5   CALIBRATION AND COMPUTATIONAL EXPERIMENTS

Kydland and Prescott on computational experiments

Standing apart from both formal econometrics, whether the 'standard view' or the view outlined in section 12.3, and the use of informal methods, is 'calibration', or the running of 'computational experiments'. Though originally developed under the label of 'computable general equilibrium theory', widely used in public finance and international economics, and introduced into macroeconomics by the supporters of real business cycle theory (Kydland and Prescott, 1982, 1986, 1990, 1991), it is a method that can be applied to any economic model, whether or not its theoretical foundations are general competitive equilibrium. The following steps are involved.

1. Formulate an economic theory suitable to answer the questions of interest. The theory needs to be 'strong' – one 'that has been tested through use and found to provide reliable answers to a class of questions' (Kydland and Prescott, 1996, p. 72).
2. Select functional forms and, where possible, parameter values based on econometric estimates taken from pre-existing *micro*economic studies and stylized facts about the data to be explained (such as constancy of the wage share in national income).
3. Set values of parameters on which there is no information so that the model 'mimics the world as closely as possible along a limited, but clearly specified, number of dimensions' (Kydland and Prescott, 1996, p. 74).
4. Run simulations using the model to answer the original questions.

Thus in their pioneering work on real business cycles, Kydland and Prescott took the neoclassical model of economic growth, calibrated it (i.e. selected functional forms, and numerical values for the parameters in the production and utility functions) so that it explained the facts of long-term growth in the US, and then used the model to answer questions concerning the contribution of technology shocks to the business cycle.

This approach involves a mixture of formal and informal methods. It is formal in that there is a clearly laid down procedure for answering economic questions, but it is informal in that rules are laid down neither for how estimates taken from the literature are to be chosen or evaluated, nor for how the validity of the resulting empirical model is to be appraised.

In defending this approach, Kydland and Prescott make several methodological claims.

1. Theories are viewed as instruments, not as statements about the economy.

> [B]y theory we do not mean a set of assertions about the actual economy. Rather, following Lucas (1980), economic theory is defined to be 'an explicit set of instructions for building ... a mechanical imitation system' to answer a question. (Kydland and Prescott, 1996, p. 72)

They are, therefore, to be judged by whether or not they are useful, not by how well they fit the data. 'Well tested' theories are thus theories that have proved useful, not theories that are believed to be true. Of the growth theory that forms the basis for the real business cycle models, they write,

> We recognize, of course, that although the economist should choose a well-tested theory, every theory has some issues and questions that it does not address well. In the case of neoclassical growth theory, for example, it fails spectacularly when used to address economic development issues. Differences in stocks of reproducible capital stocks cannot account for differences in per capita incomes. This does not preclude its usefulness in evaluating tax policies and in business cycle research. (Kydland and Prescott, 1996, p. 72)

2. Theories are of necessity abstractions and are, therefore, false.

> The models constructed within this theoretical framework are necessarily highly abstract. Consequently, they are necessarily false, and statistical testing will reject them. (Kydland and Prescott, 1986, p. 266)

3. Calibration methods are widely used in natural sciences, notably meteorology. Kydland and Prescott use the term 'calibration' is used to imply that what is involved in choosing functional forms

and parameter values is no different from what happens when a scientist calibrates an instrument, such as a thermometer, ensuring that it reads 100° when placed in boiling water, and 0° when placed in water that is on the point of freezing.

Whilst the acceptability of such methods in natural sciences is used to establish the respectability of these methods, they do not establish why economists have to calibrate their models in this way: why they cannot simply construct numerical models on the basis of rigorously estimated coefficients. Kydland's and Prescott's claim is that econometrics typically does not estimate the deep, structural parameters that will be invariant across policy regimes. These are the parameters describing preferences and production functions. In contrast, the parameters that econometricians estimate represent the interaction of these functions with constraints: they are, therefore, not invariant to changes in the policy regime. In short, calibration is essential because econometrics does not estimate the parameters that are required by the theory.

> RBC analysis turned to calibration mainly because conventional macroeconometric models do not address themselves to estimating these parameters [of the functions to be optimized]. The so-called structural models of conventional econometrics are in reality quasi-reduced forms formed by combining the first order conditions, the constraints and the forcing variable processes. Consequently they lack identification, and are prone to structural instability. (Wickens, 1995, p. 1638)

This does not, of course, mean that the parameters derived through calibration methods do in fact reflect underlying structural parameters.[28] The analogy with calibration of a thermometer is misleading, for thermometers do not more than measure – they are passive instruments. Economic models, in contrast, are used to predict.

Calibration, estimation and testing

Calibration and computational experiments are presented by their advocates as very different from estimation. The difference is that estimation is concerned with measuring parameters through

---

[28] C.f. Hendry (1995b).

constructing equations that provide the best possible fit to the data, whereas computational experiments are about deriving theories' quantitative implications. Kydland and Prescott's state explicitly that their choice of theory is dictated not by which model fits the data best, but by 'currently established theory' (Kydland and Prescott, 1991, p. 174). One reason given for this rejection of fitting the data as a criterion by which to judge theories is their view that theories are not hypotheses about the real world, but are tools. Following Lucas (1980), Kydland and Prescott define 'theory' as being:

> an explicit set of instructions for building an imitation economy to address certain questions and not a collection of assertions about the behaviour of the actual economy. Consequently, statistical hypothesis testing, which is designed to test assertions about actual systems, is not an appropriate tool for testing economic theory. (Kydland and Prescott, 1996, p. 83)

Theory is not something that can be tested using econometric methods. It is more like the hard core of a Lakatosian research programme – a set of heuristics.[29]

This view of economic theory almost implies that theories cannot be tested directly, merely by being proved reliable in repeated use. This appears to be what Kydland and Prescott have in mind. Yet if references to testing are to be more than 'passing the buck' – implying that theories will already have been tested before they come to be used – some criterion has to be provided. One possibility would be that decision makers are led to make successful decisions on the basis of conclusions drawn from computational experiments. However, though this may be implied, no evidence is provided. The other criterion is to judge the extent to which a model's predictions are confirmed. Thus when Kydland and Prescott observe that some of the questions a computational experiment is designed to answer may be concerned with testing and developing the theory, they note that 'such questions typically ask about the quantitative implications of the theory for some phenomena' (Kydland and Prescott, 1996, p. 71). At one point they go so far as to argue:

---

[29] For a much more detailed discussion of Kydland and Prescott's attitude towards models and theory, see Hoover (1995).

One way to test a theory is to determine whether model economies constructed according to the instructions of that theory mimic certain aspects of reality. Perhaps the ultimate test of a theory is whether its predictions are confirmed – that is, did the actual economy behave as predicted by the model economy, given the policy rule selected? (Kydland and Prescott, 1996, p. 83)

Given their hostility to curve fitting, one might be forgiven for thinking that they are following Friedman in viewing the prediction of novel facts as their appraisal criterion[30] – a model is calibrated in one dimension and a computational experiment is then run to test the model's ability to predict in some *other* dimension. This, however, is not what they intend. Immediately after the passage just quoted, Kydland and Prescott proceed to discuss what happens if the theory passes such tests, but they are silent as to what happens in the event of failure. The reason is that, as they had explained several pages earlier, a discrepancy between predictions and observations is only a test of the theory 'in some cases' (Kydland and Prescott, 1996, p. 74). In other cases, all that need be done is to reject the theory for answering a particular question: it may be used for other questions. In other words, they do not regard the failure of a theory's predictions as necessarily being a problem.

This refusal to admit that the failure of a theory's predictions is grounds for doubting, and possibly rejecting, the theory is tied up with Kydland and Prescott's attitude towards estimation. If they admitted that computational models should be judged by whether or not their predictions were confirmed, the difference between calibration and estimation would be virtually eliminated. It would open up the possibility of developing statistical tests by which the predictive success of computational experiments could be judged, with the result that 'calibration' would have become merely an additional estimation technique.[31] It might have advantages over other techniques, but it would nonetheless be an estimation technique.

Calibration appears, at least at first sight, to take seriously the problems with the traditional view of econometrics, discussed in section 12.3 above. Econometrics, for Kydland and Prescott as much as for Hendry, is about designing a model, the difficulties arising from economists' inability to conduct controlled experiments and the

---

[30] The phrasing of this passage is reminiscent of Friedman (1953).

[31] See Canova (1995) and Hansen and Heckman (1996).

problem that models are always oversimplifications of reality. Beyond that, however, their paths diverge drastically. Kydland and Prescott design models on the assumption that theories are correct. In the words of two of their critics,

> While Kydland and Prescott advocate the use of 'well-tested' theories in their essay, they never move beyond this slogan, and they do not justify their claim of fulfilling this criterion in their own research. 'Well tested' must mean more than 'familiar' or 'widely accepted' or 'agreed on by convention' if it is to mean anything. (Hansen and Heckman, 1996, p. 89)

They adopt methods that are, at the crucial stages, informal, without even, like Friedman, committing themselves to theories that are predictively successful or consistent with all the available evidence. The result is that the way is open to regard the economic theory component of real business cycle theory as virtually beyond question. Thus Wickens (1995, p. 1639) feels no need to hedge in any way when writing of Ramsey's model, the starting point for real business cycle theory, as 'containing a correct characterization of equilibrium'. Data are involved, but only to illustrate the theory. The idea that theories need to be tested, or that theory choice should depend, at least in the last resort, on empirical evidence, has been abandoned. In contrast, Hendry has responded to the unrealisticness of the 'traditional' view of econometric modelling by developing a methodology for ensuring that models *can* be tested rigorously, despite being constructed so that standard statistical tests will be satisfied.

12.6   DISCOVERING AND TESTING ECONOMIC THEORIES

The nature of many economic theories means that they cannot be tested directly. The best that can be achieved is to test them indirectly, where this involves:

1. Testing assumptions used in the theory.

2. Testing implications of the theory, where these can be derived with sufficient precision to be testable.[32]
3. Evaluating the extent to which models based on the theory are consistent with the data and historical evidence.

The last type of test represents an indirect test of the theory because of the difference between theories and models discussed in section 12.1 above. Furthermore, if predictions derived from a model are to be used to test a theory, they must be tested on a data set other than the one used to develop the model, for the model will, one presumes, have been constructed so as to be congruent with this data set.

The problems involved mean that the testing of many economic theories is extremely difficult and is frequently inconclusive. Econometrics can play a role, though this role is much more complex than that suggested by what was, in section 12.2 above, termed the standard view. It can be used to show whether models can be constructed that are congruent with the data, compatible with the theory, and which perform better than alternative models. It can also be used to test the extent to which models can predict novel facts. Seen in this light, the methodological chasm between Hendry and Friedman seems slightly smaller. Though they disagree strongly over: (a) the optimal degree of complexity of statistical techniques to be employed, (b) the desirability of modelling data as if generated by a single joint probability distribution across all variables, (c) whether modelling should aim at a single, best equation and (d) whether exogeneity should be defined statistically or using non-statistical information, they agree that econometrics cannot be used to test models directly. Unlike Kydland and Prescott, however, neither of them is prepared to abandon the view that theories need to be tested – econometric models are inputs into the process of testing economic theories.

One reason for this common element in the approaches of Friedman and Hendry is that they are both concerned, not simply with the evaluation of economic models, but with the process whereby models are generated. Hirsch and De Marchi (1990) have documented this for Friedman, locating his methodology of positive

---

[32] Though testing assumptions and implications are listed separately, the distinction is not clear-cut.

economics, to which he stuck throughout his career, in Dewey's pragmatism. Similarly, Summers argues that one of the values of informal empirical work is that it is more likely to suggest how alternative theories might be developed (1991, pp. 160–2).

Hendry, though he emphasizes the distinction between discovery and justification, uses it simply to make the point that a new data set has to be used in order to claim corroborated excess content (1993, p. 4). His advocacy of general-to-particular modelling strategies stems from a concern with the logic of discovery. His development of the concept of congruency stems from a recognition that statistical tests are part of the process whereby econometric models are designed, and that test statistics used for this purpose do not constitute a test of the model.

This emphasis on the context of discovery is also found in Lakatos. His ideas on informal mathematics were based on an attempt to find a logic underlying the development of mathematics. In Chapter 10 it was argued that this approach could be used to explain much that goes on in economic theory. Hendry and Friedman, in different ways, have pointed to ways in which analysis of the context of discovery can lead to a greater understanding of the relation between statistical analysis and the testing of economic theories.

12.7 CONCLUSIONS

Hendry's methodology, in which the econometric modelling is seen as constructing a simplification of the underlying data-generation process, and with its emphasis on moving from the general to the particular in order that restrictions on models are tested formally, answers several of the charges levelled against econometrics. It accepts that much econometric work involves estimation, not the testing of economic theories, and it faces squarely the problems of data-mining and of theories not yielding relationships that are sufficiently precise to be tested. Yet it has encountered much resistance.

This resistance to Hendry's methods can be ascribed in part to certain problems with the method. One of these is that, though the general-to-particular method has great attractions, it is in practice impossible to start with a completely general model. The 'general' models considered in practice assume, for example, normally-distributed, homoscedastic error terms and a limited range of lag lengths.[33] A second possible reason is that, though Hendry has used his method successfully to produce consumption and money demand equations that have (at least for substantial periods) performed well, others have found it harder to apply. The method is demanding, because finding a parsimonious representation of the data-generation process is only part of the story. Equally important is using the resulting model to generate predictions that can be tested against data not used in the construction of the theory, for it is here that the econometrician moves beyond designing a model to testing it.[34] A third possible reason is that the method, despite using theory as the basis for data selection and for specifying long-run relationships, does not provide economists with the guidance they require. Theories are not tested, and neither do the resulting empirical models provide the type of guidance that economic theorists require in building their theories.

Friedman's informal methods are open to none of these objections. However, the informality of his methods lays him open to the charges that his methods are so elastic that he could defend any theory, and that in practice he is no more open to the possibility that his theories may be wrong than are Kydland and Prescott. There are also technical problems with his approach, notably how it is possible to work with two, mutually incompatible, representations of the same data set. His scepticism about the methods used in modern econometrics, moreover, runs counter to the trend, dominant since the 1940s, towards seeking to test theories according to formal statistical criteria.

The acknowledged problems involved in using econometric methods to provide direct tests of economic theories, the failure of methodologies such as Hendry's to relate sufficiently directly to the concerns of economic theorists, and scepticism about whether informal methods can take us very far, may account, to some extent, for the recent interest in, on the one hand calibration methods, and on the other hand, various time-series techniques, such as unit-root

---

[33] See Hansen (1996).

[34] Darnell and Evans (1990), offer several criticisms of Hendry's methods, including some discussed above. However, though they makes some important points, they play down this second stage, focusing very much on the model-design aspects of the methodology.

and cointegration testing. Calibration methods simply sweep aside estimation problems, whilst some time-series methods appear to solve some of the problems that plagued econometrics for years (notably the problem of spurious correlation). More important, they offer the promise of short cuts to simple, empirical generalizations that can be used as a basis for theorizing, even if the results themselves are largely independent of theory.[35][36]

---

[35] See, for example, the use of such methods by Blanchard and Fischer (see Chapter 13 below) to summarize the main stylized facts about macroeconomic aggregates that macroeconomic theories need to explain.

[36] An explanation that has been avoided in this section is the sociological one that because econometricians are not interested in the truth, simply in publications, citations and the like, they have more interest in displaying proficiency in the latest impressive techniques than in anything else (c.f. McCallum, 1989; Colander, 1996). This is, undoubtedly an important factor in the short run, and may be important in the longer run too. However, it seems unwise to place too much emphasis on it, for several reasons. (1) Even if younger academics are under pressure to conform, the same is not true of those who are established, or of most journal editors. It is such people who set the criteria according to which newcomers have to perform. (2) There are many areas of economics, including the provision of policy advice, where being right is important. (3) If there were methods that were demonstrably superior, it is hard to believe that they would not become widely used.

13. Economic theory, empirical evidence and progress in economics

13.1 WHAT MATTERS TO ECONOMISTS?

Surveys of graduate students

Though it would surprise the layman, there is considerable evidence that facts about the real world are not central to economics as it is understood in many of the leading university departments and international academic journals. When Arjo Klamer and David Colander sought the views of graduate students at leading universities in the US, they found that 68 per cent of their sample considered 'Having a thorough knowledge of the economy' as being 'Unimportant' in putting students on the fast track. 23 per cent considered 'Being interested in, and good at, empirical research' unimportant. In contrast, 'Being smart in the sense of being good at problem solving' and 'Excellence in mathematics' were rated 'Very important' by 65 and 57 per cent of the sample respectively (Klamer and Colander, 1990, p. 18).[1]

Linguistic evidence

Such attitudes are reinforced by other evidence. One such piece of evidence comes, surprisingly, from linguistic analysis. Two linguists (whose preconceptions concerning economics had led them to expect results very different from what they found) analysed 'hedging' in a

---

[1] See also the excellent advice offered to new academic economists in Colander (1996).

sample of articles from the *Economic Journal* (Bloor and Bloor, 1993).[2] Hedging is where claims are softened, or mitigated, using phrases such as 'I wish to suggest that', 'It seems likely that', 'It appears to be the case that'. Research in biology by Greg Myers (1989) suggests that hedging us used as a politeness strategy, and is most frequently observed where scientists are making claims that concern matters central to the discipline. The rationale for this is that if one is making a knowledge claim that concerns something central to the discipline, one is threatening one's colleagues, for if the claim is accepted, those scientists whose work is affected will lose face. In contrast, if a scientist is making knowledge claims that concern peripheral aspects of the discipline, no scientist stands to lose face and politeness strategies do not have to be used.

Though it might be thought that politeness strategies might be used fairly randomly, what Myers discovered was that biologists systematically used them when making empirical claims. Theoretical claims were much less likely to be hedged. If Myers's theory is right, this is consistent with empirical evidence being seen as central to biology. In complete contrast, what Bloor and Bloor found in the *Economic Journal* was that economists systematically hedged theoretical and methodological knowledge claims, but rarely hedged claims about the real world.[3] An example of the first category is:

> The estimate of *k* *indicates* positive skewness of the distribution on the stochastic term and is highly significant, and reflects the long upper tail in the data. This *appears* consistent with what we know about the upper tail in the drinking distribution. (Bloor and Bloor, 1993, p. 162)

The italicized verbs involve hedging: it would have been quite reasonable to use unhedged verbs such as 'shows' or 'is' instead. In contrast, examples of empirical claims are:

> There are significant household composition effects on the share of spending on alcohol, with an additional man increasing the share, and additional women and children reducing the share. (Bloor and Bloor, 1993, p. 162)

---

[2] They took as their sample all eleven articles in the latest issue available when they started their research.

[3] Claims concerning propositions that are regarded as well-established, and summaries of other economists work, were excluded for these are not face-threatening.

In contrast with earlier work . . . the expected level of output is not found to be a major determinant of the level of inventories. The main effect is now seen to be the conditional variance of output and the cost of stockholding. (Bloor and Bloor, 1993, pp. 162–3)

The results are unambiguous: a decrease in the level of benefits has virtually no effect on durations. Even for unemployed individuals with a university degree a drop in benefits causes only a 1% drop in the expected duration. (Bloor and Bloor, 1993, p. 163)

Though such claims contain approximators, politeness strategies are absent. If the conclusions Myers drew from biology are correct, such claims are unhedged because they are not central to the discipline. Such an interpretation is supported by the claims of economists concerning their discipline's failure to take empirical evidence sufficiently seriously.[4] The classic example is perhaps Leontief (1971).

The use of econometric results

As Summers (1991, p. 132) has pointed out, theorists, whether in journal articles or textbooks, rarely cite econometric results. Similarly, Mirowski's observation that survey articles fail to quote means and standard deviations for estimates of what are thought to be important coefficients indicates that economists cannot regard such information as important – otherwise the authors of such surveys, or the editors of the journals in which they are published, would be under pressure to include them. Some econometricians are openly sceptical about whether econometric results have ever caused economists to change their theories, Keuzenkamp and Magnus going so far as to challenge readers of the *Journal of Econometrics* 'to name a paper that contains significance tests which significantly changed the way economists think about some economic proposition', offering a substantial reward to most convincing response (Keuzenkamp and Magnus, 1995, p. 21). Similarly, Summers challenged his readers

---

[4] When they undertook their work, Bloor and Bloor were, as linguists with no special knowledge of economics, not aware of this literature. Indeed, they found their results so surprising that they could not, initially, make sense of them.

to try and identify a single instance in which a 'deep structural parameter' has been estimated in a way that has affected the professions beliefs about the nature of preferences or production technologies or to identify a meaningful hypothesis about economic behaviour that has fallen into disrepute because of a formal statistical test. (Summers, 1991, p. 130)

These might be seen as debating points, but Keuzenkamp and Magnus, and Summers, are none the less raising doubts that many economists would endorse.

13.2   HOW DO ECONOMIC THEORISTS USE EMPIRICAL EVIDENCE?

Example 1: Diamond's *On Time*

Perhaps the best way to work out the relationship between empirical evidence and economic theory is to consider how economic theorists actually use such evidence. This can be done by considering some examples. The first example that will be investigated is *On Time*, by Peter Diamond (1994). The aim of this book is to explore how time can be modelled. In considering both the individual industry and the economy as a whole, Diamond's starting point is an atemporal model (Marshallian period analysis, and the IS–LM model) that is widely used in the literature. His objective is to replace such models with ones that take explicit account of time. At the level of the industry, for example, in place of the Marshallian distinction between the short run (where the number of firms is given) and the long run (where entry and exit takes place), each of which is an atemporal model, Diamond seeks to model entry and exit explicitly – as taking place in real time. To do this he constructs a series of simple models, distinguished from each other by the assumptions made about costs and the behaviour of demand. After this, he proceeds to consider mechanisms underlying firms' pricing behaviour.

   Though Diamond's aim is theoretical, he adduces much empirical evidence.

1. In the absence of data on entry and exit into product markets, Diamond cites evidence on job creation and job destruction,

including the fraction that is accounted for by plant start-ups and closedowns. He also claims that exit is more concentrated than entry. The point about gross flows being substantially larger than net flows is replicated in two ways: the authors of the study he cites replicated their results by analysing a range of countries; and Diamond, on the basis of his own research, argues that it is supported by data derived from interviews with workers.

2. Survey evidence is used to establish that prices vary considerably across space, different retail stores charging very different prices at the same time. This finding is backed up by evidence, obtained by different researchers, on differences in interest rates and insurance premia. Similarly, when it comes to variations in prices over time, two surveys are cited.

3. Survey evidence on the frequency of retail price changes, with prices being raised and lowered within short periods of time, is backed up by reference to other surveys conducted on a slightly different basis.

4. Price stickiness was supported by three types of evidence: a survey of prices at which large firms bought goods; evidence on news-stand prices of magazines, and mail order catalogues. In all three, price changes were infrequent.

5. Results obtained using regression analysis were used to show the effects of Federal Reserve policies on industrial production. On average, six decisions by the Fed to lower inflation, despite the consequences for output, were followed by a 12 per cent fall in industrial production 33 months later. It was pointed out that the authors of this study, Christina Romer and David Romer, had repeated the study using more recent data, obtaining 'basically similar' results (Diamond, 1994, p. 65).

6. Time series data are used to establish that (1) seasonal changes are large relative to the growth of GDP; and (2) seasonal and non-seasonal components in the growth of GDP are highly correlated. The first of these is replicated in the sense that it is found to be true for many countries.

7. Time series data are used to examine the relationship, over time, of regional to national unemployment rates in the US. Data from the UK is introduced, but this exhibits characteristics different from those found in the US data. Diamond's conclusion is that, for reasons he does not explore, regional unemployment patterns

differ across countries. UK data cannot, therefore, be used to replicate results obtained on US data.

8. Other empirical evidence is cited as common knowledge: the fact that telephone tariffs contain only a small number of rates during the day; that supermarkets give large discounts on a few goods, not small discounts on all goods; and that convenience stores do not lower their prices during large supermarkets' opening hours. Similarly, though perhaps more controversially, he argues that 'Everyone knows that a central bank can cause a recession whenever it wants.' (Diamond, 1994, p. 62).

Several points can be made concerning this, quite substantial, list of empirical evidence.[5] The first is that Diamond relies on more than stylized facts. He cites Gordon's list of stylized facts about price changes, but is not satisfied – he *is* interested in the numbers, not merely the constancy or variability of ratios and trends. But numbers are not used to test quantitative implications of his theories. They are used to establish that the phenomena his theories are concerned to model are important in practice. Thus he point out that from 1972–88, 10.1 per cent of US manufacturing jobs were lost each year but, due to job creation amounting to 9.1 per cent, the net loss of jobs was only 1.1 per cent. These numbers make the point that gross flows are substantially greater than net ones. Similarly, with price variability, Diamond points out that the range of prices found at any moment is 2:1, not because the precise number matters, but to show that the range is clearly substantial. In neither case is there a formally stated criterion for whether or not the numbers are substantial, for he assumes that once the reader is made aware of the numbers, it will be obvious. The numbers are persuasive, even though there is no formal criterion for what is 'substantial' or 'significant'.

The second point is that considerable attention is paid to providing a variety of empirical evidence to support important empirical claims. Rarely are empirical results cited without being weighed against other evidence. This could be viewed as replication, where replication takes several forms: using data from different countries, different time periods, and using different types of survey data. However, it is important to note that empirical results can be

---

[5] The book is a very slim volume.

interpreted at a number of levels of generality, which has implications for what constitutes replication.[6]

A third point is Diamond's willingness to use proxies for the variables that appear in his theories. In the absence of data on entry and exit into product markets, he uses data on the labour market. The link between these two depends on theory – that entry and exit will be correlated with the creation and destruction of jobs, and of plants – but it could be argued that this is a lower-level theory than the one Diamond is concerned to evaluate. It might be argued that this is comparable to the astronomer's treating telescopic observations as empirical facts, or the biologist's treating microscopic observations as facts, even though they depend on acceptance of the laws of optics.[7]

A fourth point is that many of the assumptions are made because, on the basis of common sense, they are considered reasonable. The existence of an upward-sloping supply curve of potential entrants is crucial for his theory, but no evidence is provided. This is one of the key assumptions in his theory, but he sees no need to justify it. Few economists (probably including heterodox ones) would question it. Similarly, the basic institutional structure that underlies the model (including concepts of entry and exit, measures of industrial production and so on) is taken for granted.

Finally, Diamond's empirical evidence is in a sense loosely tied to the models he is exploring. He motivates the section on macroeconomic empirical evidence with the following words.

> But first, I want to present some empirical studies in order to given an image of the facts about entire economies which should be kept in mind when considering theoretical models. (Diamond, 1994, p. 62)

The phrase 'kept in mind' suggests a loose usage of facts. One reason for this looseness is that the assumptions made in Diamond's theoretical models are clearly not intended to be realistic – real world firms do not, we can safely assume, fall into two categories, high and low cost firms, each of which has uniform costs. Models are used to illustrate phenomena, not to provide accurate descriptions of the real world. Empirical evidence is sometimes used to test the

---

[6] This is considered below.

[7] See page 77 above.

implications of theories, but not all a theory's implications are tested, for given the nature of the models he uses, some implications would clearly be falsified. More frequently, empirical evidence is used to establish the problems that theoretical models are to solve

In using these various pieces of empirical evidence, it is worth mentioning what Diamond regards as needing confirmation. Nowhere does he raise doubts about the survey methods, statistical tools used, the accuracy of calculations (though this is presumably because he made judgements on such matters before deciding which papers to cite, choosing simply to ignore papers whose methods he considered faulty).[8] On the other hand, where the evidence is particularly important to his argument (on entry and exit), and perhaps is also more controversial, he takes great care to describe the source of the evidence in detail. In addition, he is clearly not interested in precise numbers, though he is interested in orders of magnitude. Because he is more concerned with broader issues (the existence and characteristics of entry and exit in general, rather than creation and destruction of jobs in US manufacturing) he appears more interested in having different types of evidence bearing on the broader phenomenon, than in having additional evidence that the details of a particular study are correct. Thus he has no specific interest in the details of price-stickiness in mail-order catalogues, merely in the phenomenon of price-stickiness in general, he is happier to have evidence of some other type of price-stickiness than to have the results on mail-order catalogues replicated.

Example 2: Blanchard and Fischer's *Lectures on Macroeconomics*[9]

Virtually all the empirical evidence cited in *Lectures in Macroeconomics* (Blanchard and Fischer, 1989) is contained in two chapters: the introduction (Chapter 1) and a chapter interestingly entitled 'Some useful models' (Chapter 10).[10] Much less appears elsewhere in the book.

The introductory chapter, the aim of which is to 'introduce the major issues of macroeconomics by characterizing the basic facts that

---

[8] Goldfarb (1995) has pointed to the bias implicit in economists' publishing only regression results believed to be significant. A similar selection bias may arise with citations.

[9] This section is an abridged version of a section in Backhouse (1997c).

[10] Are the models described in the rest of the book, one wonders, not useful?

call for explanation' (Blanchard and Fischer, 1989, p. 1), highlights the following.

1. The growth of output and its decomposition into the contributions of various factors (the 'Solow' decomposition). These 'stylized facts' about growth are taken as well-established, and supported by the authors' own calculations.
2. Okun's Law that a 1 per cent decrease in the unemployment rate is associated with a 3 per cent increase in output. Blanchard and Fischer emphasize Okun's methods, pointing out that other economists have followed the same techniques, all reaching the conclusion that trend growth was lower in the 1970s and 1980s than before. Two examples of such work are cited, though the precise numbers obtained are not given. Blanchard and Fischer then estimate such a decomposition themselves, giving the equation they obtained. However, their emphasis is not on the magnitude of the coefficient in Okun's Law, but on the size of the residual variance in output. They describe it (1 per cent) as 'large' (Blanchard and Fischer, 1989, p. 10).
3. The decomposition of output into cycle and trend, using a variety of methods. They present their own work, based on the assumption that, as shocks have permanent effects, it makes no sense to look at the gap between output and a smooth trend. They cite two papers which found evidence that GDP could be described by a particular ARIMA process, whereupon they estimate such a process themselves, finding that the residual variance is similar to that derived using the technique described above. However, the significance of both this and the previous decomposition are then questioned when Blanchard and Fischer point out that it has been shown that there will in general be an infinite number of decompositions into cycle and trend. They also approach the problem through analysing the joint behaviour of output and unemployment.
4. Evidence is presented on comovements in GNP and some of its components. It is concluded that the elasticity of consumption to GNP is 35 per cent ('much smaller than 1') and that 'In those periods after 1948 when GNP declines relative to a deterministic trend, the average share of the fall attributable to a decline in inventory investment is about 50%' (Blanchard and Fischer, 1989,

p. 16). Another work is cited as evidence that if the calculation is performed slightly differently, the figure would be 68 per cent.
5. Comovements between GNP and certain relative prices are analysed in detail. The conclusion that there is little correlation between real wages and output is supported by six other studies, dating from 1938 to 1988, and using three different types of data (on the economy, industries and individual firms). These results are, they claim, reinforced by two other studies that found that, 'given nominal money, there is a positive correlation between innovations in interest rates and future innovations in GNP' (Blanchard and Fischer, 1989, p. 32).

In Chapter 10, the focus is primarily on theory, but an interesting range of empirical evidence is cited.

1. A standard CAPM describes asset returns less well than the consumption CAPM, even though the latter is theoretically superior.
2. The Lucas asset-pricing model cannot explain both the riskless discount rate and the equity premium.
3. Studies of hyperinflation (of which two, one of which has Fischer as a co-author, are cited) often stress the role of the budget deficit, which means that it is a puzzle that no correlation can be found between deficits and inflation. This is presented as a generally accepted empirical finding.
4. The tax cuts in 1981 were deflationary (a claim backed up by two sources). A macroeconometric model (the MPS model) is cited as evidence that the transmission Blanchard and Fischer have described can be used in empirical work, though no conclusions reached with the econometric model are mentioned.
5. The coefficient on expected inflation in the Phillips curve is argued to have been estimated, in the early 1970s, at between 0.4 and 0.8. This is presented as a generally accepted conclusion.
6. The Layard, Nickell and Jackman (1991) model of inflation and unemployment is discussed in detail, and the factors Layard and Nickell see as having caused rises in the actual and equilibrium unemployment rates are listed. From all this, Blanchard and Fischer draw the conclusion that the causes affecting unemployment are complex.

The first conclusion to be drawn from these examples is that the main role of empirical evidence is to suggest problems to be solved. In the main these are stylized facts about the economy. Some of these are regarded as well-established, though in several cases Blanchard and Fischer see the key issue as the techniques by which facts are established in particular cases. Once the techniques are established (for example for disentangling trend and cycle) applying them is seen as routine. A second conclusion is that although the interest is primarily in explaining stylized facts at a general level, Blanchard and Fischer do pay attention to numbers, though these rarely play an important role except in establishing broad magnitudes (usually whether a parameter is either significantly larger than zero, or whether it is close to unity). The examples of elasticities of consumption and investment to GNP were cited above. Another example, from elsewhere in the book, is the elasticity of substitution of leisure across different periods (vital to equilibrium business cycle theories) where they cite a survey as finding 'most estimates' to be between 0 and 0.45, only to qualify this by citing another survey argued that it could be anywhere between *minus* 0.3 and 14.

This point leads on to a third characteristic of the way Blanchard and Fischer use empirical evidence. It is frequently to undermine simple models – to suggest doubts, and to stop students being misled regarding hypotheses that emerge from models as certainties. There is no formal testing of opponents' theories, but there is a clear element of falsificationism involved. Perhaps even more significantly, they emphasize their commitment to the view that the causes, even of trends in macroeconomic time series, are complex.

> The reader should remember the major correlations and conclude that *no simple monocausal theory can easily explain them*. Equilibrium theories based on supply shocks have to confront the weak correlations between real wages and GNP, as well as the positive relation between nominal variables and activity. Theories in which the cycle is driven by demand shocks have to give convincing explanations for the behaviour of real wages. Theories that emphasize money shocks have to confront the correlations among interest rates, money, and output. (Blanchard and Fischer, 1989, p. 20, emphasis added)

The inadequacy of monocausal theories is almost completely unhedged. Though their methods are very different from his, this view is reminiscent of Mitchell's attitude towards explaining the business cycle.

Finally, the emphasis in the book (perhaps in part, though not entirely, because it is a textbook) the emphasis is on economic models as tools. The macroeconomic models used in the book are presented as being simplifications of reality. Some simplifications (for example the neglect of imperfect competition in considering optimal growth and the Ramsey model) are presented as being harmless. Despite all the simplifications involved, the Ramsey model is argued to be 'more than a benchmark' in that it can provide useful analysis of a small open economy (Blanchard and Fischer, 1989, p. 21). When it comes to considering fluctuations in output, however, the situation is different:

> We are sure that incomplete markets and imperfect competition are needed to account for the main characteristics of actual fluctuations. We also believe that such nonneoclassical constructs as bounded rationality ... or interdependent utility functions ... may be needed to understand important aspects of financial and labor markets. (Blanchard and Fischer, 1989, p. 27)

With business cycles, their defence of competitive equilibrium theorizing is that it provides a well-understood benchmark, from which deviations can be analysed.

This emphasis on models as tools comes out very clearly in Chapter 10. Blanchard and Fischer argue that, though the models developed in previous chapters can be used to clarify conceptual issues, to explain current events, and to help in policy design, 'almost all economists' are eclectic when considering real-world issues. Models often have to be developed in a particular direction to suit the question in hand.

> Often the economist will use a simple *ad hoc* model, where an ad hoc model is one that emphasizes one aspect of reality and ignores others, in order to fit the purpose for which it is being used.
>
> Although it is widely adopted and almost as widely espoused, the eclectic position is not logically comfortable. It would be better for economists to have an all-purpose model, derived explicitly from microfoundations and embodying all relevant imperfections, to analyse all issues in macroeconomics (or perhaps all issues in economics). We are not quite[!!] there yet. And if we ever were, we would in all likelihood have little understanding of the

mechanisms at work behind the results of simulations. Thus we have no choice but to be eclectic. (Blanchard and Fischer, 1989, p. 505)

They go on to argue that the selection of suitable assumptions is an 'art'. The good economist is one who can know which unrealistic assumptions are peripheral to a particular problem, and which are crucial. There is a trade-off between the tractability of ad-hoc models, and the insights that can be obtained from starting with first principles. Interestingly, a footnote in which they cite Friedman's essay on methodology suggests that they may have 'gone further into methodology than might be wise' (Blanchard and Fischer, 1989, p. 558, n. 3). This belief that economics is an art, in which theoretical tools are used creatively by the economist, is the way they maintain the claim that the goal of economics is empirical, whilst keeping the link between empirical evidence and their theorizing extremely loose.

Example 3: Seater on Ricardian equivalence

The third example is Seater's (1993) survey article on Ricardian equivalence. This is a very different contribution from those of either Diamond or Blanchard and Fischer, but is worth discussing because it illustrates very clearly how an economist can replicate results by bringing together pieces of empirical evidence that are genuinely independent of each other. As is made clear above, this is crucial to the problem of replication. Seater's article also illustrates some of the problems that arise when economists do this.

Seater's concern is with Ricardian equivalence – the notion that it makes no difference to the wealth, and hence the expenditure decisions, of the private sector, whether government deficits are financed by issuing debt or by taxation. Government bonds do not constitute net wealth for the private sector, the reason being that, given certain assumptions, they must eventually be repaid, and are thus matched by future tax liabilities that exactly offset the value of the bonds. His survey is valuable because he provides a systematic survey of the various types of evidence that can be brought to bear on the proposition.

1. Direct tests of the implications of Ricardian equivalence, such as the absence of any systematic effects of taxes on consumers'

expenditure or the effects of fiscal policy changes on interest rates.

Under this heading, Seater cites different types of evidence. (1a) The first, and most obvious, is econometric tests, using macroeconomic time-series data, of equations such as,

$$C_t = a_0 + a_1 + a_2 Y_t + a_3 SSW_t + a_4 G_t + a_5 T_t + a_6 TR_t + a_7 D_t + e_t,$$

where C is consumption, Y is income, SSW is the value of social security wealth, G is government expenditure, T is tax revenue, TR is transfers to individuals, and D is government debt. e is an error term. If Ricardian equivalence holds, we should find that

$$a_4 < 0, a_3 = a_5 = a_6 = 0, a_2 = a_7.$$

(1b) The second type of direct evidence on the predictions of Ricardian equivalence comes from 'natural experiments'. One such experiment was conducted when Reagan cut taxes without being able to achieve any reductions in public expenditure, thus raising the government deficit as a fraction of national income. The effects of this on variables such as interest rates, the saving ratio and consumption can be used to test the predictions of Ricardian equivalence.

2. Indirect tests – tests of the propositions that need to be true if Ricardian equivalence is to hold (tests of the theory's assumptions).

Indirect tests fall into three categories. (2a) Seater cites econometric studies of the permanent-income/life-cycle hypothesis that is central to Ricardian equivalence, finding that, during retirement, households save less than the theory would imply, and that responses to announcements of policy changes are delayed. (2b) There are also tests based on 'natural experiments', such as changes to the social security system which resulted in rises in the level of benefits being paid. (2c) Finally, Seater cites extensive casual evidence on the assumptions made in the theory of Ricardian equivalence. For example: bequests are not always made for altruistic motives; 20 per cent of couples have no children and should therefore not care about tax liabilities that fall on future generations; 12 to 18 per cent of households are liquidity constrained, implying that they cannot readjust their borrowing to compensate for fiscal policy changes; many people do not even understand what the government deficit is.

The main feature of this list evidence is that, especially when it comes to indirect tests, or tests of assumptions, Seater brings a variety of independent pieces of evidence to bear on the problem. Microeconomic studies of the effects of benefits on household consumption, or on the proportion of childless couples, are completely independent of the aggregate macroeconomic time-series data that underlie the direct tests of Ricardian equivalence. It could be argued that Seater is attempting establish Ricardian equivalence through a process that does involve replication. Notice, however, that when Seater uses the term replication, he uses it in the sense conventional amongst econometricians: to refer to macroeconometric time-series studies that 'replicate' earlier (essentially similar) work. In contrast, the argument put forward here is that replication arises when different types of evidence are brought together.

Replication is, however, very difficult, because so few of the studies are in any sense conclusive, even in establishing isolated parts of the larger picture. Take, as an example, the macroeconometric studies of debt, interest rates and consumption. Not only are there standard econometric problems (lags, treatment of serial correlation, omitted variables, simultaneity, and so on) but there are serious measurement problems. Total government debt held by households is not easy to measure, and it is not clear which of the various possible measures is, theoretically, the correct one. Saving should take into account capital gains, and not simply be the difference between personal disposable income and consumption.

The main problem Seater faces is that the evidence does not all pull in the same direction. It would be entirely legitimate to read the survey and conclude that Ricardian equivalence does not hold – though there are some studies that are consistent with it, the evidence against is sufficiently strong to undermine it. At the very least, the evidence is so contradictory that it is impossible to claim strong support for Ricardian equivalence. On direct econometric tests, he writes, 'An initial reading of that literature is both confusing and disheartening, suggesting that such tests are uninformative about Ricardian equivalence' (Seater, 1993, p. 174). On indirect evidence, Seater concludes,

> For the most part, the indirect evidence on Ricardian equivalence is inconclusive, either because it is contradictory of because crucial pieces are missing. There are hints that Ricardian equivalence might not hold – the evidence of non-negligible inadequacies in the PILCH [permanent-income/life-cycle hypothesis] framework regarding the timing of policy changes, the apparent importance of nonaltruistic bequest motives, the many childless families, and the existence of liquidity constraints. However, nothing is at all definitive. (Seater, 1993, p. 160)

He resolves this conflict in two ways. First, he removes the ambiguity in the message from direct econometric studies by arguing that 'virtually all the confusion arises from problems with econometric methodology' (Seater, 1993, p. 174). When attention is confined to sound studies, the data almost all fail to reject Ricardian equivalence. The second is that, he argues that, though Ricardian equivalence does not hold exactly (that it is rejected by the evidence), the evidence also rejects the traditional view of government debt. The answer, he contends, is that Ricardian equivalence holds as a close approximation. Whether or not one wishes to regard Ricardian equivalence as true, depends on the type of question in which one is interested.

This raises several issues concerning the nature of any replication going on.

1. There is a serious attempt to replicate results by bringing in a variety of types of evidence.
2. The overall message is inconclusive, even when a variety of data is introduced. The contradictory nature of the evidence means that it is hard to conclude that the data supports Ricardian equivalence, whilst the inconclusive nature of individual pieces of evidence means that it is hard to apply the falsificationist rule that one piece of contradictory evidence is sufficient to disprove a theory.
3. One could reasonably claim that the failure of Ricardian equivalence to hold exactly has been replicated, in that there is a wide variety of evidence against it; but that neither the inadequacy of the traditional view, nor Seater's conclusion that it holds approximately has been replicated. His statement that 'I

think it reasonable to conclude that Ricardian equivalence is supported by the data' (Seater, 1993, p. 181) seems grossly over-optimistic.

This situation, of an economist seriously trying to bring a variety of pieces of evidence to bear on a problem and being over-optimistic in drawing definite conclusions when confronted with very serious problems, is not uncommon. Replication of positive results is much less frequent than negative ones.

Replication as an *economic* problem

Diamond's use of empirical evidence provides a good counter-example to the generalization that economists do not care about whether or not empirical evidence can be replicated. *Reference is frequently made to several studies that can be regarded as replicating each other.* Diamond regularly attempts to find different types of evidence to support claims that the phenomena he is seeking to model are important. Unlike the studies cited in the Pencavel survey, criticized by Cartwright,[11] these studies do provide independent evidence on the phenomena at issue. Several points follow from this.

1. Replication can be seen as an *economic*, not a purely econometric problem. Even if none of the studies cited had been replicated in the sense discussed in Chapter 11, it would be true that the conclusions Diamond drew from these studies had all been replicated. In other words, the significance of econometricians' failure to replicate each others' work depends crucially on the use that is made of such work. For some purposes, failure to replicate precise econometric results may matter less than it does for other purposes.
2. The process of replication is very informal. It involves no systematic attempt to verify empirical results, but simply users of empirical results comparing alternative studies which they consider relate to a problem.
3. Replication can be, and frequently is, only partial. Indeed, partial replication may, for some problems, be all that is required. Consider the study, cited by Diamond, concerning labour

---

[11] See page 144 above.

turnover in US manufacturing. This 'fact' can be tested at a number of levels: (a) Are the precise numbers correct – was the study was undertaken correctly? (b) Are the orders of magnitude for labour turnover correct? (c) Is it correct that entry and exit are much more important problems that the relatively stable behaviour of macroeconomic aggregates might suggest. By and large it is the more general statements that economists wish to test, *not* the precise numbers.

It follows that, when we consider not only the production of econometric results, but also the use of such results by economic theorists, replication becomes much more complex. It may be that, for some purposes (a theorist wanting evidence on price stickiness) a result is replicated, but for another purpose (an applied economist predicting the quantitative effect of a policy change) it is not. An equally fundamental point is that replication is not a purely econometric problem, but an economic one. It concerns the nature of economic theory as much as econometric practices, for a key issue is the relationship of economic theory to generalizations that can be tested.

Theories are about causal mechanisms, or generic structures. They are rarely sufficiently specific that one can identify specific constants that play a crucial role, the values of which are believed to be stable and sufficiently important to quantify with a high degree of precision. Why?

1. Economists generally believe that the numbers attached to parameters will be different at different times and places. The aim, therefore, is to find common structures beneath this variety, into which different sets of numbers can be placed.
2. Models are approximations, frequently because of aggregation. Theories typically refer to individual agents, yet theories refer to the behaviour of groups of individuals.
3. Parameters are normally dependent on the precise functional form being used, something for which there is frequently no theoretical justification.
4. The values of economic parameters are frequently irrelevant to understanding the processes involved, even if there is good reason for choosing a specific functional form. In physics, there are good reasons why gravity involves an inverse square law

rather than, say, an inverse cube law. There are no comparable reasons why, for example, we might need to know whether the incremental capital output ratio is 3 or 4.

Thus where the numerical value of a constant does matter, economists generally explore the consequences of a range of values rather than seeking to establish precisely what the 'true' value is.

The role played by empirical evidence in economic theory

The examples of Diamond and Blanchard and Fischer show that, for all the problems discussed in earlier in this section, facts *do* matter in economics. But how is such evidence used? What role does it play in the process whereby economic theories are developed?

For both Diamond and Blanchard and Fischer, empirical evidence is used primarily to establish the facts that theories should explain. This task is performed very carefully. A second use of empirical evidence, particularly marked in Blanchard and Fischer, is to undermine competing theories. They do this, not by arguing directly for the superiority of their own specific theories, but by using empirical evidence to show that simple theories are inadequate. In contrast, there is a notable absence of any systematic attempt to use empirical evidence either to support the assumptions made in the authors' own theoretical models, or to test their conclusions in any formal way.

Clearly, there are many examples of economic theory for which empirical evidence is irrelevant,[12] but the two examples discussed above are, I conjecture, typical of much contemporary economic theory, both micro and macro. Much contemporary theorizing starts with an empirical observation and proceeds to demonstrate how the phenomenon concerned can be derived from optimizing behaviour under a carefully defined set of circumstances. Empirical observations are as frequently institutional features (long-term wage contracts or incomplete contracts) as statistical regularities. Where they are empirical regularities, these frequently take form of 'stylized facts' rather than precisely-stated econometric results.

---

[12] The obvious example is Debreu's *Theory of Value* (1959). Such work, however, it not representative of economic theory, even microeconomic theory.

The role of facts in economic theorizing fits well with the role of facts in the discussion of informal mathematics in section 10.2. In Lakatos's view of informal mathematics, progress is theoretical, but regulating this process is an informal, intuitive concept of what certain mathematical structures mean. It is these in empirical concepts that are determine what the theorems are to prove and which are the source of the counter-examples which force mathematicians to reconsider their proofs. In the same way, in economics, empirical evidence provides the stylized facts that determines the results that economic theorists seek to explain, and that cause them to reject some theories in favour of others. For example, the emergence of stagflation in the 1970s caused a change in the stylized facts that labour-market theories were expected to explain, with the result that Phillips-curve theories were abandoned in favour of natural-rate theories. Similarly, in the 1980s, the persistence of high unemployment produced further changes in the stylized facts, necessitating modifications to natural rate theories.

13.3   EMPIRICAL PROGRESS IN ECONOMICS

The limitations of economic theory

Economics has not exhibited the degree of empirical progress that was once expected. Given that there would appear to have been significant theoretical progress, and that the hopes entertained of econometrics in the 1950s and 1960s have certainly not been fulfilled, it is tempting to lay the blame for this with econometrics. If we accept the picture of economic theory having developed as informal mathematics, we might argue that econometrics has failed to pin down the nature of the reality that theorists are seeking to model. To reach this conclusion would, however be a mistake.

The mathematicians seeking a proof of Euler's conjecture could assume a common intuitive understanding of the concept of a polyhedron. In economics, in contrast, such common understanding is much more difficult to achieve, for three main reasons.

1. We cannot 'see' many economic concepts in the same sense as we can see a polyhedron.

2. The continually changing nature of the economic world makes it harder for a consensus to emerge, for by the time one begins to emerge, the world will frequently have changed.
3. The need, by virtue of the extreme complexity of the economic world, to work continually with assumptions that are unrealistic.
4. Lack of agreement on the basic concepts that economics should be seeking to explain.

In addition to making it harder for a consensus to become established, the changing nature of the world causes other problems. Runs of data become shorter, as older data come to be regarded as generated by a different model, and replication becomes more difficult. More important than this, however, continual change has caused economists to retreat into theory. The reason is that they want to produce general, if not universal theories, which militates against applied work. As Marshall put it, the 'engine' of economic analysis is the only part of economics that can claim universality – that has no dogmas. Seeking universal theories, economists have failed to heed Marshall's warning that 'pure theory' is not economics 'proper' (1925, p. 437).[13] It is interesting to speculate that as economics has become an increasingly internationalized discipline, this problem has increased enormously: applied work on the British motor industry or the Belgian steel industry will never be published in the leading international journals, unless it illustrates a novel theoretical or econometric point.

The fact that economists are continually having, of necessity, to work with models that are clearly unrealistic, has arguably weakened any natural instinct towards wanting assumptions to be as realistic as possible, or of wishing seriously to test whether the unrealism of specific assumptions has serious consequences for the theory. This problem has been increased as economic theory has become more formal, with assumptions becoming less and less realistic. The result has been that theorists have been allowed

---

[13] The full quotation is, 'In my view "Theory" is essential. No one gets any real grip of economic problems unless he will work at it. But I conceive no more calamitous notion than that abstract, or general, or "theoretical" economics was economics "proper". It seems to me an essential but a very small part of economics proper: and by itself even – well, not a very good occupation of time.'

enormous freedom in the way they have developed theories.[14] This freedom has been exacerbated by the absence of any consensus as to what phenomena need to be explained – in the absence of such a consensus, theory has played the major role in determining the questions to be answered. The door has been open for mathematical values to become dominant at the expense of empirical-science ones. What Mayer (1993) has called 'formalist' values have acquired excessive importance in the discipline.

Given such freedom, economic theory has developed in a way that is far from ideal for empirical testing. For whatever reason,[15] economists have become committed to theories based on individual agents making choices on the basis of their beliefs and preferences. These preferences are defined in the most general terms possible. This creates immense problems for testing, because the parameters of individuals' utility functions cannot be measured. Preferences and beliefs are near impossible to disentangle.[16] Models of behaviour are often grounded only very loosely on empirical generalizations which, in turn, are frequently not very securely established. Neither do models always lead to testable predictions – rather, most theories are frequently, to use Fisher's apt terminology, exemplifying theories. They say what *might* happen, not what *must* happen.

This change in the nature of economic theories is reflected in economists' idiosyncratic use of the terms 'theory' and 'theorist'. Theory has, for economists, ceased to mean a body of propositions about the world, but has come to mean a set of mathematical theorems. In some quarters, the term is even reserved for those working on mathematically rigorous theories of individual optimizing behaviour. Keynes's theory of the consumption function, for example, though a generalization about the real world, including an explanation, would no longer count as theory. To see theory in this way is to accept that it is not generating testable hypotheses about the world.

---

[14] This freedom is felt not at the level of the individual theorist, who is constrained to undertake work that meets the standards imposed by her peers, but at the level of the community as a whole.

[15] There are many possibilities: the desire draw welfare conclusions; physics envy (Mirowski, 1989); the argument that people should be modelled as behaving as they ought to behave (Hausman, 1992).

[16] See Rosenberg (1992), Chapter 5.

The limitations of econometrics

Perhaps the major reason for econometrics appearing to have failed is the excessive optimism that once prevailed. In the words of a leading econometrician,

> The infant had a lofty ambition: to find a quantitative resolution of the mysteries of the economic universe, or at least some parts thereof. Were there empirical counterparts to the graceful demand and cost curves, which adorned the economics treatises? Could the Greek letters in the mathematical constructs of the more sophisticated economic theorists be replaced by numbers? Were there laws of motion of the economic system waiting to be discovered? Could the path of the economic system be changed by purposive action, based on sound empirical research, so that the economist might advise the Chancellor of the Exchequer not just in what direction he should move, but approximately what distance down the recommended road he should travel? (Johnston, 1991, p. 51)

Now that computing power has increased beyond what most economists imagined even 20 or 30 years ago, making it possible to employ a far wider range of econometric techniques, the problem appears rather different. Though much work does not fall into this category, Johnston speaks for many when he writes that, due to these developments,

> It is thus all too possible for someone to activate an econometric software package, of which he has only a dim understanding, to apply it to data of whose nature and provenance he is ignorant, and then to draw conclusions about an economic situation, whose historical and institutional realities he has, perhaps, not studied in any depth. (Johnston, 1991, p. 52)

The problem, arguably, is that the application of econometric techniques has, to a substantial extent, displaced rather than supplemented alternative, more informal ways of undertaking empirical research. This has, perhaps, arisen because learning complicated techniques, whether in economic theory or econometrics, requires time, and has displaced the learning of less technically-demanding skills. Handling data, relating data to institutions, and pattern recognition are craft skills, less amenable to textbook treatment than more formal modelling and testing techniques.

There is also the problem that elaborate econometric techniques have not, by and large, been particularly good at revealing the type of robust empirical generalizations that are vital to economic theory, both as puzzles to be explained and, perhaps even more important, as constraints on theorizing. Such empirical generalizations are usually simple in form (theorists need to be able to understand and use them in a variety of models) and are not usually precisely stated, this being an almost necessary price of robustness. Closely linked to such generalizations are classification and the development of conceptual schemes into which data can be fitted. Had economics modelled itself on medicine or biology, disciplines that rival economics in the complexity of their subject matter and the limitations of our knowledge, there might have been a much greater emphasis on pattern recognition.[17]

Though expressed slightly differently, this is substantially the case argued by Summers when he argues that econometrics has failed to make a significant impact on the development of economics, whereas informal empirical methods have. Robustness to incorrect model specification and to errors in the data are crucial characteristics of useful generalizations.

To say this is not to argue that econometrics is fruitless, or that formal econometrics is pointless, or that ignorance of relevant econometric techniques is defensible.

1. Tests need to be as rigorous as possible if spurious results are to be exposed.
2. Forecasting is an important activity, which may demand techniques different from those involved in testing and developing theories.

To illustrate this last point consider a remark of Hendry's, intended to illustrate the value of the econometric techniques he employs.

> [I]f a model based on sensible theory and designed on pre-1978 data continues to perform as anticipated for the following 20–30 quarters, then the theory-based critical assertions of Lucas and Sims or the statistical objections of Leamer seem irrelevant: it behoves them to explain why such an event occurred given that other models do not have good track records over a similar period. This is especially true in the UK since the Thatcher experiment

---

[17] See O'Brien (1992), pp. 111–12.

seems to have perturbed the economy more than any other domestic regime succeeded in doing since 1921. (Hendry, 1985, p. 76)

Being able to make such a claim is evidence that a powerful equation has been developed. For forecasting purposes an equation that can perform in this way is clearly superior to rough, less formally tested generalizations, and the ability to develop such models clearly represents progress. On the other hand, in the life of a theory, 5 to 6 years is a short time.[18] The theorist, therefore, wants to know what, if any, generalizations will survive when such an equation breaks down. For this a different type of evidence is needed.[19]

To be of use to theorists, the most important characteristic of an empirical generalization is arguably that it is robust, not tied closely to a particular theoretical model. Given the degree of uncertainty attached to most economic phenomena, it is hardly surprising that Summers felt able to argue that, 'formal econometric work where elaborate technique is used to either apply theory to data or to isolate the direction of causal relationships where they are not obvious *a priori* virtually always fails' (Summers, 1991, p. 146).

The institutions of the profession

Blaug's interpretation of this situation is that economists are failing to practice the falsificationist methodology that they preach. 'The working philosophy of science of modern economics,' he contends, 'may indeed be characterized as "innocuous falsificationism"' (Blaug, 1992, p. 244). Rather than submitting theories to empirical tests, and abiding by the results, they prize other virtues: 'analytical elegance, economy of theoretical means, and the widest possible scope' (Blaug, 1992, p. 243). The remedy is clear: economists should try harder to live up to their professed falsificationist methodology.

Even if one accepts this explanation – as is reasonable if one interprets falsificationism fairly loosely as shorthand for a hard-headed empiricism, without necessarily implying a strict Popperian position, and whether one accepts Hendry's or Summers's diagnosis of the remedy – it is not the whole story. Economists are part of a community in which individuals respond to incentives. If they are

---

[18] It is also longer than many econometric results survive.

[19] The fact that particular equations are successful, even if for limited periods, is of course an important fact to be explained.

not sufficiently empirical, not testing their theories sufficiently, an explanation has to be found at the level of the community. Such an explanation was offered by Leontief (1971) who argued that the structure of incentives in the profession had become seriously distorted. Too little prestige, he argued, was attached to vital empirical work such as the development of new statistical sources and detailed empirical work, and too much prestige to mathematical theory and the development of more sophisticated econometric techniques. Because of such incentives, theory has flourished, the result being a 'fundamental imbalance' in the discipline.

> The weak and all too slowly growing empirical foundation cannot support the proliferating superstructure of pure, or should I say, speculative economic theory. (Leontief, 1971/77, p. 25)

Leontief emphasized the need for improved data, but important as this is, the problem does not end there. Scientific communities are characterized by mechanisms whereby facts are established: whereby speculative results, first published in journal articles, gain acceptance first within a narrow circle of specialists, and eventually become generally accepted facts, quoted in the textbooks through which newcomers are introduced to the discipline. Such mechanisms, through which potential new facts are systematically evaluated, would appear to be much better developed for economic theory than for empirical results. The structuring of textbooks round theory, with empirical evidence being introduced sparsely (especially in microeconomics) and in a comparatively unsystematic way, is not simply a symptom of an imbalance in the discipline: it is part of the problem.

The difficulties economists have in assimilating empirical evidence are part (admittedly only a part) of what Solow is referring to in a remark that many economists will strongly endorse.

> If I feel oppressed by anything it is by the NBER and that flood of yellow-covered working papers. None of them contains an existence theorem. Most of them are empirical. They do indeed test hypotheses. The trouble is that so many of them are utterly unconvincing, utterly forgettable, utterly mechanical, and there is no way of knowing in advance which are and which not. That is more of a threat. (Solow, 1991, p. 30)

Such views are consistent with Hausman's view that, when faced with a conflict between theory and empirical evidence, economists are frequently well-justified in having greater confidence in the theory than in the empirical evidence (Hausman, 1992). Rather than seeing 'innocuous falsificationism' or a conflict between economists' explicit and implicit rhetoric, we should see economists as responding rationally to the situation they face, for many theories, both theoretical and empirical, are based on auxiliary assumptions that are known to be false. Such an attitude is reinforced by the great problems inherent in collecting and analysing economic data, the underdevelopment of the empirical base, and the great merits of theories based on rational behaviour.

It could also be argued that the current state of economics reflects a prisoners' dilemma. Whilst all economists would be better off if the discipline became more empirically focused, so long as the majority undertake theory, the payoffs to individuals from doing more empirical work are low, with the result that the profession remains trapped in a sub-optimal equilibrium.

The successes of economics

For all these problems, there are undeniably instances where economics has seen empirical progress. The claim that empirical evidence can never settle disputes is far from true. To discover the factors that contribute to such successes, it is best to consider some examples: finance, industrial economics and labour economics.

The economics of finance has made significant progress, for which a variety of reasons would appear to have been responsible.

1. The quality of the data, which corresponds precisely to the data available to decision makers.
2. Detailed knowledge of market structures and the way markets operate. This is possible because of the tightly-structured way in which most financial markets are forced to operate by the regulatory authorities.
3. Agents objectives are relatively straightforward. Though risk aversion may occur, profit maximization is a viable working assumption.

Truth and Progress in Economic Knowledge

4. Technology is simple and transactions costs very small, with the result that the assumption of arbitrage is sufficient to generate many results.
5. Transactions are dominated by professional traders who are well-informed.
6. Information can be found out directly from market participants about how decisions are taken and the factors that are taken into account.
7. The assumption of perfect markets means that separation theorems apply: many (though not all) financial transactions can be analysed independently of real activities in the economy.
8. There exist well-established empirical generalizations which, given the other characteristics of financial markets, have direct implications for economic theory.

Simply to list these characteristics makes it clear that finance is promising territory for economic analysis.[20]

In the field of industrial economics, the structure–conduct–performance paradigm appeared, at one time, to offer similar prospects in the field of industrial economics. There was a clear theoretical model and seemingly good opportunities to measure at least market structure and firms' performance. Detailed microeconomic data were available. There was, however, less success, for published data did not necessarily measure the variables relevant to the theory. Structure and performance were, in practice, hard to measure. Yet even in industrial economics, there are well-established empirical results, such as the failure of mergers to improve company performance. The key factor here is the availability of a large quantity of reliable data. Firms fall into two clearly-identifiable categories (bidders and targets) and relevant data (the history of share prices, bid prices and dates) are all known. Though theoretical explanations can be provided, it is a result that is not dependent on a specific theory.

Another example, cited by Leontief, is agricultural economics which, he claims, provides

---

[20] There is also the point that economic theory may have a direct and substantial payoff if it is successful.

An exceptional example of a healthy balance between theoretical and empirical analysis and of the readiness of professional economists to cooperate with experts in the neighboring disciplines. (Leontief, 1971/77, p. 30)

Good data sets, notably cross-section and cohort studies, have also been important in progressing arguments in the field of labour economics. Such microeconomic analysis, though some of the variables are motivated by rational choice theory, always involves a numerous variables to measure individuals' personal characteristics. The theory underlying these is generally informal, and the resulting coefficients come close to simply identifying patterns in the data.

The main feature in all these areas are the availability of good-quality data that can be directly related to variables that appear in the corresponding economic theories, awareness of the details of the institutional structures, and the derivation of robust relationships that can guide theory.

References

Backhouse, Roger E. (1985) *A History of Modern Economic Analysis*. Oxford and New York: Basil Blackwell.
Backhouse, R. E. (1990) 'Competition' in J. Creedy (ed.), *Foundations of Economic Thought*. Oxford: Basil Blackwell.
Backhouse, Roger E. (1992a) 'Should we ignore methodology?', *RES Newsletter* 78, July, pp. 4–5.
Backhouse, Roger E. (1992b) 'How should we approach the history of economic thought, fact fiction or moral tale?' *Journal of the History of Economic Thought* 14(1), pp. 18–35. Reprinted in Backhouse (1995).
Backhouse, Roger E. (1992c) 'The constructivist critique of economic methodology', *Methodus* 4(1), pp. 65–82.
Backhouse, Roger E. (1992d) 'Why methodology matters', *Methodus* 4(2), pp. 58–62.
Backhouse, Roger E. (1992e) 'Lakatos and economics', in S. Todd Lowry (ed.), *Perspectives on the History of Economic Thought* VIII. Cheltenham and Brookfield, VT: Edward Elgar.
Backhouse, Roger E. (1993) 'Rhetoric and methodology', in R.F. Hébert (ed.), *Perspectives in the History of Economic Thought* IX. Cheltenham and Brookfield, VT: Edward Elgar.
Backhouse, Roger E. (1994a) 'The fixation of economic beliefs', *Journal of Economic Methodology* 1(1), pp. 33–42.
Backhouse, Roger E. (1994b) *New Directions in Economic Methodology*. London and New York: Routledge.
Backhouse, Roger E. (1994c) 'The Lakatosian legacy in economic methodology', in Backhouse (1994b).
Backhouse, Roger E. (1995) *Interpreting Macroeconomics: Explorations in the History of Economic Thought*. London and New York: Routledge.
Backhouse, Roger E. (1997a) 'The changing character of British economics', in A. W. Coats (ed.) *The Post-War Internationalization of Economics*, (*History of Political Economy*, 28, Annual Supplement), pp. 31–58.
Backhouse, Roger E. (1997b) 'Novel facts', in John Davis, D. Wade Hands and Uskali Mäki (eds), *Handbook of Economic Methodology*. Cheltenham and Brookfield, VT: Edward Elgar.
Backhouse, Roger E. (1997c) 'How do economic theorists use empirical evidence? Two case studies', in Sheila C. Dow and John Hillard (eds), *Beyond Keynes*. Cheltenham and Brookfield, VT: Edward Elgar.
Backhouse, Roger E. (1997d) 'An inexact methodology of economics', *Economics and Philosophy* 13(1), pp.
Blanchard, Olivier Jean, and Fischer, Stanley (1989) *Lectures on Macroeconomics*. Cambridge, MA and London: MIT Press.
Blaug, Mark (1991) 'Introduction', in *Pioneers in Economics, Volume 1: The Historiography of Economics*. Cheltenham and Brookfield, VT: Edward Elgar.

Blaug, Mark (1992) *The Methodology of Economics*. Second edition. Cambridge: Cambridge University Press.

Blaug, Mark (1994) 'Why I am not a constructivist: confessions of an unrepentant Popperian', in Backhouse (1994b).

Bliss, Christopher J. (1986) 'Progress in economic science', in M. Baranzini and R. Scazzieri (eds), *Foundations of Economics: Structures of Inquiry and Economic Theory*. Oxford and New York: Basil Blackwell.

Bloor, D. (1984) 'The strengths of the strong programme', in J.R. Brown (ed.), *Scientific Rationality: The Sociological Turn*. Boston: Reidel, pp. 75–94.

Bloor, Meriel, and Bloor, Thomas (1993) 'How economists modify propositions', in Henderson, Dudley-Evans and Backhouse (1993).

Boland, Lawrence (1994) 'Scientific thinking without scientific method: two views of Popper', in Backhouse (1994b).

Booth, Wayne (1974) *Modern Dogma and the Rhetoric of Assent*. Notre Dame: University of Notre Dame Press.

Bresnahan, Timothy (1991) Comment on Fisher (1991), *Brookings Papers on Economic Activity: Microeconomics 1991*, pp. 226–31.

Buiter, Willem, and Miller, Marcus (1981) 'The Thatcher experiment: the first two years', *Brookings Papers on Economic Activity*, 2 pp. 315–79.

Caldwell, Bruce (1990) 'Does methodology matter? How should it be practised?' *Finnish Economic Papers* 3(1), pp. 64–71.

Caldwell, Bruce (1991) 'Clarifying Popper', *Journal of Economic Literature* 29(1), pp. 1–33.

Canova, Fabio (1995) 'Sensitivity analysis and model evaluation in simulated dynamic general equilibrium economies', *International Economic Review* 36(2), pp. 477–501.

Cartwright, Nancy (1983) *How the Laws of Physics Lie*. Oxford: Clarendon Press.

Cartwright, Nancy (1991) 'Replicability, reproducability, and robustness: comments on Harry Collins', *History of Political Economy* 23(1), 143–55.

Coats, A. W. (1969) 'Is there a "structure of scientific revolutions" in economics?' *Kyklos* 22, pp. 289–96.

Colander, David C. (1991) *Why Aren't Economists as Important as Garbagemen?* Armonk, NY and London: M.E. Sharpe.

Colander, David C. (1996) 'Surviving as a slightly out of sync economist', in Steven G. Medema and Warren J. Samuels (eds), *Foundations of Research in Economics: How Do Economists Do Economics?* Cheltenham and Brookfield, VT: Edward Elgar.

Collins, Harry (1985) *Changing Order: Replication and Induction in Scientific Practice*. London and Los Angeles: Sage.

Collins, Harry (1991) 'The meaning of replication and the science of economics', *History of Political Economy* 23(1), pp. 123–42.

Collins, Harry, and Pinch, Trevor (1993) *The Golem: What Everyone Should Know about Science*. Cambridge: Cambridge University Press.

Darnell, Adrian C., and Evans, J. Lynne (1990) *The Limits of Econometrics*. Aldershot and Brookfield, VT: Edward Elgar.

Debreu, Gerard (1959) *The Theory of Value: An Axiomatic Analysis of Economic Equilibrium*. New Haven and London: Yale University Press.

Debreu, Gerard (1986) 'Theoretic models: mathematical formalism and economic content', *Econometrica* 54(6), pp. 1259–70.

Debreu, Gerard (1991) 'The mathematization of economic theory', *American Economic Review* 81(1), pp. 1–7.

De Marchi, Neil, and Blaug, Mark (eds) (1991) *Appraising Economic Theories: Studies in the Methodology of Research Programmes*. Cheltenham and Lyme, NH: Edward Elgar.

Devitt, Michael (1991) *Realism and Truth*, second edition. Oxford: Basil Blackwell.
Dewald, William G., Thursby, Jerry G., and Anderson, Richard G. (1986) 'Replication of empirical economics: the *Journal of Money, Credit and Banking* project', *American Economic Review* 76, pp. 587–603.
Diamond, Peter A. (1994) *On Time: Lectures on Models of Equilibrium*. Cambridge and New York: Cambridge University Press.
Dornbusch, Rudiger (1976) 'Expectations and exchange rate dynamics', *Journal of Political Economy* 84, pp. 1161–76.
Dow, Sheila C. (1992) 'Postmodernism and economics', in J. Doherty, E. Graham and M. Malek (eds), *Postmodernism and the Social Sciences*. London: Macmillan.
Feyerabend, Paul K. (1988) *Against Method*, revised edition. London and New York: Verso.
Fish, Stanley (1980) *Is There a Text in this Class?* Cambridge, Mass.: Harvard University Press.
Fish, Stanley (1985) 'Consequences', *Critical Inquiry* 11, pp. 433–58.
Fisher, Franklin (1989) 'Games economists play: a noncooperative view', *Rand Journal of Economics* 20(1), pp. 113–24.
Fisher, Franklin (1991) 'Organizing industrial organization: reflections on the *Handbook of Industrial Organization*', *Brookings Papers on Economic Activity: Microeconomics 1991*, pp. 201–40.
Fisher, Robert M. (1986) *The Logic of Economic Discovery: Neoclassical Economics and the Marginal Revolution*. New York: New York University Press.
Friedman, Milton (1953) 'The methodology of positive economics', in M. Friedman (ed.), *Essays in Positive Economics*. Chicago: Chicago University Press.
Friedman, Milton (1957) *A Theory of the Consumption Function*. Princeton: Princeton University Press.
Friedman, Milton, and Schwartz, Anna J. (1963) *A Monetary History of the United States, 1867–1960*. Chicago: University of Chicago Press.
Friedman, Milton, and Schwartz, Anna J. (1982) *Monetary Trends in the United States and the United Kingdom*. Chicago and London: University of Chicago Press.
Friedman, Milton, and Schwartz, Anna J. (1991) 'Alternative approaches to analyzing economic data', *American Economic Review* 81(1), pp. 39–49.
Gerrard, Bill (1991) 'Keynes's *General Theory*: interpreting the interpretations', *Economic Journal* 101(2), pp. 276–87.
Gilbert, Christopher L. (1986) 'Professor Hendry's economic methodology', *Oxford Bulletin of Economics and Statistics* 48, pp. 283–307. Reprinted in Granger (1990).
Goldfarb, Robert S. (1995) 'The economist-as-audience needs a methodology of plausible inference', *Journal of Economic Methodology* 2(2), pp. 201–222.
Granger, C.W.J. (ed.), (1990) *Modelling Economic Series: Readings in Econometric Methodology*. Oxford and New York: Oxford University Press.
Haavelmo, Trygve (1944) 'The probability approach in econometrics', *Econometrica*, 12, Supplement.
Hacking, Ian (1983) *Representing and Intervening*. Cambridge and New York: Cambridge University Press.
Hahn, F.H. (1984) *Equilibrium and Macroeconomics*. Oxford: Basil Blackwell.
Hahn, Frank (1992a) 'Reflections', *RES Newsletter*, 77, April, p. 5.
Hahn, Frank (1992b) 'Answer to Backhouse: Yes', *RES Newsletter* 78, July, p. 5.
Hamminga, B. (1983) *Neoclassical Theory Structure and Theory Development*. Berlin: Springer.
Hamminga, B. (1991) 'Comment', in De Marchi and Blaug (1991).

220   *Truth and Progress in Economic Knowledge*

Hands, D. Wade (1990) 'Second thoughts on "Second Thoughts": reconsidering the Lakatosian progress of *The General Theory*', *Review of Political Economy* 2, pp. 69–81.

Hands, D. Wade (1991) 'The problem of excess content: economics, novelty and a long Popperian tale', and 'Reply' in De Marchi and Blaug (1991).

Hands, D. Wade (1993) *Testing, Rationality and Progress: Essays on the Popperian Tradition in Economic Methodology*. Lanham, MD: Rowman and Littlefield.

Hands, D. Wade (1994) 'The sociology of scientific knowledge: some thoughts on the possibilities', in Backhouse (1994b).

Hansen, Lars Peter, and Heckman, James J. (1996) 'The empirical foundations of calibration', *Journal of Economic Perspectives* 10(1), pp. 87–104.

Hausman, Daniel M. (1992) *The Inexact and Separate Science of Economics*. Cambridge: Cambridge University Press.

Henderson, Willie, and Dudley-Evans, Tony (eds.) (1990) *The Language of Economics: The Analysis of Economics Discourse*, ELT Documents, 134. London: Modern English Publications in association with the British Council.

Hendry, David F. (1985) 'Monetary economic myth and econometric reality', *Oxford Review of Economic Policy* 1(1), pp. 72–84.

Hendry, David F. (1993) 'The role of economic theory and econometrics in time series econometrics', Nuffield College, unpublished.

Hendry, David F. (1995a) *Dynamic Econometrics*. Oxford and New York: Oxford University Press.

Hendry, David F. (1995b) 'Econometrics and business cycle empirics', *Economic Journal* 105, pp. 1622–36.

Hendry, David F., and Ericsson, Neil (1991) 'An econometric analysis of U.K. money demand in *Monetary Trends in the United States and the United Kingdom* by Milton Friedman and Anna J. Schwartz', *American Economic Review* 81(1), pp. 8–38.

Hendry, David F., and Mizon, Grayham E. (1978) 'Serial correlation as a convenient simplification, not a nuisance: a comment on a study of the demand for money by the Bank of England,' *Economic Journal* 88, pp. 549–63.

Hendry, David F., and Morgan, Mary S. (1995) *The Foundations of Econometric Analysis*. Cambridge and New York: Cambridge University Press.

Hendry, David F., and Richard, Jean-François (1982) 'On the formulation of empirical models in dynamic econometrics', *Journal of Econometrics* 20, pp. 3–33. Reprinted in Granger (1990)

Henrion, Max, and Fischhoff, Baruch (1986) 'Assessing uncertainty in physical constants', *American Journal of Physics* 54(9), pp. 791–8.

Hirsch, Abraham, and De Marchi, Neil (1990) *Milton Friedman: Economics in Theory and Practice*. Hemel Hempstead: Harvester Wheatsheaf.

Hookway, Christopher (1990) *Scepticism*. London and New York: Routledge.

Hoover, Kevin D. (1994) 'Pragmatism, pragmaticism and economic method', in Backhouse (1994b).

Hoover, Kevin D. (1995) 'Facts and artefacts: calibration and the empirical assessment of real-business-cycle models', *Oxford Economic Papers* 47(1), pp. 24–44.

Houser, N., and Kloesel, C. (eds) (1992), *The Essential Peirce: Selected Philosophical Writings, Volume I (1967–1893)*. Bloomington and Indianapolis: Indiana University Press.

Hutchison, Terence W. (1938) *The Significance and Basic Postulates of Economic Theory*. London.

Hutchison, Terence W. (1977) *Knowledge and Ignorance in Economics*. Oxford: Basil Blackwell.

Hutchison, Terence W. (1992) *Changing Aims in Economics*. Oxford and Cambridge, MA: Basil Blackwell.

Johnston, Jack (1991) 'Econometrics retrospect and prospect', *Economic Journal* 101(1), pp. 51–6.

Keuzenkamp, Hugo A., and Magnus, Jan R. (1995) 'On tests and significance in econometrics', *Journal of Econometrics* 67(1), pp. 5–24.

Kincaid, Harold (1996) *Philosophical Foundations of the Social Sciences*. Cambridge and New York: Cambridge University Press.

King, Mervyn (1992) Letter to the editor, *RES Newsletter* 79, October, p. 2.

Klamer, Arjo (1987) 'The advent of modernism', mimeo, University of Iowa.

Klamer, Arjo (1990) 'The textbook presentation of economic discourse', in Warren J. Samuels (ed.), *Economics as Discourse: An Analysis of the Language of Economists*. Boston, Dordrecht, London: Kluwer Academic Publishers.

Klamer, Arjo, and Colander, David (1990) *The Making of an Economist*. Boulder and London: Westview Press.

Knapp, Steven, and Benn Michaels, Walter (1982) 'Against theory' *Critical Inquiry* 8, pp. 723–42.

Knight, Frank H. (1940) '"What is truth" in economics?' *Journal of Political Economy* 48(1), p. 1–32.

Knight, Frank H. (1941) 'The significance and basic postulates of economic theory: a rejoinder', *Journal of Political Economy* 49, pp. 750–3.

Kuhn, Thomas S. (1962/70) *The Structure of Scientific Revolutions*, 2nd. enlarged edition. Volume 2(2) of International Encyclopaedia of Unified Science. Chicago: University of Chicago Press.

Kuhn, Thomas S. (1977) *The Essential Tension*. Chicago and London: University of Chicago Press.

Kydland, Finn E., and Prescott, Edward C. (1982) 'Time to build and aggregate fluctuations', *Econometrica* 50, pp. 1345–70.

Kydland, Finn E., and Prescott, Edward C. (1986) 'Theory ahead of business cycle measurement', *Federal Reserve Bank of Minneapolis Quarterly Review*. Reprinted in Miller (1994).

Kydland, Finn E., and Prescott, Edward C. (1990) 'Business cycles: real facts and a monetary myth', *Federal Reserve Bank of Minneapolis Quarterly Review* 14, pp. 3–18. Reprinted in Miller (1994).

Kydland, Finn E., and Prescott, Edward C. (1991) 'The econometrics of the general equilibrium approach to business cycles', *Scandinavian Journal of Economics* 93(2), pp. 161–78.

Kydland, Finn E., and Prescott, Edward C. (1996) 'The computational experiment: an econometric tool', *Journal of Economic Perspectives* 10(1), pp. 69–85.

Lakatos, Imre (1967) *Proofs and Refutations*. Cambridge: Cambridge University Press.

Lakatos, Imre (1970) 'Falsificationism and the methodology of scientific research programmes', in *Criticism and the Growth of Knowledge*, edited by I. Lakatos and A. Musgrave. Cambridge: Cambridge University Press. Reprinted in Lakatos (1978).

Lakatos, Imre (1971) 'History of science and its rational reconstructions', in R.C. Buck and R.S. Cohen (eds) *PSA 1970, Boston Studies in the Philosophy of Science*, 8, pp. 91–135. Reprinted in Lakatos (1978).

Lakatos, Imre (1978) *The Methodology of Scientific Research Programmes: Philosophical Papers, Volume I*. Cambridge: Cambridge University Press.

Laudan, Larry (1977) *Progress and its Problems*. London: Routledge and Kegan Paul.

Laudan, Larry (1984) *Science and Values*. Berkeley, Los Angeles and London: University of California Press.

Laudan, Larry (1990) *Science and Relativism: Some Key Controversies in the Philosophy of Science*. Chicago: University of Chicago Press.

Lawson, Tony (1994) 'A realist theory for economics', in Backhouse (1994b).

Layard, Richard, Nickell, Stephen, and Jackman, Richard (1991) *Unemployment: Macroeconomic Performance and the Labour Market*. Oxford: Clarendon Press.

Leontief, W.A. (1971) 'Theoretical assumptions and nonobserved facts', *American Economic Review* 61, reprinted in W.A. Leontief *Essays in Economics*, Volume 2. Oxford: Basil Blackwell, 1977.

Levy, David, and Feigenbaum, Susan (1993) 'The market for (ir)reproducible econometrics', *Social Epistemology* 7, pp. 215–32.

Lucas, Robert E. (1980) 'Methods and problems in business cycle theory', *Journal of Money, Credit and Banking* 12, pp. 696–715.

Machlup, Fritz (1955) 'The problem of verification in economics', *Southern Economic Journal* 22(1), pp. 1–21. Reprinted in B. Caldwell (ed.), *Appraisal and Criticism in Economics*. London: Allen and Unwin, 1984.

Mayer, Thomas (1980) 'Economics as a hard science: realistic goal or wishful thinking?' *Economic Inquiry* 18, 165–78.

Mayer, Thomas (1993) *Truth versus Precision in Economics*. Cheltenham and Brookfield, VT: Edward Elgar.

Mayer, Thomas (1995) *Doing Economic Research*. Cheltenham and Brookfield, VT: Edward Elgar.

McCallum, Bennett (1986) 'On real and sticky price theories of the business cycle', *Journal of Money, Credit and Banking* 18, pp. 398–414.

McCallum, Bennett (1995) 'New classical macroeconomics: a sympathetic account', *Scandinavian Journal of Economics* 91, pp. 232–52.

McCloskey, D.N. (1983) 'The rhetoric of economics', *Journal of Economic Literature*, 21, pp. 481–517.

McCloskey, D.N. (1986) *The Rhetoric of Economics*. Brighton: Wheatsheaf Books.

McCloskey, D.N. (1988a) 'Two replies and a dialogue on the rhetoric of economics: Mäki, Rappaport and Rosenberg', *Economics and Philosophy* 4(1), p. 150–66.

McCloskey, D.N. (1988b) 'Thick and thin methodologies in the history of economic thought', in Neil de Marchi (ed.) *The Popperian Legacy in Economics*. Cambridge and New York: Cambridge University Press.

McCloskey, D.N. (1991) 'Economic science: a search through the hyperspace of assumptions?', *Methodus* 3(1), pp. 6–16.

McCloskey, D.N. (1994) *Rhetoric and Persuasion in Economics*. Cambridge and New York: Cambridge University Press.

McCloskey, D.N., and Ziliak, S.T. (1996) 'The standard error of regressions', *Journal of Economic Literature* 34(1), pp. 97–114.

Miller, Preston J. (1994) *The Rational Expectations Revolution: Readings from the Front Line*. Cambridge, MA, and London: MIT Press.

Mirowski, Philip (1989) *More Heat Than Light: Economics as Social Physics, Physics as Nature's Economics*. Cambridge and New York: Cambridge University Press.

Mirowski, Philip (1994) 'A visible hand in the marketplace of ideas: precision measurement as arbitrage', *Science in Context* 7(3), pp. 563–89. Reprinted in M. Power (ed.) *Accounting and Science: Natural Inquiry and Commercial Reason*. Cambridge and New York: Cambridge University Press.

Mirowski, Philip (1995) 'Three ways of thinking about testing in econometrics', *Journal of Econometrics* 67, pp. 25–46.

Mirowski, Philip, and Sklivas, Steven (1991) 'Why econometricians don't replicate (although they do reproduce)', *Review of Political Economy* 3(2), pp. 146–63.
Mitchell, W.C. (1925) 'Quantitative analysis in economic theory', *American Economic Review* 15, pp. 1–12. Reprinted in Mitchell *The Backward Art of Spending Money*. New York, 1937.
Morgan, Mary S. (1988) 'Finding a satisfactory empirical model', in N. De Marchi (ed.), *The Popperian Legacy in Economics*. Cambridge and New York: Cambridge University Press.
Morgan, Mary S. (1990) *The History of Econometric Ideas*. Cambridge and New York: Cambridge University Press.
Morishima, Michio (1991) 'General equilibrium theory in the twenty-first century', *Economic Journal* 101, pp. 69–74.
Munz, Peter (1984) 'Philosophy and the mirror of Rorty', *Philosophy of Social Science* 14, pp. 195-238.
Myers, Greg (1989) *Writing Biology: Texts in the Social Construction of Scientific Knowledge*. Madison, WI: University of Wisconsin Press.
O'Brien, Denis P. (1974) 'Whither economics?' Inaugural lecture, University of Durham. Reprinted in D.P. O'Brien *Money, Methodology and the Firm: The Collected Essays of D.P. O'Brien, Volume 1*. Cheltenham: Edward Elgar, 1994.
O'Brien, Denis P. (1992) 'Economists and data', *British Journal of Industrial Relations* 30(2), pp. 253–85. Reprinted in D.P. O'Brien *Money, Methodology and the Firm: The Collected Essays of D.P. O'Brien, Volume 1*. Cheltenham: Edward Elgar, 1994.
Pagan, Adrian (1987) 'Three econometric methodologies: a critical appraisal', *Journal of Economic Surveys* 1(1), pp. 3–24. Reprinted in C.W.J. Granger (ed.) *Modelling Economic Series*. Oxford: Clarendon Press.
Peirce, C. S. (1877) 'The fixation of belief', *Popular Science Monthly* 12, pp. 1–15. References are to the reprint in Houser and Kloesel (1992).
Peirce, C. S. (1878) 'How to make our ideas clear', *Popular Science Monthly* 12, pp. 286–302. References are to the reprint in Houser and Kloesel (1992).
Pencavel, John (1986) 'Labor supply of men: a survey', in O. Ashenfelter and R. Layard (eds) *Handbook of Labor Economics*. Amsterdam: North Holland.
Petley, B. W. (1985) *The Fundamental Physical Constants and the Frontier of Measurement*. Bristol and Boston, MA: Adam Hilger.
Popper, Karl (1959) *The Logic of Scientific Discovery*. English translation, 1959, revised 1980. London: Unwin Hyman.
Popper, Karl R. (1983) *Realism and the Aim of Science*. London: Hutchinson.
Reder, M. W. (1982) 'Chicago economics: permanence and change', *Journal of Economic Literature* 20(1), pp. 1–38.
Robbins, L. C. (1933) *An Essay on the Nature and Significance of Economic Science*. London: Macmillan.
Romer, Christina D., and Romer, David, H. (1989) 'Does monetary policy matter? A new test in the spirit of Friedman and Schwartz', *NBER Macroeconomics Annual 1989*. London and Cambridge MA: MIT Press, pp. 124–70.
Rorty, Richard (1980) *Philosophy and the Mirror of Nature*. Oxford: Basil Blackwell.
Rorty, Richard (1982) 'Pragmatism and philosophy', in *The Consequences of Pragmatism*, Minneapolis: University of Minnesota Press; reprinted in *After Philosophy*, ed. Kenneth Baynes, James Bohman and Thomas McCarthy, 1987.
Rorty, Richard (1991) *Objectivity, Relativism and Truth: Philosophical Papers, Volume I*. Cambridge and New York: Cambridge University Press.

Rosenberg, Alexander (1985) 'Methodology, theory and the philosophy of science', *Pacific Philosophical Quarterly* 66, pp. 377–93.
Rosenberg, Alexander (1986) 'Lakatosian consolations for economists', *Economics and Philosophy* 2, pp. 127–39.
Rosenberg, Alexander (1992) *Economics – Mathematical Politics or Science of Diminishing Returns*. Chicago: Chicago University Press.
Seater, J. (1993) 'Ricardian equivalence', *Journal of Economic Literature* 31(1), pp. 142–90.
Smith, Adam (1776) *An Inquiry into the Nature and Causes of the Wealth of Nations*.
Snowdon, Brian, Vane, Howard, and Wynarczyk, Peter (1994) *A Modern Guide to Macroeconomics: An Introduction to Competing Schools of Thought*. Cheltenham and Lyme, NH: Edward Elgar.
Solow, Robert M. (1970) *Growth Theory: An Exposition*. Oxford and New York: Oxford University Press.
Solow, Robert M., (1988) 'Comments from inside economics,' in Arjo Klamer, Donald N. McCloskey and Robert M. Solow (eds.) *The Consequences of Economic Rhetoric*. Cambridge: Cambridge University Press.
Solow, Robert M. (1991) 'Discussion notes on "Formalization"', *Methodus* 3(1), pp. 30–1.
Summers, Lawrence H. (1991) 'The scientific illusion in empirical macroeconomics', *Scandinavian Journal of Economics* 93(2), pp. 129–48.
Suppe, Frederick (1977) 'The search for philosophic understanding of scientific theories', in *The Structure of Scientific Theories*. Chicago and London: Chicago University Press.
Toulmin, Stephen (1958) *The Uses of Argument*. Cambridge: Cambridge University Press.
Vint, J. (1994) *Capital and Wages: A Lakatosian History of the Wages Fund Doctrine*. Cheltenham and Lyme, NH: Edward Elgar.
Walras, Leon (1874/1954) *Elements of Pure Economics*, translated by W. Jaffé. London: Allen and Unwin.
Weintraub, E. Roy (1985) *General Equilibrium Analysis: Studies in Appraisal*. Cambridge: Cambridge University Press.
Weintraub, E. Roy (1988) 'The neo-Walrasian research program is empirically progressive', in N. de Marchi (ed.), *The Popperian Legacy in Economics*. Cambridge: Cambridge University Press.
Weintraub, E. Roy (1989) 'Methodology doesn't matter, but the history of thought might', *Scandinavian Journal of Economics*; reprinted in *The State of Macroeconomics*, ed. Seppo Honkapohja. Oxford: Basil Blackwell, pp. 263–79.
Weintraub, E. Roy (1991) *Stabilizing Dynamics: Constructing Economic Knowledge*. Cambridge and New York: Cambridge University Press.
Weintraub, E. Roy (1992) 'Roger Backhouse's straw herring', *Methodus* 4(2), pp. 53–7.
Wendt, Paul (1990) 'Comment' on Amariglio (1990), in Warren J. Samuels (ed.), *Economics as Discourse*. Boston, Dordrecht and London: Kluwer.
Wible, James R. (1994) 'Charles Sanders Peirce's economy of research', *Journal of Economic Methodology* 1(1), pp. 235–60.
Wickens, Michael (1995) 'Real business cycle analysis: a needed revolution in macroeconomics', *Economic Journal* 105, pp. 1637–48.
Ziman, John (1994) *Prometheus Bound*. Cambridge and New York: Cambridge University Press.

Index

228   *Truth and Progress in Economic Knowledge*

Hacking, Ian vii, 26, 76–8, 80, 138, 141
Hahn, Frank 4, 8, 9, 15, 19, 48, 50, 99, 109, 121, 129, 131, 133
Hamminga, Bert 120, 123–4, 125, 133–4
Hammond, Daniel xi
Hands, D. Wade xi, 42, 47, 84, 86, 114, 115, 171
Hansen, Bruce 181–2, 185
Hard core, hardening of 124
Hausman, Daniel M. vii–ix, xi, 23, 82, 158, 208, 213
Heckman, James 181, 182
Hedging 187–9
Heidegger, Martin 26
Henderson, Willie xi, 33
Hendry, David F. xi, 14, 116, 144, 164, 166–9, 171, 172–4, 176, 179, 183–5, 210–11; comparison with Friedman 172–5, 183
Henrion, Max 151
Heuristic novelty 114, 119
Heuristics 91–3, 124–5
Hirsch, Abraham 183
Historical evidence 175
Hobbes, Thomas 3
Holism ix
Hooke's Law 104
Hookway, Christopher xi, 44
Hoover, Kevin D. xi, 64, 180
Hume, David 11
Hutchison, Terence 37, 47, 108–9, 114
Hypothesis tests 119
Hypothetico-deductive method 23, 29

Imperfect competition 130
Incommensurability 2, 13, 60, 75
Inconsistency, elimination of 102
Indirect tests, of Ricardian equivalence 200–201
Induction 38, 84
Industrial economics 19–22, 130, 214

Informal empirical work 175–6, 178, 184–5, 210
Informal mathematics 206
Informality, of replication 203
Inquiry, *see* Belief, fixation of
Instruments, theories as 178
Internal and external history, Lakatosian definition 95
Interpretation, of texts 32, 33–4
Intervention 78–80, 81, 141
Intuititive concepts 128–9
Invisible hand theorem 128–30, 133
Irreversible change, as criterion for progress 99

Jackman, Richard 196
James, William 97
Johnston, Jack 209
Joint probability distribution 161, 173, 183
Journal of Money, Credit and Banking study 143, 144, 148, 150
Journals 61
Jury, verdict of 87

Kaldor, Nicholas 37, 48, 50, 79, 80
Kant, Immanuel 27
Kelvin, William 11
Keuzenkamp Hugo A. 189–90
Keynes, John Maynard 32, 37, 208
Kincaid, Harold vii, ix–x, 113
King, Mervyn A. 8
Klamer, Arjo 12, 33, 43, 187
Knapp, Steven 35
Knight, Frank 108–9
Knotty problems, solving 8, 14
Knowledge, and communities 41, 43, 44–51, 67; as accurate representation 27–8; foundations for 82–3; growth of viii, 87–8; hypothetical nature of 82–3; justification of 45
Koopmans, Tjalling C. 14, 122–3, 125, 131, 132
Kuhn, Thomas S. vii, ix, 1–2, 6, 42, 47, 53–62, 71, 72, 74, 77, 88, 94, 98